1911 OHIO DOMINICAN COLLEGE

LIBRARY

1216 SUNBURY RD.
COLUMBUS, OHIO

The Readable People of
GEORGE MEREDITH

The Readable People of
GEORGE MEREDITH

By Judith Wilt

Princeton University Press
New Jersey

823.8
M 559 W
1975

Library of Congress Cataloging in Publication Data will
be found on the last printed page of this book

Publication of this book has been aided by a grant from
The Andrew W. Mellon Foundation

This book has been composed in Linotype Monticello

Printed in the United States of America
by Princeton University Press,
Princeton, New Jersey

74 — 25610

Contents

99119

Acknowledgments

Fruitful readings of these chapters were given me by Professors Mary Burgan, Donald Gray, Malvin Zirker, and Martha Vicinus at Indiana University, and Professor E.D.H. Johnson at Princeton University, and I am heartily grateful to them. I owe thanks, too, for wonderfully humane technical help to Anthony Shipps at Indiana University Library and Joanna Hitchcock at Princeton University Press.

The Readable People of
GEORGE MEREDITH

"Character must ever be a mystery! . . ."
"In a plain world, in the midst of such readable people!"

Debate of the narrators, *The Amazing Marriage*

Introduction

THERE IS SOMETHING OF A MEREDITH RENAIS-
sance going on in the seventies, it seems. Publication
of C. L. Cline's three-volume complete edition of the *Letters* in 1970 and of Ioan Williams' *Meredith: The Critical
Heritage* in 1971 shows scholarship stirring; volumes like
Gillian Beer's *Meredith: A Change of Masks*, published in
1970, and the essays edited by Ian Fletcher under the title
Meredith Now (1971) show criticism moving into a new
cycle of revaluation—though hedging its bets somewhat.
"Most of the contributors," Fletcher "dares say" in his preface, "would argue that he [Meredith] is a major if flawed
artist."

How might a revaluation and rereading of this late Victorian novelist be a proper product of this decade of the
twentieth century? Well, to some readers even the "flaws"
first pinned down in the counterreaction of early twentieth-
century critics are beginning to look good; his so-called
intellectuality, the knotty, mind-disciplining complexity of
his language, the healthy sanity of his balanced optimism.
But another connection suggests itself as well. It is not too
far-fetched to say, I think, that the extreme, manic view
with which the writing persona of most Meredith novels
regards his story, his enterprise, his readers, and himself,
his awareness, awe, pugnacity, and doubt, puts this Victorian sage somewhere in the same column of narrative
history as today's Barth, Borges, and Nabokov.

George Meredith was obsessed with the real and the
fictional Reader.[1] Writing at perhaps the most self-

---

[1] I am attempting to use the words reader and writer, or author,

3

conscious and self-questioning period in the history of the
novel, he made his obsession one of the foundations of his
style and his ambivalence part of the material of his fictions. Driven by the diverse and contradictory aspects of
his genius to try to integrate into the novel such alien elements as poetry, philosophy, and verbal "play," Meredith
is a reader's novelist, not least because he had the reputation of being "unreadable." Concern with the real and the
fictional reader is a living principle in work after work of
his, growing as the whole matrix of his aesthetic grows.
The struggle to define, distinguish, understand, and finally
to shape and change the reader becomes in various subtle,
often exciting—sometimes damaging ways—the very core
and content of his novels.

Meredith's aesthetic has its psychological roots in the
profound ambivalence that the man Meredith felt about
being "accepted" in the England he loved and hated not
like a son but like a foreigner turned Anglophile, as one
critic phrased it. He craved public acceptance, but not
from the public as he knew it—divided, contradictory,
whimsical, petulant, gifted, straying child that he saw it
to be. The public, of course, returned the compliment. So
extravagantly praised and condemned was Meredith by his
contemporary readers that his work was held by one critic
to demonstrate the very "futility of criticism," so utterly
contradictory were the responses even to the same passages
in Meredith novels.

Meredith came to expect, even to invite, such responses.
He even depended on them, making them part of the content of his novels. His stories in a crucial sense are always

---

in several ways in this study, both to draw attention to the qualities of Reader and Writer when they approach the status of fictional characters and to refer to the living persons involved. My
tendency has been to capitalize as sparely as possible, after the
distinctions are initially established, and leave to the reader the
necessary discriminations. The same principle holds for major
Meredithian concepts, like Egoism, which are occasionally capi-
talized by Meredith to strengthen a rhetorical point.

4

stories in which different readers are pitted against each other, with the Civilized Reader—the sanctioned reader of the comic convention developed, as we shall see, by Fielding—appearing to win out. Again and again, by every device of tone and style, structure and rhythm, by every trick of metaphor and turn of narrative persona, Meredith demonstrates his sensitive and aggressive awareness of the presence at the heart of his creative act of the reader— that formidable, inert piece of wayward human individuality who must be shaped, animated, "ensouled" by the novel.

It is crucial to point out Meredith's creative attention to the reader in his novels because such attention contradicts part of the Meredith Legend, which holds that he despaired of his contemporary readers and proceeded according to his ideal of his art, in lofty disregard of criticism. Meredith did often talk of such despair and such disregard, especially toward the end of his career. The lionized author of the letters and the dinner table conversations came quite close to maintaining Percy Lubbock's definition of the new ideal novelist, one having "the single-minded attitude of the artist before his work, his unqualified homage to it and it alone."[2] The "historical" Meredith often sounds like the ideal Jamesian artist. And yet the implied author of Meredith's novels is so clearly in the presence of his recalcitrant, aggravating, mysterious, and powerfully important reader that one is reminded of Sartre's mystical picture of the reader as the true Creator of the artwork:

> There is no art except by and for others. . . . The literary object, though realized *through* language, is never given *in* language. On the contrary, it is by nature silence and an opponent of the word. Nothing is accomplished if the reader does not put himself from the very beginning and almost without a guide at the height of this silence; if in short, he does not invent it, and does not then place there,

[2] In "Review: The Collected Novels of George Meredith," *Quarterly Review*, 1910, rpt. in *Meredith: The Critical Heritage*, ed. Ioan Williams (London: Routledge and Kegan Paul, 1971), p. 509.

and hold on to, the words and sentences which he awakens.[3]

Meredith's frequent rages at the lack of attention and the lack of "real" criticism of his novels are clearly traceable to a kind of artistic despair and fury that nothing has been accomplished, that the critic has declined the difficult role of reader and so the book has fallen dead, out of Being entirely. On the other hand, while Meredith's reader is certainly invited and meant to work as hard as Sartre's, awakening the words, Meredith does absolutely give his literary object *in* language, testing and twisting that language mercilessly and deliberately to challenge the reader. And he gives his reader not silence in which to place the language of the book, but sound, argument, conflict. For he assumes that the implied author and many of the kinds of readers in his prose audience are in serious conflict over how to regard the literary object.

In the dramatization, the admitting and welcoming of this conflict, Meredith parts from Fielding and others of the English comic tradition of the characterized reader. Fielding, too, interposes that extra action, that attention to the fictional reader and writer, between the man reading and the experiences portrayed, depriving the reader of that silence in which, Sartre says, the reader can really encounter the story. But Fielding seems quite certain what sort of people he means the fictional writer and reader to be, how they are made that way, and why it is a good thing to be a certain sort of Writer and Reader. When we come to look at the process of characterizing the reader in *Tom Jones* more closely, we will see how soothing and confident a hum of voices there is between writer and reader in the interpolated world between the story and the man reading the story, a world that Wayne Booth calls the "subplot" of novels. By Meredith's time many of Fielding's human and

[3] In *What Is Literature?* 1950, trans. as *Literature and Society* by Bernard Frechtman (New York: The Citadel Press, 1962), p. 30.

artistic certainties were fading, and the very act of writing a novel, or of reading one, was becoming an existentially vulnerable, perhaps even morally questionable, act.

It is this latter quality of exhilarated, fascinated, horrified exploration of the crimes and triumphs of being a writer and a reader that is partly responsible for the renewal of the tradition of the characterized reader in contemporary literature. Writers like Barth and Nabokov use it, I think, in a sort of hilarious and grumpy surrender to the convolutions of self-awareness that edify and cripple contemporary man. Meredith could never make such a surrender openly, let alone joyfully. He was, after all, the self-proclaimed champion and fountainhead of "Philosophy in fiction"; his liberal and comic aesthetic called for a writer and a reader to get on top of life, to marshal awareness and self-awareness in orderly patterns, to see life as a whole organism with unity, system, and direction. But this very stance is undercut in several crucial ways in Meredith's novels by portraits of philosophers whom philosophy has made less than human. There was in Meredith a tendency toward the seemingly irresponsible ellipticism of a Barthelme, the sly sleight of personality of a Nabokov, the open play with literary and real worlds of a Borges. I see this tendency—one of the first and most significant appearances of the contemporary "comic" stance—working itself out in Meredith's continuing wrestle with the fictional reader and the philosopher in his novels. This conflict, it is crucial to say, is evident on two levels of his fiction, the level of story and theme and that of "reader-making," the activity of the subplot.

On the level of story, it seems clear that Meredith's fictions were from start to finish governed by a fascination with three ideas or processes (or rather an interlocking matrix of ideas or processes) which he called sentimentalism, egoism, and civilization. All these ideas are evident in each of these novels, but *Sandra Belloni* makes a direct effort to deal with the human consequences of sentimentalism, *The Egoist* with those of egoism, and *One of Our*

7

Conquerors with the philosophical basis of, and flaws in, the idea of civilization. I therefore want to single these novels out for special attention.

Sentimentalism and egoism are Meredith's names for diseases of the human spirit which promote isolation, solitariness. Sentimentalism is man in pleased contemplation of his own states of feeling, and egoism is man bemused by the fact of his own individual being. Both states are unhealthy first because they are unreal, and then because, being unreal, they are destructive. Reality, "comic" reality, is connection, the impingement of one being upon another, the flow of one man's feeling toward another for the sake of the other's response. Denial of this reality on anyone's part brings him destruction by chaining him firmly to abstraction; it also spreads destruction through the whole situation he inhabits, as far as his being impinges, as widely as his feelings touch others. Steps in the direction of abstract idealization (of oneself or of another, it is the same sentimentalism) or of abstract contempt (here again, as demonstrated powerfully in the story of Willoughby Patterne, contempt for others is contempt for oneself) are for Meredith the source of human distress. Since for Meredith reality is connection, integration, since for him the evolutionarian civilization is an organism maturing as its intradependent elements grow and change, this concession to unreality at the individual level is felt as civil and social distress too. Civilization is distorted by sentimentalism and egoism; and then the social distress feeds and confirms unreality back on the personal level.

Meredith has a prescient sense of the inevitability of these temptations into the unreality of overvaluing one's individual states. In fact, he shows a profound insight into the source of the energies drawing man into the unreal. Man, he feels, at his earliest primitive vulnerable stages needed all the dark brutality of egoism, all the blinding brilliance of sentimental, even superstitious, ideal feeling to jolt himself into the long slow journey toward the state of civilization. But the task is different now. Reality itself

8

has changed, become community, civilization, and the self survives or is destroyed now according to the nourishment it receives and gives to others in that context. Men and societies are all still in a semiprimitive state, Meredith observes, and men and societies may both be counted on to move tentatively back and forth to sentimentality or egoism. There are tolerable and intolerable, culpable and nonculpable, surrenders to these unrealities in Meredith's world, and the explorations of sentimentalism in *Sandra Belloni*, of egoism in *The Egoist*, and of civilization in *One of Our Conquerors* show that keen eye for "moral distinctness" that Meredith says distinguishes the comic writer from the satirist.

What is most interesting about these novels for my purpose, however, is that the author plays in the subplot with the temptation that the characters feel in the plot, so that the reader is made to feel these temptations too. For the kinds of sentimentalism and egoism Meredith explores are exactly those subtle kinds of hypnotized self-worship that the civilized sensitive man is prey to and that he may conceal behind the facade of the "philosophic" outlook. In each of these novels the narrative strategy can be seen as a game in which the author and reader meet the same sort of temptation as the characters to "unreality," self-worship, idealization, and contempt. Each time Meredith draws back from the temptation, leaving the civilized reader to find his own way either deeper into unreality, abstraction, superiority, dissociation, or back again to community and comedy—the "centre of the world," as Meredith calls it in *One of Our Conquerors*.

The form of this author-reader game is interestingly different in each of these three novels, which is another reason for their being chosen for study. In *Sandra Belloni* the narrative voice is openly split between two narrative characters who struggle to control the story and the reader's attitude toward it. In *The Egoist* there is one narrative voice, but it creates several sorts of reader attitudes, "looks" on life, characterized as the Comic Spirit, the

9

Comic Muse, the Satiric Imps, and the tone of the book varies among these attitudes. In *One of Our Conquerors* a striking proto-stream-of-consciousness narrative technique enables the narrator's voice to diffuse itself convincingly through many of the characters' looks on life, and allows Meredith to reconcile inside his diffused, enlarged, compassionate implied author the problem of *Richard Feverel*'s Adrian Harley, here restructured, matured, and rounded into the character of the satirist cynic, Colney Durance.

Meredith's last published novel, *The Amazing Marriage*, is at once a summing up and a bursting asunder of Meredith's philosophy, and makes an indispensable final chapter for any study of the artist. In it he returns to the shadowboxing with fever, fate, and philosophy that marked *Richard Feverel*, to the open narrative dualism he experimented with in *Sandra Belloni*, to the examination of the peculiar flaws of the civilized reader, sentimentalism and egoism, to the psychoses, the internal detachments and deaths that are charted in *Sandra Belloni*, *The Egoist*, and *One of Our Conquerors*. In this novel more than any, on the levels both of story and subplot, he finally dramatizes his agonizing conclusion that the shadow, the sickness, the very principle of duality and disintegration is somehow inherent in, coherent with, the truly human integrationist philosophy of fiction and of life.

1. The Reader and the Editor

I T IS EASY, BUT NOT VERY PROFITABLE, TO SEE THE activities of the writer and reader of a work as somehow mutually exclusive—that is, to regard the absolute power over what happens in the communication that is literature as either the writer's or the reader's. The statements of Lubbock, that a work exists solely in the writer's fidelity to his private vision, and of Sartre, that it sleeps in an almost nonexistent state until awakened by the unique touch of each reader's private vision, seem true, but somehow not "the truth." We sense that however flawed, however inevitably "re-made," however elusive the communication, the pivotal fact about literature, especially the novel, is that it unites rather than disjoins. The novel, like all works of art, speaks of many aspects of the real, speaks of everything-at-once if it is a great enough novel, but essentially, when all has been said about the novel's vindication of the individual and its direct address to the private self, we still feel that the novel speaks to community rather than alienation. Most literary theoreticians seek to regard the literary object as appealing from the human individual freedom of the writer to an equally important and respected and necessary freedom in the reader, somehow making the writer and the reader sharers in one continuous freedom, performers of one equal, almost simultaneous co-creating act, rather than as battlers for the title of whom art is *by* and *for*.

When we look at attempts to analyze the writer-reader continuum in prose fiction, a central process seems to stand out. The analyst first breaks down the continuum into a cast of characters, who are in the rhetoric of the analysis "alive" and who act upon each other in a variety of ways. The most pervasive metaphor used in these analyses is "distance"—the fictional reader "stands back from" the action, the fictional writer is "behind" the narrator, the co-creators of the fiction are "above" the characters and their crisis. These are all spatial metaphors, designed to do justice to our sense of a third dimension somehow caught in the regular length and width of the prose line. A human space containing an action is what the rhetoric of these analyses says of the writer-reader continuum; the space provides a stage, a drama, in Wayne Booth's term, a subplot.[1]

Booth's familiar and influential study, *The Rhetoric of Fiction*, provides a continuum of six in the distance between the person who writes and the person who reads, like a cast of six characters in the subplot of novels. Onstage are the narrator, who may be any of a dozen shades of "reliable," and the "reader" or "readers" addressed in the book, who are first of all characters imagined by the narrator. Behind or maybe slightly "above" these are the implied author, whose values, embedded particularly in stylistic choices, govern the book, and the implied reader,

---

[1] Booth uses the term, with quotations, in his discussion (*The Rhetoric of Fiction* [Chicago: The Univ. of Chicago Press, 1961], pp. 213-17) of the narrator-reader relationship in *Tom Jones*, hesitating a bit about extending the meaning of the term: "It may be extravagant to use the term 'subplot' for the story of our relationship with this narrator. Certainly the narrator's 'life' and Tom Jones' life are much less closely parallel than we expect in most plots and subplots. . . . In *Tom Jones* the 'plot' of our relationship with Fielding-as-narrator has no similarity to the story of Tom. . . . Yet somehow a genuine harmony of the two dramatized elements is produced." My own analysis of the subplot of *Tom Jones* departs from Booth's in proposing that there is indeed a similarity in the plot of our relationship with Fielding-as-narrator and the story of Tom. I am therefore emboldened to extend the term still further to suggest that many novels, certainly all those with characterized Writer and Reader, pre-eminently those of Meredith, can be profitably viewed as containing such a linked subplot.

whose assumed and sanctioned values help govern the book *and the choices of style* (this is a particularly important point to remember with Meredith). Beyond these are the historical or "real" writer and the individual reader, whose private vision or world of values is always, Booth says (and I agree), altered or transformed somewhat in the actual act of writing-reading and reading-writing. The action of this subplot of novels, Booth goes on to affirm, is a rhetoric, that is, a persuasion-to-value. But it is a peculiarity of the novel that the writer's act of persuasion is camouflaged to look like the reader's act of discovery. The drama of the novel's subplot chronicles the reader's discovery—in that charged space between the fictional story and his own personality—of values he shares with the writer of the book. Or, more precisely, the subplot reveals the reader's seeming recovery of those shared values from their submersion in the everydayness of his own story. There is drama in the reader's finding of his real self and in the restoration of his freedom to act from his real self without the distractions of his time-bound life.

The disguising of the writer's attempt to persuade as the reader's independent choice would not seem to be an easy trick. It would seem particularly hard to achieve in a novel, because the fictional reader of the novel seems to be clearly distinguished from other generic readers by his painful skepticism toward the "invitation" of the writer of the novel, which is always essentially an invitation to step out of the "audience" of the fiction and join the writer in analysis of it. There are, of course, quite positive, even seductive reasons for accepting the invitation, for to do so is to turn the "audience," with which the reader is at first physically and psychologically continuous, into "society," an abstraction, an object, whose relationship to and implications for himself the reader can mentally manipulate.[2]

---

[2] Raymond Williams (*The English Novel from Dickens to Lawrence* [London: Chatto and Windus, 1970], pp. 11-18) distinguishes between relationship, community, and society, with the first term connoting the acme of personal freedom and involve-

The consequences for a fuller and solider ego experience for the reader are deep and seductive. On the other hand, the dangers of accepting the invitation are correspondingly great, and account for the peculiar skepticism of the reader of the novel.

In the first place, the releasing of the reader's ego, the reader's personality, through individual separation from the "audience" is accompanied by a powerful attraction toward the personality of the writer. Anything strong enough to break the old assumed orientation of the fictional reader within the audience of the fiction threatens to engulf him in a new one prepared by the writer. But the hardening, abstracting, objectifying of audience may also undercut the subjectifying, the independent selfing, of the individual reader in a more subtle and damaging way. For if Marshall McLuhan is right, the real "message" of this archetypal product of the Gutenberg Galaxy, the novel, is in the sinister equation that the mode of printing makes between the values of individuality, mobility, and flexibility, and the more dubious qualities of segmentation, homogeneity, and repeatability. That equation assaults the psyche in ways too deep for defense, but not too deep for anxiety—producing, McLuhan argues, two equal and opposite historical responses by readers to novels. On the one hand, "a basic aspect of any literate audience is its profound acceptance of a passive consumer role in the presence of book or film." On the other, "Western man fought the harder for individuality as he surrendered the idea of

---

ment, and the last connoting (to the individual) the blind, solid, dead, threatening object he may become, the state that threatens him most. It is as if society were history with all the individual personality bleached out, and relationship (sometimes) were simply the naïve exchange of personalities with history left out, and community the middle state where personality and history equally animate the individual. Williams goes on to argue that "the problematic of the knowable community" is more deeply and conveniently etched in the Dickens-to-Lawrence novel "than anywhere else in our recorded experience" (p. 19). But he leaves out Meredith.

unique personal existence," achieving, McLuhan concludes somewhat rhapsodically, "transcendence of the Gutenberg technology at the moment of surrender to it."[3]

In other words, the peculiarity of the act of reading a novel stems from the fact that the novel exists, from its generic beginning, as an invitation delivered in identical form to thousands of individuals, each of whom is simultaneously invited to objectify all the others. A man reading a novel about "society" and the individual is in the Sartrean dilemma of anxious alienation, purchasing his selfhood by the unselfing of the Other, and doomed to suffer the same objectivization from the Other unless he restores subjectivity to the Other, and thus to himself, by an act of his own freedom. Sartre, in his nice awareness of the multiplicity of "reader," points to this radically disturbing quality of the mass-printed word in his discussion of novels in *What is Literature?*: "If you name the behavior of an individual you reveal it to him: he sees himself. And since you are at the same time naming it to all others, he knows that he is seen at the moment he sees himself. After that, how can you expect him to act in the same way?" *(Pp. 12-13.)* The nature and position of the "audience" of the novel, then, is important. The cast in Booth's continuum, his subplot, is missing one set of characters. Crucially present in the reading space somewhere between the individual reader of the novel and the implied reader, the sharer-discoverer of the novel's world of values, is this audience of other individuals, who stand in a challenging or threatening relationship to the reader just as the writer does.[4]

[3] *The Gutenberg Galaxy: The Making of Typographic Man* (Toronto: Univ. of Toronto Press, 1962), pp. 235, 277.

[4] I do not mean to say that the "invitation" of other genres, the drama or the poem for instance, contains no element of this threat, this seeming competition for psychic freedom, for dominance. The Other is present in the drama. But his presence is diluted, scattered in the great physical and psychic independence of his characters, an independence intimately associated with their unembeddedness in narrative. The Other is present in the poem. But his

15

It seems, then, as though the invitation that the novel offers us may contribute not to community but to separateness. The novel is addressed to its reader not as man but precisely as he differs from men—and he is invited and assumed to differ from "men" really rather as the writer differs. Thus there is a peculiar rhetorical tension in the novel; it is much stronger, of course, in novels where the conflict is pointed up by characterized readers and writers, but it is present to some degree in any novel. The audience, man, becomes men, an abstract object to be studied. On the one hand, this rhetoric invites the fictional reader to become an independent, creative personality in the act of literature. On the other, he leaves the audience only to answer an invitation from the writer that clearly reads "Be yourself—which is *me*," and that is a threat to the reader's independence. And so the act of leaving audience, of helping the writer to transform it into "society," becomes both indispensable and perilous to the reader. The invitation, especially where the subplot is supplied with characterized reader and writer, will have its air of pugnacious defensiveness. The reader's response, the identification-with-Writer, will be tentative, and slightly hostile.

The subplot of the novel, then, is distinguished by three presences, in all cases implied, to recall Booth's terminology, but in many cases actually characterized, given typical personalities. These are the reader, who is conceived in the traditional English comic novel as having a certain set of traits which make me call him the civilized reader; the writer, whose stance I will call for reasons to be discussed later that of an editor; and the readers, or the audience, the implied audience of the work whom the civilized reader is called on to characterize as "society" or an abstract "them." A tension all along the shifting axis between the man who wrote and the man who reads resolves itself into

---

presence is rendered less threatening by his vulnerability, or his indifference. His back is partly turned. Poetry, in Mill's great phrase, seems not heard but overheard.

16

that complication of the strategy of presentation in the form of multiple frames, angles of vision, masks, roles, inversions, subversions, diversions, which is—beyond all variety of peculiarities in characterization or description or action—the quintessential quality called novelistic.

I. The Civilized Reader

If the novel has a generic subplot complete with characters, then we may legitimately explore the possibility of its having a generic theme, one that emerges precisely from this novelistic complicating of the strategy of presentation, this engaging of the fictional reader in more or less covert "game" relationships with the writer. It is the child-like hide-and-seek in the traditional subplot for which, in his suavely petitioning way, Thackeray speaks at the end of *Vanity Fair*: "Which of us has his desire, or having it, is satisfied?—Come, children, let us shut up the box and the puppets, for our play is played out." My feeling is that the typical theme of the novel's subplot is the education and civilizing of the reader, and that in the teacher-writer's bag of tools games-playing has as significant a use as instruction. All major fictions in the tradition of the characterized reader partake of this manipulated, game-like quality, including those whose authors claimed, or had claimed for them, the distinction of at last writing "novels for grownup people."

The phrase is used by Virginia Woolf of George Eliot,[5] and it points to one of the most interesting areas of crisis in the history of the novel, that period in the last third of the nineteenth century when the novelists first began to feel the popular audience, democracy's children, moving out from under them. The children seemed to be following the Pied Piper of romance, of adventure, of the happy ending, while to write for the grownups was to question,

[5] In her respectful and convincing essay "George Eliot," *The Common Reader* (New York: Harcourt, Brace and Co., 1925), p. 237.

reflect, explore the failures and defeats of the spirit, and hold out the narrower promise of "psychological" happy endings, the achievement of a modest understanding or the acceptance of the basically incomprehensible. To continue his teaching function, the novelist either had to abandon that audience in the childhood of readership, or to abandon the concept of a real, present, common public, or to make new, sometimes clumsy adjustments to those paradigm writer-reader relationships evolved in what was then the central tradition of the English novel, the tradition of the characterized reader, which is almost the same as to say, of the "comic" novel.

Among the novelists consciously writing for adult people in that period was George Meredith. His first mature and perhaps best-known work, *The Ordeal of Richard Feverel*, was published in 1859, a year called *annus mirabilis* by more than one critic because in *Feverel* and *Adam Bede*, not to mention Darwin's *Origin of Species* and Mill's *On Liberty*, they find a new maturity of outlook for the maturing race of readers. *Feverel* was not Meredith's first novel, however, but his third. If *Feverel* is characteristically Meredithian in its serious exploration of neurosis, its complicated syntax, and the Chinese-box-intricacy of its structure, *The Shaving of Shagpat*, his first novel, is equally Meredithian in its love of the romantic action tale, and most of all in its confident, childlike delight in its own original voice. *Shagpat* was written with a precocious and genuine glee upon the model of the *Arabian Nights* and published in 1855 when Meredith was twenty-seven, before the trials of a mismated marriage and an equivocal reception as a poet and writer had turned him into a professional grown-up. After *Feverel* he wrote no more fantasies; rather he turned an adept psychologist's eye on the fantasies of his characters, and attempted to teach the reader of his novels the methods by which a civilized man or woman abandons or integrates those fantasies in an adult life, and the methods by which a civilized reader abandons or reforms the tastes he acquired in his reading childhood. But the fantasies examined in Meredith's novels live because the love of the fantastic remained alive in the brain of the psychological novelist. In the typical teacher-author of Meredith's works we can sense the instructively brilliant presence of the child, distracting but often very effective as pedagogue for the reader.

The new Meredith, however, officially favored the sophisticated man, the civilized reader, the balanced, judicious temperament. The encomium he sought, as well as the place in the dividing stream of the serious and the popular novel he appeared to seek, is evident in the response to *The Egoist* of another civilized reader, Virginia Woolf: "Meredith pays us a supreme compliment to which we as novel readers are little accustomed. We are civilised people, he seems to say, watching the comedy of human relations together. . . . He imagines us capable of disinterested curiosity in the behaviour of our kind."[6]

This statement reads rather as though this cozy partnership of "civilised people" were an invention of the late nineteenth-century psychological novelists. It was not, in fact. The theme of the traditional novel's subplot from the beginning was precisely the education, the raising up, of the civilized reader. The subplot, as well as the plot of many of the most influential novels in the English tradition, can profitably be looked at as a *Bildungsroman*. Meredith did not invent the convention of the civilized reader; he inherited it, used it brilliantly, and modified it according to his rising doubts about the human value of "disinterested curiosity." He inherited this particular convention of reader-education, reader-creating, from Fielding, whose subplot in *Tom Jones* I take to be the paradigm of all subplots that deserve to be called novelistic, the center of the genre that all novels echo even as they move away from it. Fielding's subplot is basic to the convention, and an understanding of its action and its theme is basic to an understanding of Meredith's stance toward his Reader.

[6] "The Novels of George Meredith," *The Second Common Reader* (New York: Harcourt, Brace and Co., 1932), p. 253.

19

Bernard Bergonzi usefully reminds us that the novel was distinguished at its origin precisely by a sense of freedom from "genre" and from established literary conventions generally,[7] a fact quite evident in *Tom Jones*, where the display and the validation of that freedom is one of the main subjects of the novel. Whatever else may be said of Fielding's famous Prefatory Chapters, it is clear that they serve to focus attention on his pugnacious defensiveness about the seeming circularity of the novel's subject: novels are about the writing and reading of novels.[8] This last is important. If Fielding's chapters insist that the writer be allowed freedom from conventions, they insist at least as strongly that the reader free himself from conventions, habits, all prejudgments whatever, and read each book as a new creation with a unique design. The describing, perfecting, and legitimizing of this freedom is one of Fielding's central concerns in *Tom Jones*. Looked at as an allegory for human action, as a lesson about life, writing-reading a novel is in fact Fielding's major concern there. For the villain of the piece, whether his name is Blifil or Square or Thwackum, is precisely "the clerk who began to invade the power and assume the dignity of his master," the men "of shallow capacities who easily mistake mere form for substance," the small spirit whose mission is to fetter the large of heart and great of spirit by means of "rules and laws which have not the least foundation in truth or nature, and which commonly have no other pur-

[7] *The Situation of the Novel* (London: Macmillan, 1970). He adds disapprovingly: "In the last few decades the novel has, I think, abandoned freedom for genre. . . . The categories of recent American fiction suggest a truly neo-classical strictness and diversity of genres: the Negro novel, the Jewish novel, the depression novel, the beat novel, the campus novel" (p. 20).

[8] Obviously, I do not mean here simply the deliberate position taken in Gide's *The Counterfeiters*, Mann's *Death in Venice*, Joyce's *Portrait of the Artist as a Young Man*, or Meredith's *Diana of the Crossways*. I mean it also in the wider sense implied in the remark of a teacher of mine that *Emma* is about how Emma Woodhouse learned to stop writing bad novels and start writing good ones.

pose than to curb and restrain genius"[9]—in a word, the "critic." All these phrases describe one of Fielding's major subplot characters, the critic; the action of his paradigm subplot, as in many Meredith novels, is a war between writer and critic for the allegiance of reader among readers. The translation of this action into terms of plot is obvious. Tom has a kind of genius for humane contact which is threatened by the rules-as-traps set by small-minded or false-minded men. He is also confronted with the variousness, the unpredictability, and the sheer energy of his own nature. The task as the fictional writer sees it is for Tom to find and live the laws of his nature, to arrive at his own natural prudence, while avoiding the nets that the laws of other men's natures would fling over him—or rather, the laws that the shallow-minded clerks have, with numerous errata and great misemphasis, transcribed from observing other men's natures.

If we consider, for a moment, that the fictional writer, reader, and critic in the subplot of *Tom Jones* are the types of writer, reader, and audience in the traditional subplot of the novel, then we will look for a controlled and self-conscious plenitude in Fielding's writer, a not fully controlled nor yet fully discovered or educated plenitude in his reader, and a sort of blind, instinctual stinginess in his critic. These qualities will reflect the dynamic relationship among the triad. They reflect the purposeful capaciousness of self out of which the invitation of art comes, the potential, educable capaciousness of self to which the invitation is always addressed, and the sort of blind, instinctual state of arrested growth, anti-education, petrifaction, solidity-with-audience, in the light of the reader's assumed attachment to which the invitation of the novel takes place.

The plenitude of Fielding's writer is expressed in a many-sided narrator whose basic manifestations are, briefly, the entertainer, the historian, and the epic poet. All

[9] All quotations from *Tom Jones* are from the Penguin edition, ed. R.F.C. Mutter (Harmondsworth, Middlesex, England: Penguin Books Ltd., 1966). This one is from bk. v, ch. 1.

three are personae solid enough to receive capitalization several times in the novel, although the entertainer—who interestingly has always been the self-aspect that novelists live with most uncomfortably—appears in three subroles, discernible as innkeeper, public conveyance traveler, and drama director. The entertainer-innkeeper calls attention to the hard cash facts of the writing-reading relationship: "An author ought to consider himself, not as a gentleman, who gives a private or eleemosynary treat, but rather as one who keeps a public ordinary at which all persons are welcome for their money. . . . Men who pay for what they eat will insist on gratifying their palates" *(bk.* i, *ch. 1).* The entertainer-traveler calls attention to the sort of undifferentiated simple-minded human warmth of the novel relationship: "As we have therefore travelled together through so many pages, let us behave to one another like fellow-travellers on a stage coach who have passed several days in the company of one another and who, not withstanding any bickerings or little animosities which may have occurred on the road, generally make up all at last" *(bk.* xviii, *ch. 1).* The entertainer-drama director calls attention to the minor errors of communication that may prevail in a novel, even among fellow travelers: "I ask pardon for this short appearance, by way of chorus, on the stage. It is in reality for my own sake, that while I am discovering the rocks on which innocence and goodness often split, I may not be misunderstood to recommend the very means to my worthy readers by which I intend to shew them they will be undone. And this, since I could not prevail on any of my actors to speak, I was obliged to declare myself" *(bk.* iii, *ch. 7).*

The two other aspects of the narrator are the historian and the epic poet, writers-within-the-writer, subauthors, whose ethical and stylistic concerns, fussily illustrated time and again, are narrowly generic. The crucial point to note in the play of these two writing selves is that invariably they are dramatized as being controlled by—*not* manipulated by—a larger, wider, freer, writing self whose freedom is expressed by simultaneous drives towards simplicity of expression and complexity of feeling. Thus epic poet is forever tripping over his rhetoric, but not before its uses as well as its dangers can be shown:

> Now the little trembling hare, whom the dread of all her numerous enemies, and chiefly of that cunning, cruel, carnivorous animal, man, had confined all the day to her lurking place, sports wantonly o'er the lawns: now on some hollow tree the owl, shrill chorister of the night, hoots forth notes which might charm some modern connoisseurs in music: now in the imagination of the half-drunk clown, as he staggers through the churchyard, or rather charnel-yard, to his home, fear paints the bloody hobgoblin: now thieves and ruffians are awake and honest watchmen fast asleep: in plain English, it was now midnight. . . . *(bk.* x, *ch. 2)*

The historian, with his pedantic, ridiculous, and ambiguously quite useful insistence on "the facts"—"It is our province to relate facts, and we shall leave causes to persons of much higher genius" *(bk.* ii, *ch. 4)*—sets up for the larger, controlling writing self the whole problem of the transformation of "the facts" into "the truth" which properly constitutes that "realism" which is another peculiarly novelistic quality. The search for "the truth" is "novelistic" when it is rendered, not simply asserted, in terms of the multitude of perceiving selves in the seeker and in his effort to align and shape these perceivers into a whole, steady vision.

If this novelistic sensitivity to the multiplicity of perceivers obtains with respect to the implied writer of a work, it obtains even more with respect to the implied reader, who is quite clearly portrayed in Fielding's novel as a man living among men, women, fox-hunters, lovers, gourmands, servants, and university graduates. The presence of this audience of readers, with these kinds of information and attitudes, is not simply implied by virtue of the scenes and settings of the novel; it is dramatized, constantly alluded to, in ways that make apparent the writer's

sense of his work as immersed in a real sea of individuals—
"my worthy readers . . . my fair readers . . . you men of
intrigue." Indeed, many of Fielding's most telling effects
depend exactly on our sense of others, of individuals half-
known, half-understood, reading the novel at the same
time as we are. Sophia is "accidentally" following Tom
through inns on his way to London, and the narrator comments: "Partridge, to use the Squire's expression, left everywhere a strong scent behind him, and he doubted not
in the least but Sophia travelled, or as he phrased it, ran,
the same way. He used indeed a very coarse expression
which need not be inserted here, as fox hunters, who alone
would understand it, will easily suggest it to themselves"
(bk. x, *ch. 9).* And a hundred pairs of ears strain to catch
the gamy expression just uttered, barely audibly on a
choke of laughter, somewhere in the audience of the novel.

Thus Fielding establishes in his subplot the message of
the medium of the print-novel: like a hundred coughs in
a dark room, the picking out of different readers by Fielding reveals to the fictional reader that he is not alone, that
he is one of many minds absorbing and recasting the book,
minds all mysterious and dark and perhaps threatening in
their homogeneous lack of identity until the author lights
them up by reference to individual characteristics. The
manner of the addresses to various readers anticipates the
reader's wish to identify and differentiate himself, and it
provides as well the way of doing so—by measuring himself, favorably, against certain groups of readers whom the
author alludes to unfavorably and whom he lights up lurid-
ly next to the Reader.

Perhaps the most memorable of such readers, lighted up
again and again throughout *Tom Jones,* are those whose
attitude toward life—as well as toward novels—is governed strictly by appetite. Fielding muses to these readers,
"love may probably, in your opinion, very greatly resemble
a dish of soup, or a sir-loin of roast-beef" *(bk.* i, *ch. 1).*
This gourmandizing reading attitude is also greatly ex-

ploited by Meredith, who is, however, careful to point out that a realistic appreciation of the sensual basis of all perception, even of all aspiration, is a good basis for a reader to build a philosophy on, and for a writer to build a novel on—and for a teacher to build a lesson on. Sensual appetite is only damned by these writers when it is the whole form of a character rather than his foundation: Blifil's attitude toward Sophia, resembling that of "an epicure for an ortolan," is damning not because of its sensuality but because of its narrowness, its diminishment of person, its clerkly stinginess.

The group of readers from whom the fictional reader of *Tom Jones* is urged strenuously and ominously and pre-eminently to differentiate himself is the group of critics. The critic, we recall, is the short-sighted, dull-brained, heavy-handed clerk who copies, inaccurately, the rules genius makes for itself and then turns those rules into straitjackets for the next generation of geniuses. The critic is irretrievably small-minded; impotent himself, he would master and harass the fecund with the limitations of the past.[10] This person, this "little reptile of a critic," may be next to us in the audience of the fiction. He may *be* us: "those readers who are of the same complexion with [Tom] will perhaps think this short chapter contains abundance of matter; while others may probably wish, short as it is, that it had been totally spared as impertinent to the main design" *(bk.* xv, *ch. 8).* But these "others" are clearly in the wrong, for Fielding warned critics "not too hastily to condemn any of the incidents in our history as impertinent

[10] One of the more interesting allusions to the essential impotence of the Critic is in Fielding's conviction, which novelist after novelist repeats, including Meredith, that the novel will seed responses in posterity, while criticism has no sons and dies in the winds of the times. This is partly a reference to the immortality of the printed book and the mortality of journalism, to which Fielding alludes in bk. xviii, ch. 1: "However short the period may be of my own performances, they will probably outlive their own infirm author, and the weakly productions of his abusive contemporaries."

and foreign to our main design, because thou dost not immediately conceive in what manner such incident may conduce to that design" *(bk. x, ch. 1).*

This warning of Fielding's, his claim to total freedom for the novelist to make up his own design, his claim that nothing is necessarily impertinent or foreign to the novel so long as the designer holds it to be part of his design, is crucial to an understanding of Meredith's fictions. Critics who note, either with horror or with glee, that Meredith "introduced" poetry into the novel, or "added" philosophy to its concerns, or "superimposed" Welsh cadences or French abstractions or German locutions upon his Anglo-Saxon would do well to remember how close Meredith was to Fielding in his assumption that the novel was the genre of freedom-from-genre. My main impulse is to look at Meredith as one of the first of the "moderns," but in this respect it is interesting to view him as the last of the eighteenth-century *enfants terribles* of the new form, the precocious designers in the childhood of the genre. That is how Percy Lubbock saw him. Lubbock's classic and perceptive review of Meredith's collected works in 1910 began as an elegy not for a man but for an age of the novel, the age of freedom:

> Fiction must follow, and is already following, the line of development that carries it from its first expansive thoughtlessness to self-conscious deliberation. It must run its course; like other forms of art it must lose certain qualities and assume others; it must submit to maturity and make the best of it without trying to reproduce the essentially youthful graces of its past. It must pay the penalty of its prolonged predominance by learning to "know itself" and its principles. Such a process implies loss in a hundred ways, loss perhaps of the very qualities for which we most incline to value the art, but if the sacrifice is inevitable, it is only the sharper challenge to the novelist. *(Critical Heritage, p. 503)*

The reader in Fielding's paradigm subplot here would inevitably see such a statement as "clerkly" in the extreme, its profound rhetoric of penalty, loss, and submission merely an envious pruning and confiscation of genius by one who can no longer achieve or even appreciate the free graces of youth. The reader in *Tom Jones* cannot but know that maturity beckons, and is inevitable. But he will have learned in his reading that maturity is not only inevitable, but desirable, and desirable precisely because it involves not loss but acquisition—the acquiring of that purposeful freedom of the designer which the writer of *Tom Jones* has claimed both for himself and for the reader. In a sense, he has first created it in the reader he creates, and then claimed it for himself from that reader. By connecting this theme of maturity as freedom in the subplot with the education of Tom Jones in the plot, Fielding has proposed to us the lesson on the human alignment of values he wants to remain embedded when we turn from our existence as his fictional reader back to our own stories: "If we judge according to the sentiments of some critics, and some Christians, no author will be saved in this world, and no man in the next" *(bk.* XI, *ch. 1)*.

Thus Fielding's reader discovers himself to be both mature and free—freedom, it is proposed, is at both ends of growth. But what is the nature of this mature freedom? What sort of persons, implied writer and implied reader, are created to find themselves in the field of this freedom? "Civilized people," to use Virginia Woolf's phrase, capacious of spirit, benign, tolerantly full of "disinterested curiosity" in the behavior of the not-so-civilized, readers who have been pleasantly breathed, not winded, by the mental exercise involved in the withdrawal from audience, from "readers," which parallels the withdrawal from story that has always been inherent in the novel and openly so in the comic novel. "Gallant squires, have amongst you," is the spirited opening of one of the earliest novels, Nashe's *The Unfortunate Traveller* (1594), "A mumchance I mean not . . . but a *novus, nova, novum,* which is, in English, news of the maker." There we have the novel, not simply "the news," but news of the maker, not simply story, but

27

covert instructions on how to make, and how to take, the story. Since the reader is co-maker of the news, it is of himself that he learns. What he learns is that he is a new man, a novel man, an evolving human being risen out of mass into individual, out of story into story-making, out of action into reflecting about action, out of audience into reader—out of barbarism into civilization, says George Meredith quite directly in his "Essay on Comedy": "A perception of the Comic Spirit gives high fellowship. You become a citizen of a selecter world, the highest we know of in connection with our old world. Look there for your unchallengeable upper class! You feel that you are one of this our civilized community, that you cannot escape from it, and would not if you could" *(p. 48).*[11]

That is what you learn of yourself, reader of the novel— so Meredith says, so Fielding believes. You learn that your freedom consists of your civilized capacity for the reading of life, lessons for which are available in the proper reading of books:

> The chief consideration for us is, what particular practice of Art in letters is the best for the perusal of the Book of our common wisdom. . . . Shall we read it by the watchmaker's eye in luminous rings eruptive of the infinitesimal, or pointed with examples and types under the broad Alpine survey of the spirit born of our united social intelligence, which is the Comic Spirit? Wise men say the latter. *(The Egoist, i, 3)*

Meredith seeks to unite fictional writer and reader in the "broad Alpine survey" of the comic perception or reading of life, to bring you and me to the mature freedom of the civilized reader in that unchallengeable upper class. He

[11] All references to Meredith's works are to *The Works of George Meredith: Memorial Edition*, 27 vols. (New York: Charles Scribner's Sons, 1910-11), especially vols. XXIII, *An Essay on Comedy and on the Uses of the Comic Spirit*, XVI, *Diana of the Crossways*, II, *The Ordeal of Richard Feverel*, III and IV, *Sandra Belloni*, XIII and XIV, *The Egoist*, XVII, *One of Our Conquerors*, and XIX, *The Amazing Marriage*.

exploits this inherited and distinguishing convention of the novel matchlessly, making the action of his subplots, like Fielding's, the education of the civilized reader. But he is not always comfortable with this convention. For the smooth impregnable Alpine profile of the civilized reader harbors a flaw. He may be the hero of the subplot, but like all heroes he is prone to pride, and the particular brand of hubris that waits for the civilized reader, the man singled out from audience, from society, by his intelligent response to the novel's value world, is contempt for the classes of readers he has just left. It is a vice that Meredith calls the original sin of the Comedian; it involves an immediate fall from comic grace into "satire." Satire is out of place in "this our civilized community" because it paralyzes action, it teaches nothing. But a form of contempt enters even this "selecter world," and as we watch Meredith play with it, struggle with it, sidestep it, sometimes fall into it, we shall have occasion to recall that strange wayward flutter in the center of his most confident assertion of the convention of the civilized reader: "You feel that you are one of this our civilized community, that *you cannot escape from it*, and would not if you could" (italics mine).

II. The Editor

As the hero of the *Bildungsroman* of the novel's subplot, the civilized reader is seen by writers, especially those of the comic tradition, as having to grow "up" not only out of the general prose audience of readers, but also out of his attachment to what the novel clearly implies is the childhood of narrative, the tale. He also has to control or sublimate his adolescent urges to lyricism or historicism. We have seen in Fielding's subplot for *Tom Jones* the self-conscious freedom with which the novel established itself as an attack form, attacking established modes like the history, the epic, the drama, even the romance by subsuming them, turning the old media, or "environments" in McLuhan's terminology, into the content of the new; turn-

29

ing the makers of the old forms, the historian and the epic writer of *Tom Jones*, into the characters of the new form. The novel's equivocal fame as a jackdaw genre results from this curious fact, that the forms attacked and seemingly discarded by grownup writer and matured and civilized reader are in some transformed way always crucially present in and necessary to the novel.[12]

The germ of any narrative is the tale, the action, and since the tale is present in the novel the novel has always within it a struggling element of the romance. The teller of the tale is also essential to narrative, and this element of voice, of temperament, of individual bias is present in the novel too. But the tale and the teller are distinguished in the form of narrative called the novel by their intimate relationship with language-as-written rather than with language-as-spoken or sung. Where in narrative proper the tale exists as speech and the telling is shaped by a second speaking, in the novel the tale, the germ of story, quite often exists as written language. The teller's role, and his problem, is that of a reader-translator of that written language, a second writer, a re-writer, in fact, an editor. The first reader in the novel is the novelist himself; the novel is the result of a reading on the part of the teller of the tale. An act of reading had somehow to take place in the writer before the novel could be written. Recall, for instance, the crucial narrative "conceit," or structural metaphor, which governs perhaps the first and most influential novel in this tradition, *Don Quixote*:

> I was standing one day in the Alcana, or marketplace, of Toledo, when a lad came up to sell some old notebooks and other paper to a silk weaver who was there. As I am

[12] David I. Grossvogel (*The Limits of the Novel: Evolutions of a Form from Chaucer to Robbe-Grillet* [Ithaca: Cornell Univ. Press, 1968]) uses this quality to define "the novel," sweeping in Chaucer's *Troilus and Criseyde*, among others: "In creating out of the formal structure of this romance an antiromance, [Chaucer] anticipates his reader in his withdrawal so as to use that very withdrawal as a new form of involvement" (p. 73).

30

extremely fond of reading anything, even though it be but the scraps of paper in the streets, I followed my natural inclination and took one of the books, whereupon I at once perceived that it was written in characters which I recognized as Arabic. I recognized them, but reading them was another thing. . . .[13]

Here in Cervantes' characterization of the author as a young reader is what I take to be the central narrative conceit of the traditional novel. At the heart of the novel the tale is embedded as the Book, the notebooks and scraps of paper picked up in the marketplace. Recognizable but not easily *readable*, expressed in written language and organized as a book yet basically unsophisticated, mysterious, needing reorganization and editing, the tale that forms the germ of the novel exists to be read, and Cervantes the editor warns his reader over and over that reading a book is a dangerous business. There is life and truth, experience, reality, *in* the Book, that is, in the tale, but the expression of that reality in language is not fully trustworthy, not fully intelligible. The reader has to fill in gaps, disregard obvious errors in fact, speculate about opinions, compensate for the human bias in Cid Hamete Benengeli's history. The Book that the novelist finds in the marketplace on mysterious scraps of paper calls out to him to be translated, interpreted, re-created, tamed, and balanced by a matured mind. It is a hot medium crying out for the cooling apparatus of footnotes, interpolations, prefaces, chapter titles, marginal white space[14]—the whole mosaic of print technology under

[13] *Don Quixote*, in *The Portable Cervantes*, ed. Samuel Putnam (New York: The Viking Press, 1949), ch. 9, "The Second Sally," p. 122.

[14] Cervantes has a splendid little parable on the novel as marginal note in the chapter "Second Sally": the author asks an Arab speaker to look at one of the notebooks, and

he opened it in the middle and began reading and at once fell to laughing. When I asked him what the cause of his laughter was, he replied that it was a note which had been written in the margin. I besought him to tell me the content of the note, whose aegis the entirely new role of the editor came into the gallery of the characters of literature. The editor is the character in whom the interdependence of reading and writing is seen, in whom the two roles are fused to become that of "novelist."

Here we lay another basis for the strange contrariness of the writer-reader-audience relationship in the novel. What is in fact dramatized in the novel of this tradition started by Cervantes is the enthusiastic but thoughtful response to the written word: a fundamental act of the genre for the writer too is not writing but reading. From Malory's retouching of "the French book" and Defoe's edition of Moll's biography to Richardson's compilation of Clarissa's letters, from Carlyle's translations of Teufelsdrockh and Monk Jocelyn and Meredith's expurgation of the Book of Egoism to Nabokov's marginal notes on Kinbote on Shade and Barth's memo on Publishers ABCD on Johnbarth on Giles, Stockton—all up and down this tradition the message of the medium is "here is how to read the Book." Writer and reader theoretically start out equal before the Book, but the writer found it first, and has risen from reader to editor. The Book was already a reading of life, the novel is a revision of it by the editor, and the civilized reader he creates in the novel is revising the revision according to the editor's guidance. Now, is this process of revision distancing the life and truth originally in the Book? Or is it somehow correcting the original bias of the Book by passing it through various analytic minds, thus bringing out its original life and truth? Or is the act of revising, of following the analysis of another mind, first submitting to it, and then challenging it, of watching both in the editor and in ourselves the very process of analysis, of enthusiasm being tempered by thought—is this act of

---

and he, laughing still, went on, "As I told you, it is something in the margin here: 'This Dulcinea del Toboso, so often referred to, is said to have been the best hand at salting pigs in all La Mancha' " (p. 123).

reading, that is to say, the very aspect of life and truth the novel intends to explore and convey?

The latter, I would say. The novel explores and criticizes, even while it promotes and even preaches, the new truth about man's life in the Gutenberg Age: he is, and he should be, a reader. The novelist-editor exemplifies the dangers of readerhood even while he draws the individual into that mode of being. For it is of the essence of editor to be mistrusted. When Cervantes and Defoe and Richardson took on that fictional title they used as its basis the real position of editor just becoming important in civilization. An editor has a bifocal vision of art not simply as intuition-expression (the term is, of course, Croce's), but as intuition-expression-communication. For Croce the work of art does not exist until it has made itself real and physical; as for Lubbock it exists while the artist-craftsman is forging it in homage to the intuition he has had. But for Sartre, and I think for Meredith, the work of art has only marginal and dead existence until "something has been accomplished" through a "reading" of it. Likewise, the novelist-editor holds, without cynicism if he is truly an artist, an aesthetic of market in whose terms the unread or unreadable masterpiece is a contradiction verging on an abomination; in these terms the reading is all-important, the accomplishing or co-creating of the novel by the reader being crucial to the existence of the novel.

The question is what is to be accomplished by the reader? Or indeed what can possibly be accomplished in a revision of a revision of the Book? The Book is Cid Hamete Benengeli's intuition-expression, but that is lost to us, altered forever by "Cervantes'" reading. Receiving the altered Book from the novelist-editor for its second reading, a second reading which is in fact several hundred simultaneous readings, the reader may be forgiven for feeling uneasily the vulnerability of the Book itself, let alone the Book's truth or life, to the editor, to himself, to other readers. The touch of mind, of human attention, has already shivered the fragile object, the original intuition, into splinters. The splinters reform obligingly, with untrustworthy solidity, into patterns differently solid in each reading, as if the Book, containing the fragments of the first intuition, were a kaleidoscope. That intuition, that truth of life, reality, experience, being, primary intuition— whatever one takes to be the ground of life and art—seems not solid, not ground at all, but rather, to move to another important metaphor in the criticism of art and life, sea, shifting and heaving, energetic but formless.

The metaphor is Sartre's, and with it he launches one of the most interesting and important of modern attacks upon the tradition of the comic English novel, and especially upon its subplot character, the editor. Since Meredith uses this character directly or indirectly in most of his work, he is vulnerable to Sartre's criticism, and, since much of my reading of Meredith is based on the assumption that Meredith in fact does in his own way what Sartre accuses the writers in this tradition of not doing, it seems appropriate to comment on Sartre's criticism.

For Sartre, the fact of existence is terrifying and the process of existing authentically is most difficult. The basic condition of human existence is "nausea," a sort of threatened sensitivity to the capricious, ferocious roll and swell of the energies of being that may leave one emptied at any moment. The basic condition of social existence stems from this and is described as "alienation," the result of the irresistible rush of one's being, one's subjectivity, toward the vacuum of the gaze of the Other, since human existence is subject to the same dreadful contingency and formless sealike rolling and oozing as all existence. From such a sense of "the truth," Sartre builds both his philosophy and his aesthetic; any type of art that denies or ignores this truth and its terror betrays life, and what it accomplishes is illusion and falsehood.

Not really surprisingly, Sartre's most famous expression-communication of this intuition is a novel, whose hero, Roquentin, is driven back and back through the veils of perception and the harder but ultimately quite breakable

forms of literature and art until he finally confronts existence as a "paste . . . soft, monstrous masses, all in dis-
order."[15] At the edge of madness his hero turns upon "existence," the unbearable flux and roll of living, "this time
in which the world has fallen" *(p. 34)*, with the intention
of driving it out of himself, purifying himself of the two
elements of "living," contingency and superfluity, which
the billows of existence continuously roll through him. He
wants the silence, the spareness, the solidity, the invulnerable "quidditas" of the "to be" as an end to the absurdities,
the veritable sickness, of existence. But "to be" is really to
"have been," as Roquentin muses about himself early in
the novel: "he tried to live his own life as if he were telling
a story. But you have to choose, live or tell. . . . I wanted
the moments of my life to follow and order themselves like
those of a life remembered" *(p. 58)*. In the end Roquentin
establishes an aesthetic that makes the novel the "to be" of
life, the fixed point where the individual settles down out
of time and is strained out of existence into essence. He
looks forward to his own achievement of this quidditas
through the novel he plans to write.

We must align this rather anticlimactic and solipsistic
aesthetic with Sartre's passionate defense in *What is Literature?* of a literature *engagé*, deeply committed to the communication bands of the intuition-expression-communication spectrum, in order to see what it means for the position
of the editor in the novel: "The writer has chosen to reveal
the world and particularly to reveal man to other men so
that the latter may assume full responsibility before the
object which has thus been laid bare. . . . The function of
the writer is to act in such a way that nobody can be ig-
norant of the world and that nobody may say that he is
innocent of what it is all about" *(p. 14)*. We must also align
it with his powerful appreciation of the activity of reading
quoted above, of reading as directed creation: "There is no
art except for and by others. . . . The literary object,

[15] *Nausea*, trans. L. Alexander (London: Purnell and Sons, Ltd.,
1949), p. 171.

though realized *through* language, is never given *in* language. On the contrary, it is by nature silence and an opponent of the word. . . . Nothing is accomplished if the reader does not put himself from the very beginning and almost without a guide at the height of this silence; if, in short, he does not invent it, and does not then place there, and hold on to, the words and sentences which he awakens" *(p. 30).* In this alignment it seems to me that W. J. Harvey is right when he argues that the autonomy aesthetic of Roquentin, like that of Stephen Dedalus, is "a still imperfect partial notion . . . a fresh point of departure,"[16] the resting place of the character, not of the fictional writer nor of the reader, of Sartre's novel. Sartre's own aesthetic seems rather to position the work of art, and above all the literary object, as the very expression and arousal of the nausea of existence, where the reader is forced to "invent a silence" to dispel the howling winds of Time amidst which he lives his own story, and then is forced to "hold on to" the words and sentences given him out of the queasy ebb and swell of language. A victory in such an enterprise does have something of the heroic about it. Sartre's phenomenology of the creating of the literary object celebrates the reader in images evocative of what I take to be Cervantes' archetypal portrait of the progenitor of the novel, man in the screaming marketplace irresistibly drawn to the Book and simultaneously faced with the task of an editor-translator: "I recognized [the characters], but reading them was another thing."

The reader-hero Sartre is describing here is the reader of the *novel*; essentially what I am trying to do is extend his description to the reader of the Book at the heart of the novel, to the reader of the tale, who, having read it, becomes its editor, the writer of the novel. His struggle with the Book, the material of the story and the primary intuition it contains, has been just as difficult as Sartre's reader's, and it was of the same order: an attempt to sup-

[16] *Character and the Novel* (Ithaca, N.Y.: Cornell Univ. Press, 1965), p. 158.

press the roaring of his own Time, his own tale, long enough for primary intuition, noncontingent truth, to enter his hard-won silence and take shape as words and sentences. This struggle may take place in the mind of every writer; it may be evident to all his biographers. But for Sartre unless the struggle is evident in the work of art itself, unless the contingency, the flux, the Nauseating unsettledness of existence is actually dramatically present, the work of art is a betrayal of truth.

The traditional comic English novel is guilty of this betrayal, Sartre continues, a double betrayal because it perpetrated the falsehood of tranquillity, absoluteness, the noncontingency of existence right at the crucial period of the forming of the bourgeoisie and hence became its tool, promoting the editing or reading of experience rather than experiencing itself; providing in the morally stable, morally certain editor-novelist the very type of the self-satisfied burgher; and seducing the common people into admiring and emulating his confident, rational, compassionate, non-mystical, anti-"revolutionary" liberalism. This technique was a betrayal, Sartre charges, of the "integrating and militant" function of literature in society and consisted in this technical distancing of story from narration, of experience from analysis, of terrifying existence from blandly coherent assimilation of existence that I have described as the distinction of the editor's novel from the Book.

Sartre's sense of the "illegitimacy" of the traditional novel is based first of all on his view that that distance is an unnecessary complication of the contact between the story and the audience, a contact which ideally has the immediacy, the continuousness, of the folk-epic-being-narrated-among-the-folk. Sartre's philosophy of man tells him that we are, still and always, potentially a "folk," a community made by the freedom with which each man wills to negate the isolation of all men, a community in which each man is responsible for the freedom of all men. Thus his negative response to the differentiating qualities of the technique of the novel, that invitation addressed neither to the individual

37

nor to the group but to the individual-in-the-group, is not surprising, although his naïve expectation that one man can actually experience the existence, the story of another man or character is surprising. Surely the best we can do is to experience truly and wholly our own response to another man's existence. An editor who chooses to acknowledge his own really unhidable presence in the written prose of a novel is not simply "interfering" with the reader's experiencing of the story, he is rather presenting the reader with two stories, two existences, to which to respond.

Sartre's second major complaint about the nature of the editor in the traditional novel is more serious. He argues that the presence of the novelist's "almost guilty solitude" in the very fabric of the story involves a certain steadiness of point of view that carries a message about the solidity, the saneness, the essential at-homeness of man in the universe that is reassuring to "the bourgeoisie" even if the point of view dramatized in the narrative is antibourgeois. The technique of the traditional novel, resting as it does in the solitary subjectivity rather than in the collective identity of the tale, "considers from a viewpoint of absolute rest the absolute movement of a relatively isolated partial system" (p. 106). The novelist as editor, choosing to dramatize himself as thinker-about, or translator-of, or interpreter-of a Book already written, makes the real event of the novel, the presentation of the editor, a static one, and thus speaks a message of rest instead of revolution, of peace where there is no peace. This is the case, Sartre maintains, even when the novelist, who is the "primary subjectivity," is attempting to communicate the revolutionary or terrifying experience of his narrator, who is inevitably a "secondary subjectivity": "He wants to drag the reader along with him into his terror. But the twig is bent; lacking a technique adapted to madness, death, and history, he fails to move the reader" (p. 121). This failure, says Sartre, is a sort of guilty collaboration between the novelist and his historical readers, who do not want to be moved to terror, to the truth of existence, but only moved to the celebration of the narrative consciousness which has seen, interpreted, and assimilated terror for them.

Sartre's analysis, contained in *What is Literature?* in the chapter titled "For Whom Does One Write?" is, as he says, "incomplete and debatable." The grounds on which I would debate him are the very ones he provides in the earlier pages of the book. He thinks that "nothing is accomplished" if the reader is created primarily to meet the writer instead of the story-experience. Sartre looks forward to the invention of a new technique of fiction that will "make the reader contemporary with the story." This, it seems to me, is impossible, if we take "story" to mean the Book, the primary experience of characters who have been created, read, and then edited by a writer. But if, as I have been saying, there are two stories in every novel, plot and subplot, the story of an experience and the story of the interpreting, then the traditional novel does make the reader contemporary with one of these stories, perhaps the most important one. The traditional novel's subplot makes the reader contemporary with the writer's reading of experience, an act sufficiently fraught with terror, madness, and history, as Sartre describes it, to carry the most revolutionary of implications. For the novel tells us that we cannot know the story, we can only know the knower. We see that the writer in reading the experience or existence he has chosen to look upon is essentially coming to know himself. We realize that we, in reading the writer's knowing of himself through story—which is the novel—come essentially to know neither the story nor the writer but the reader, that is, ourselves. The novel tells us all this most clearly in those very works with characterized editors and readers that Sartre deplores, but almost every novel tells us so to some degree. Under that message hums the still more revolutionary and terrifying possibility that there is no story at all, only the reader-editor, a possibility just as alive in the winks of the editor of *Moll Flanders* and the purposeful grins of the puppet master of *Vanity Fair* as in the solemn shams of Pynchon's Cryer of Lot 49 or the encyclopedists

39

of *Tlon, Ukbar; Orbis Tertia*. Carrying those epistemological implications, the novel merits that special place as an event in the history of ideas that Ian Watt describes in the earlier chapters of *The Rise of the Novel*, and in the history of technologies that McLuhan gives it; it merits these places precisely as it celebrates the looker-on, the figurer-out, the wrestler-with-an-obscure-text, who symbolically stands for the new man in the novel universe, the reader-editor.

Sartre's main complaint about this epistemological message is that it does not "incite," move to action, contain "efficacity." This may be true for some readers: the discovery of oneself as creator of one's own perceptions may seem rather more conducive to sitting in corners than to storming the barricades. This is the dilemma that faces one of the great contemporary reader-characters, Jake Horner, in Barth's *End of the Road*. Barth's hero comes to a dead stop in the middle of his young life, his educated brain so watchful of all the action around him, so dizzily cognizant of all possibilities, so contemporarily aware of the contingency and unpredictability of Time, that his choice-making apparatus has frozen. But little Jake Horner is not John Barth nor the reader of his novel, and *End of the Road* does not bring the message that action and choice are impossible, only that these are, to quote Sartre again, terrifying, mad, and vertiginously historical.

The problem of action is one that haunts all of George Meredith's work, since the struggle to deal with one's contradictory and perhaps illusory perceptions is open in many of his subplots. He is constantly playing editor in ways both direct (*Sandra Belloni, The Egoist, Diana of the Crossways*) and indirect (*Richard Feverel, One of Our Conquerors, Beauchamp's Career*). In fact, Meredith comes close sometimes to describing romance itself as simply the addiction to action and the novel as an addiction to thought, promoting the latter at the expense of the former out of some naïve faith that the simple multiplication of thoughtfulness in the world would solve problems, even national and international problems. But Meredith is increasingly aware of the possible consequences of the spread of thought from the editor himself to his readers as an addiction. He salts all through his works warnings to the readers both in his stories and of them, about the destructive consequences of becoming too safe and civilized a reader, too judicious and balanced an onlooker. In these warnings, these under-cuttings of the very process he has most faith in, lies much of the action of a Meredith novel, much of its "efficacity," much of what is humanly accomplished. And in this action, engaging the reader for perhaps the first time in a real and continuing review of the excellences and dangers of read-ing, lies much of his originality too.

III. The Community of Literacy

Meredith, like many another artist, was convinced that he was at the expanding frontier of a civilization ready in the near future to fulfill itself. He thought of the novel as a leaven for that great fulfillment. The reader he creates to complete his fictions is listening to Meredith with one ear, but the other is cocked to catch and to transmit back to a grateful Meredith echoes from that future when posterity will almost literally be one civilized reader, so well will the novel have done its work:

> At present, I am aware, an audience impatient for blood and glory scorns the stress I am putting on incidents so minute. . . . An audience will come to whom it will be given to see the elementary machinery at work, who, as it were, from some slight hint of the straws, will feel the winds of March when they do not blow. To them nothing will be trivial . . . and they will perceive, more-over, that in real life all hangs together, the train is laid in the lifting of an eyebrow, that bursts upon the field of thousands.
>
> *(The Ordeal of Richard Feverel, p. 280)*

This too is a very Sartrean sort of vision for such a "traditional" novelist. For another of Sartre's complaints about the tradition in which Meredith worked is that it

41

had addressed itself to questions of one class and "covered up those of other milieus"; his discussion of this notion suggests that the reader is the "ground" of the novel in a concrete human social sense as well as in the philosophical and structural sense that I have been talking about. Says Sartre:

> *Actual* literature can only realize its full *essence* in a classless society. Only in this society could the writer be aware that there is no difference of any kind between his *subject* and his *public*. For the subject of literature has always been man in the world. However, as long as the virtual public remained like a dark sea around the sunny little beach of the real public, the writer risked confusing the interests and cares of man with those of a small and favored group. *(What is Literature? p. 116)*

His point is, of course, well taken, although the additional point he makes by implication, that other literary genres have been less guilty than the novel of a parochial attention to special class questions, seems dubious. Still, if the novel invites its fictional reader to help its writer make the rest of the readers into a "subject," then it does at first seem as though the novel, especially the traditional comic novel, promotes class and destroys community. Or at least it promotes the class of reader, and concerns itself with that class's particular cares, since the novel is both practically and thematically an invitation to those who can read. How, then, might one possibly get from the novel to a classless society, from the audience of Meredith's day that is to be rejected to that future audience that is "one" in its civilized awareness of the interconnecting movement of all events?

Let us say for the sake of argument that the man who chooses to write a novel has at least equal concern with the dramatist, the poet, or the epic singer for the virtual public. In that case, how dares a man like John Bunyan, sedulously committed to the community of man in the saving Blood of Jesus Christ, address his fable on the follies of man-in-the-world to the reading Christian? How if not in the faith that all men are, or may be, reading Christians? Now, the faith that all men are or may be (or should be) Christians was open to debate even at the birth of the novel. But what was not open to debate then, what became an article of faith in the formative years of the novel, perhaps the initial article in the religion of progress, the philosophy of liberalism, was the fact that all men are, or may be, and ought to be, and certainly will be one day, readers. Fears of content and consequences aside, the faith that the reading public was encompassing the virtual public seems to me to provide the clearest, solidist, and most uniform basis for the "act" of the novel up to modern times. Artists knew that man-in-the-world, the virtual public, would be troublesome in the future, even that he would continue to be troubled—but he would be a reader, and be troublesome and troubled precisely because he was a reader. It is a provocative view of reader-in-the-world that opens and dominates *The Pilgrim's Progress*, for instance:

> As I walked through the wilderness of this world, I lighted on a certain place where was a Den, and I laid me down in that place to sleep: and as I slept I dreamed a dream. I dreamed, and behold I saw a man clothed with rags, standing in a certain place, with his face from his own house, a book in his hand, and a great burden upon his back. I looked, and saw him open the book and read therein, and as he read, he wept and trembled; and not being able longer to contain himself, he brake out with a lamentable cry, saying, what shall I do?[17]

Bunyan's linking of the Book and the Burden provides a memorable paradigm for the sort of sketch of the peculiarly novelistic reader that I have in mind. It is a paradigm of the emergence of the knowledge of good and evil into the world, of the most famous Western plot of the *Bildungsroman*, with the reader playing Adam and the Book ambiguously figuring as the Tree, in both the Old Testa-

[17] *The Pilgrim's Progress* (New York: Holt, Rinehart and Winston, 1968), p. 9.

43

ment and the New Testament meanings of the word. The paradigm is laid out in an encounter between reading Christian and Mr. Worldly Wiseman, or, in one of those forced marvels that print technology afforded Bunyan in 1678 and has always been repeated by Editors, in an encounter between reader and World:

World. How camest thou by the burden at first?

Christian. By reading this book in my hand.

World. I thought so: and it is happened unto thee as to other weak men, who, meddling with things too high for them, do suddenly fall into thy distractions; which distractions do not only unman men, as thine, I perceive, has done thee, but they run them upon desperate ventures to obtain they know not what. *(P. 19)*

Thus World, to all the Emma Bovaries and Ursula Brangwens and Artur Sammlers[18] who bear a Burden as a result of the Book, all the great reader-characters who ran themselves upon desperate ventures to obtain they knew not what. World is the Serpent here, but in reverse. He would have no meddling, no knowledge of good and evil, no suffering and Fall, but no consciousness and redemption either, no confrontation with the terrifying truth of man's flawed but mysteriously Saved existence, no readings. He would have man remain dark and unconscious of himself. Bunyan would have him come to consciousness and embark on desperate ventures which do first, in a sense, unman him, and then re-man him, as readers first shatter and then re-create the Book.

The Book is an instrument in this re-manning, but so is the novel. Bunyan sees himself as carrying on the work of

[18] Note, for instance, Saul Bellow's splendid opening line in *Mr. Sammler's Planet*: "Shortly after dawn, or what would have been dawn in a normal sky, Mr. Artur Sammler with his bushy eye took in the books and papers of his West Side bedroom and suspected strongly that they were the wrong books and the wrong papers."

the Book, but he also sees the novelist's editing of the
Book, the telling of the dream, as an exercise in co-creation
between writer and reader which is bound to be a continuing struggle:

> Now, reader, I have told my dream to thee:
> See if thou canst interpret it to me.
> . . . But if thou shalt cast all away as vain,
> I know not but 'twill make me dream again.
>
> *(P. 169)*

Bunyan's novel is thus a very serious struggle of minds
over interpretations, with the novelist admitting his very
interpretation to be a dream, terrifying, mad, and historical,
that is, tied to his Time, "situated," in Sartre's term, and
subject to re-dreaming even by the novelist himself in another part of his Time. The faith that keeps him dreaming
is the faith that the reader will keep interpreting, that there
will always be readers to continue that work. The novelist
makes his commitment on the basis of his assumption that
whatever else dies—the Christian, the Man of Feeling, the
Gentleman, God—the Reader lives.

The reader will live; whatever values he holds, whatever interpretations he makes, the reader will be there, and
he will share with all men, despite the individualization of
values and value worlds that the novel also promotes, the
commitment to the value of reading, the power and the
disposition to interpret. Thus the novelist, using his main
narrative conceit about the interpretation of the dream
about the Book, considers himself part-architect of a new
kind of community even while he is espousing the individual discovery of social or moral values. This kind of social
or moral value world is mortal, it is clear. Robert Alter
observes of Fielding's mixture of styles and fragmentation
of narrative character that a tacit assumption of a shared
outlook between writer and reader guides the logic of the
choice of a vivid but varied persona, but then Alter quali-
fies: "Perhaps it might be more precise to say that he
creates rather than reinforces this shared autlook, for Fiel-

ding is clearly aware that in his age the community of values, like the community of men, has lost much of the intactness it may once have had—this is, from one point of view, why he had to write comic-epic novels and not serious epic poems."[19]

This remark of Alter's has pertinence to my thought in two directions here. In the first place, it points again to the source of the peculiarly novelistic pugnacity with which authors address readers: an ambiguity about the fact of community as well as the need for community is built into the novel, stemming from the novel's place in history at the apogee of the movement for the independent self-awareness of every mind, common and uncommon, and at the center of the advance of print technology and the *private but not solitary* reading that print provides. To the liberal mind (I follow Harvey in calling the traditional novel's philosophic-structural basis liberal) Reading isolates and validates the individual's world and his responsibility to it and for it. But liberalism assumes that what the individual will responsibly discover is his will-to-community. The question is, what kind of community? The community of unconsciousness, the dark sea that flowed through Sartre's virtual public, will disappear with universal literacy, so the liberal mind expects. What will replace it?

Timid, evasive, or strident assertions of one sort or another abound. Lamentation and elegy on this issue hover over many of the important novels in the tradition—one thinks of *Persuasion, Bleak House, Middlemarch, The Rainbow*. The epic of the disappearance of old communities, of the notion of community itself, could be and has been, a serious epic poem. But those who write novels cannot write that epic tragedy because they celebrate the reader in the very act of despairing of men; they speak, furtively and sometimes clownishly it is true, of the community of literacy even in the teeth of the fragmenting winds of change. This is the second point that needs to be

[19] "Fielding and the Uses of Style," *Novel*, i (Fall 1967), 59.

struck off Alter's remark. Confidence that the novel is the multiplicand of reader into readers until the virtual public *is* the actual public is the basic motive of the traditional novelist and is the secret of the "comic" stance of all novelists. Like Dante, the reader may travel through hell with the writer, but, if he sits down to write about it, it can only be because he has come out the other side, temporarily at least; it can only be because he has succeeded in inventing that "silence" in which a creation and organization of intuition or story can take place. When he writes it can therefore only be a comedy, a resting together, a mutual perception of a whole. Novelists with characters in their subplots take this stance more openly than those without, but my feeling is that any novelist, however "undercut" his values, however dispersed his writer and reader, however open, contingent, and terrifying his picture of experience, writes on the wave of a splendidly naïve faith that man is essentially organized as *homo legens*, reading man.

Q. D. Leavis, for instance, touchingly begins her disapproving picture of *Fiction and the Reading Public* on this wave: "In twentieth century England not only everyone can read, but it is safe to add that everyone does read."[20] This sounds rather like the Parousia of the religion of progress: state education has elevated the virtual public into the actual public, the waters have receded and all mankind is jostling together on the "sunny beach" of literacy. Leaving aside the question of whether universal literacy has been achieved, the state of affairs as Mrs. Leavis's book presented it in 1932 was clearly to be deplored rather than celebrated. All men are readers and the reader is indeed supreme, but he is too many, too vulgar, and, most distressing of all, he is segmented into stratas of the Reading Public. And he loves it! He values his difference from the highbrows or lowbrows or middlebrows

[20] London: Chatto and Windus, 1932, p. 3. Cultural historians argue convincingly that by no means everyone could read in 1932—nor can they in 1975, for that matter.

(depending on what he considers himself, of course); he positively revels in the varied kinds of snobbery that literacy affords him; or he has with "hearty goodfellowship" demeaned the novel by supinely agreeing with "the herd" that "anyone who denies the P. G. Wodehouses and Edgar Wallaces a place in literature along with Milton and Donne is mean spirited as well as arrogant" *(p. 196).* The virtual public has been reached, but there is no community, certainly no community of civilized readers all alike.

Mrs. Leavis's book is that sort of serious girding for the Armageddon of Fiction versus the Reading Public—"All that can be done, it must be realised, must take the form of resistance by an armed and conscious minority"—which is a constitutional disease of the civilized reader. Meredith was not entirely immune himself. And the Lowering of Standards and the Coming of Anarchy are certainly knotty problems for the liberal mind promoting universal literacy. But what is really interesting about such discussions of the divergencies and diversities of the Reading Public is that they too are celebrations of community, in spite of themselves. For the novel taught the public to read, the novel and its wicked stepmother, the journal. That much is clear from the history of both. The novel might have taught the reader that he was isolated, interchangeable, homogeneous with his fellows, unchanging, and passive. So McLuhan argues. What has the novel produced instead? A hotly argumentative, emotionally cliquish, absolutely unhomogeneous, hilariously sentimental, wildly suspicious, surly exhilarated cantankerous electrifying mosaic of a real public full of sharp edges. This is a victory over the technology that robotizes, surely? Yet it is not so very much of a surprise. McLuhan points out that the novel began both as a reinforcement of *and* as a contradiction to print—a contradiction especially in its unwearying attempt to reproduce speech, voices, by whatever subterfuge of dialogue, emphasis, exclamation, italics, mixture of style, argumentative pattern of tone writers could discover. For writers and for readers homogeneity and solipsism are essentially the same, and both are found unacceptable over and over again. The tense in-between, the individual in the group of individuals whose independence of interpretation is the mutually shared value, the reader in his circle of light surrounded by, arguing with, differing from, other readers, including the editor-writer who was the original reader—and that gives him the advantage but not, certainly, the match— here is the image of reader-in-the-world that the novel projects and creates. A virtual public becomes real in response to the Book, becomes a community of individuals, an orthodoxy of heterodox readers. But a homogeneous public, even of civilized readers? Not while the novel lives!

The public is rather a mosaic of publics all energetically differentiating themselves as men while they unite as readers. Indeed, it sometimes seems that each reader is really his own public. Talking about the writing of novels, for instance, Wayne Booth testily asserts that "this is not the place to attempt a reconciliation between the half-truth that all good works are *sui generis* and the undeniable fact that we cannot engage in practical criticism at all without grouping works according to kinds of effects," but admits in the next breath that "readers may be troubled by the suspicion that I have sneaked general criteria in the back door while denouncing them from the front stoop."[21] I can make the same assertion about the widely held half-truth, of which Walter Allen's comment that "real readers, like poets, are born, not made"[22] is a good example, that all good readings are *sui generis*. It is only a half-truth, and I frankly do not know how to define the error; I have only been attempting to define the other half of the truth. But as I turn from theoretical to "practical" criticism, where one must speak of the fictional readers that are made, not born, I make three assumptions about the novel's making of readers which, viewed together, constitute a pattern, a convention

[21] *The Rhetoric of Fiction*, p. 377. Booth, of course, being the first reader of his book, was the first to be troubled.

[22] *Reading a Novel*, rev. ed. 1949 (rpt. London: Phoenix House, 1956), p. 10.

of the civilized reader, by whose light many, perhaps most, novels can be opened up to interesting effect.

The first assumption underlying this convention is that the anticipated community of *homo legens* represents to authors a wholly new and welcome, if not fully predictable, civilization. The second is that this civilization is anticipated to consist of minds quite different in value orientation but similar in that stance that we have seen the novel creating, a stance whose qualities are capaciousness born of distance, sympathy born of analysis, skepticism born of the experience of the malleability of reality, the story, the intuition, the Book. This is the mind that Meredith calls philosophic, and of which he asserts in *Diana of the Crossways*: "The forecast may be hazarded that if we do not speedily embrace Philosophy in Fiction, the art is doomed to extinction" *(p. 19)*. My third assumption, crucial in practical criticism, is that the subplots of novels, especially of novels with as complex a narrative strategy as Meredith's always are, will yield interesting dramas of the making of the new civilization and its minds, and that these dramas are always necessary to the understanding of the whole work. They support or expand the plot, so-called, and may in fact hold the real key to the single work, or even to a large body of an author's whole work.

Meredith is an author whose work embodies these assumptions. Where I remarked earlier that the plot and the subplot may be similar in novels, I find that in Meredith they are usually directly related. They are related in the self-conscious attention to the evolution of civilization and the novel's production of the civilized reader that I have seen operating in the plots and subplots of pivotal novels in the comic tradition. Meredith sees "making philosophers" through the act of writing-reading and reading-writing as the business of fiction as well as of life. His wrestle with the dark side of that activity, with the hidden dragons of contempt and moral paralysis that wait to tempt the civilized reader, is the source of my fascination with him, and its exploration is the object of this study.

2. The Meredithian Subplot

> Next to fighting the world, fighting oneself is the
> prime luxury, and to put yourself in such a position
> that you will have to do the latter, because you
> have done the former, is genius. (Letter to Frederick
> Maxse, *Letters*, I, 333)[1]

> I have had a letter from a stranger, calling on
> me to be up with the pen "second only to Shake-
> speare's." There are maniacs who would send us
> about with a feathered Indians head. (Letter to
> Louisa Lawrence, *Letters*, II, 762)

> To be out of the world is delightful, so long as
> the world continues to show itself attached. Other-
> wise it is uncomfortable coquetry. (Letter to Marie
> Meredith, *Letters*, I, 398)

GEORGE MEREDITH MET "THE WORLD" IN HIS LIFE
the way he met it in his novels, with a grimace and a
metaphor; he and his readers were rarely satisfied with one
another even when they were praising each other. But co-
quet as he sometimes did, the novelist never lost his attachment to the world, even while he fell in and out of the good
graces of several publics over a writing life spanning more
than sixty years. The attitude of the man toward the world,
especially the world of readers and critics, was often hostile, sometimes even paranoid; but underlying the rhetoric
of disdainful or despairing distance there was always a
healthy sense of himself as part of the world and of his
reciprocal need of readers and critics—so long as they
really did read and criticize. It was a difficult reciprocity

[1] Meredith's letters are quoted from *The Letters of George Meredith*, ed. C. L. Cline, 3 vols. (London: Oxford Univ. Press, 1970).

51

to state, and Meredith was not always graceful in stating it nor in coping with the pressures of obscurity and the equally disturbing pressures of fame. In his life Meredith sometimes surrendered to the temptation of playing roles that set him against the world—Martyred Prophet, Unconcerned Hermit, Grand Old Man of Letters. Sometimes he would even don the feathered Indian's head and play the "Sage of Box Hill," though to do him justice it must be admitted that the world tempted him most awfully and persistently with this role. Still, Meredith had a keen enough eye for the line that separates a diseased apprehension of the world from a healthy one, and we have only to meet one of the pursued-or-ignored-by-the-world figures in his novels to know him, as Meredith does, for a fool or a villain.

Meredith hoped initially to make his mark on his chosen world as a poet. Having no money and no name, he launched himself in 1851 with a book of poems published at his own expense. Critics duly noted his resemblances to Keats and the early Tennyson, patted the book gently and dismissed it, laying the groundwork for Meredith's lifelong conviction that the world he wanted to enter had no room for new voices, only for reiterations of the old, especially where poetry was concerned. Talking about an obscure line in Tennyson, he observed to Frederick Maxse: "If *I* had written such a line, what vehement reprobation, what cunning efforts to construe, and finally, what a lecture on my wilfulness! In Tennyson it is interesting. . . . But George Meredith, who is not known, not acknowledged, he shall be bounced if he offers us a difficulty—we insist upon his thinking in our style" *(Letters*, i, *336).* His early novels were better received, and gained notices from most of the major reviewers and from some readers. But notices did not pay the bills, and Meredith remained for the first thirty years of his writing career unable to wrest a living from his readers. With *Beauchamp's Career* (1876), *The Egoist* (1879), and *Diana of the Crossways* (1885), Meredith's reputation was established and a measure of financial comfort was assured with the additional help of a reversion from an aunt. But his reputation remained controversial; almost without exception criticism of his work showed that relish for exaggeration and bias that critics feel when they are in hot argument. When his works began to create a coterie of disciples in the seventies and eighties the warfare in the journals sometimes reached ludicrous proportions and Meredith withdrew from it, annoyed alike with both sides. As he wrote the books of his final period, *One of Our Conquerors* (1891), *Lord Ormont and His Aminta* (1895), and *The Amazing Marriage* (1895), he harbored a growing sense that to be called "the second Shakespeare" by his friends was just as ridiculous a judgment, based on just as incorrect and narrow a reading of the works, as to be called a despoiler of young minds by Mudie and the British Matron who complained about prurience in *Richard Feverel*.

On the other hand, nothing was more personally and aesthetically ridiculous and hateful to Meredith than not to be called anything—to be ignored, to be, as he once bitterly prophesied, an old fellow stitching books nobody buys. Meredith had many hard things to say about readers and to the readers in his novels precisely because he knew how necessary they were to his idea of a writer, to his idea of himself. The wish to make a living from his own works, from his readers, was a drive not simply for economic stability but for fundamental self-identity too. Neither the intuition—the impulse that created the stories—nor the expression—the manuscripts and the printed books—really sufficed to stabilize Meredith's vision of himself as a writer. Only the reader, communicating back to Meredith in the monthly sales lists his confirmation of his existence as writer, could stabilize that vision.

A coterie reader, a class reader, however, could not do this for him. He wanted all of them—the university graduates, the second assistant bookkeepers, the young maidens, the pork butchers, the cooks, and the baronets; he even coveted the British Matron with her tattling to Mudie, not merely because he wanted to be popular but because he wanted to be, in the Sartrean sense, "efficacious." He relished the differences among men with an artist's eye: the classless society was not for him if it meant the homogeneous society. But he looked, as a liberal always looks, to education to solve the most visible human deficiencies in a society of classes, the tyranny, the narrow horizon, the poverty of mind and body. He intended his novels to promote that education, to reveal nobility, narrowness, philosophy, egoism, and sentimentalism in all their forms high and low, social and psychic, male and female. More than that, he intended his novels to *be* that education, to turn men into Readers, civilized readers, so that they would carry back into their own stories and their society all the qualities for which "reading" is a metaphor. As his career went on, he tended increasingly to treat "reading," that metaphor with its products and its dangers, directly in his novels, producing in his nineteenth-century readers the unmistakable sense that it was they, and not the characters in the stories, who were being mercilessly examined and urged and molded in his works.

This sense of scrutiny found vent in a pervasive and curious metaphor of physical anguish and attack in the contemporary critical readings of Meredith. "He must be an enthusiast indeed who does not shut his aching eyes and hold his throbbing brows," groaned Edmund Gosse about *The Amazing Marriage (rpt. Critical Heritage, p. 430).* "After one has been stung with whips or battered on the brain with a quarterstaff, it is not the pretty wristplay nor the artful bludgeoning that gets the praise," warned James Stuart reviewing *Lord Ormont and His Aminta:* "before praise is mentioned there is something to say of the smarting wales, of the aching bumps on the skull" *(rpt. Critical Heritage, p. 391).* The "stylization" in such critical wit points, as Susan Sontag would have it, to an ambiguity of response to the subject, in this case Meredith's own style, and the ambiguity is neatly summed up in W. E. Henley's remark to Sidney Colevill about the Meredith who wrote

The Egoist: "The devil will surely damn him hot and deep. I hate and admire him."[2]

The critical world explained its own ambiguous reception of Meredith by analyzing his motives, attributing to him the desire to revenge his early neglect by transferring his own pain and humiliation to the reader of his novels. His admirers were seen by many critics to be victims of a sinister and false elitism by which appreciation of Meredith's novels, like admiration of the Emperor's new clothes, became the measure of a man's pretense to culture. J. M. Robertson in an article damning "preciosity" and published, singularly enough, in *The Yellow Book*, scolded: "The prompt appreciation of a few good readers did not teach him to look on the reading public as what it is, a loose mass of ever varying units in which even the dullards have no solidarity; he rather entrenched himself in the Carlylean and Browningesque manner, personifying the multitudes as one lumpish hostile entity."[3]

Thus do the hostile readers of Meredith's own world, feeling themselves attacked for insensitivity, laziness, and narrowness in their reading personalities, reply to him whom they feel to be their attacker. The battle that was joined in the critical periodicals, at lectures and meetings and in the London salons, finds its way increasingly into the novels themselves as Meredith attempts to clarify and intensify his education of the reader.

This series of ripostes by Meredith's adversary readers is almost from the first anticipated and met, if not always parried, as a major action in the typical Meredithian subplot. The thrust and counterthrust between narrator and the flawed audiences he sees himself as addressing can be pinned down to three main areas. In the first place, critics,

---

[2] Quoted in Lionel Stevenson, *The Ordeal of George Meredith* (New York: Scribner's, 1953), p. 233.

[3] Rpt. *Critical Heritage*, p. 455. Robertson's article also harbors "a misgiving . . . as to whether much of Mr. Meredith must not inevitably go the way of Donne," another of his sufferers of linguistic "preciosity."

obligingly behaving just as the narrator expects them to behave, charge Meredith with contempt for the "common reader" and suggest that he uses his novels to create an elitist reader to be his accomplice in sneering at the multitudes. In the second place he is thought to personify all readers as "one lumpish hostile entity"; he is accused of a Manichean view of the reading universe, with the many personified as one gross devil, and himself and his assenting fictional reader portrayed as unflawed angels of mystic intellectual power and rapport. Thirdly, and most interestingly, he is seen as doing all this through *style*, in "the Carlylean and Browningesque manner." I want to explore these charges with a look first at the theory of comedy by which Meredith wanted his work with readers to be judged, secondly at the subplot of *Diana of the Crossways* and the varieties in Meredith's imagined audience and reader there, and thirdly at Meredithian style and its effect.

I. The Struggle to be Comic

By his own theory the charge of contempt, if true, would have disqualified Meredith as a comic novelist, his own self-definition. Indeed, as I have said, the problem of being comic, not realistic or satiric, is the subject of many of Meredith's novels in the same way as it is of *Tom Jones*. For Meredith, as for Fielding, who first defined the novel as "a comic epic in prose . . . a comic Romance," comedy, properly understood, is the great genre. The "comic poet" whom Meredith praises in several of his works may write a drama, a verse, or a novel (and Meredith tried all three); he may mix his elements of lyricism, dramatic action, analysis, character, type, and idea with the freedom that Fielding claimed for his work and his descendants. He may, if he wishes to write a novel, even follow all the "rules" that in the century since Fielding had come to circumscribe that freedom, "certain broad and obvious tests which it is both pertinent and natural to apply," as one hostile critic of Meredith put it: "Is he great at construction? Is he great

as a master of narrative? Is he great as an artist in dialogue? Is he great as a creator of character?"[4] But for Meredith, one of the greatest of Fielding's descendants, if a man
has all this and has not "comedy," he has not yet made a
novel. Fielding, whom Meredith called England's only
comic poet, fixes for an example of his method of comedy
on the shallow lawyer who is Parson Adams' traveling
companion in book II of *Joseph Andrews*; the lawyer is
"taken from life," yes, but not copied from Fielding's acquaintanceship. He is an example of "manners," not men;
he is "real" with a typological reality that calls on the
reader's acquaintanceship for much of his detail: "His appearance in the World is calculated . . . not to expose one
pitiful Wretch, to the small and contemptible Circle of his
Acquaintance; but to hold the Glass to thousands in their
Closets, that they may contemplate their Deformity, and
endeavour to reduce it." In Fielding's view, nothing should
interfere with this active participation of the reader in
character, with this facing and finding of himself and his
actual world in the glass of fiction—especially not a mar-
veling at the author's dexterity in mimicry or his range of
sympathy or his depth of thought. All that does not directly
contribute to the reader's finding of himself in the fiction
is, Fielding says, self-indulgence on the author's part, pan-
dering to the chaos of his own brains.

Thus the comic artist works with a kind of paradox of
presentation, that the "real" is not necessarily the fictionally
"living." If Fielding were to describe minutely the lawyer
of his acquaintance, "one pitiful Wretch," the man he
knew, that description would be a lifeless object, one which
the reader may marvel at but will not enter into, because
it does not need him or challenge him. But if the comic
writer pulls the real slightly out of shape—underarticu-
lates the feeling, unfleshes or universalizes the situation,
shadows or highlights the personality of the character—
then life enters: the reader is called into the action first to

[4] William Watson, "Fiction-Plethoric and Anemic," *National
Review*, Oct. 1889 (rpt. *Critical Heritage*, p. 319).

recognize and position himself with respect to the writer's distorting presence, and then to recognize and contribute his detail to the feeling, the situation, the character. In those actions of the reader are hidden the lessons that the comic writer wants to teach, or more properly the skills he wants to impart. For if the writer has been skillful in his construction of the mirror character, what the reader sees there, beyond all difference of detail from period to period, from writer to reader, is "nature," the living radicals of character which are always recognizable if one man, the writer, has the ingenuity to distinguish and present them, and another man, the reader, has the courage to look at and acknowledge them. In many cases the accumulation of "realistic" detail and the massive surface pressure of "the small and contemptible Circle" of our acquaintance may obscure from us the presence and operation of these radicals, in which cases the "real" is not the natural. Apply to the "real" the comic distortion, the comic dislocation, the comic universalization, and the reader, jolted, will see and reach for, re-invent, the natural—which, in the comic artist's philosophy, the reader has already within him.

Yet, while claiming distortion as his medium in a sense, the comic artist is careful to distinguish himself from the caricaturist, the satirist, and the burlesquer. Fielding, defining the novel in the preface to *Joseph Andrews* as "a comic romance" and "a comic epic poem in prose," spends only a sentence or two separating his new art from the romance and the epic, proposing to admit into "the sentiments and the diction" of the novel the "low," the "light," and the "ludicrous." Not only are these elements now to be part of the subject of the new art, but they are also allowed into the sentiments of the author, that is, into the author's own value world, into the shape of his belief about reality,[5] and,

[5] I borrow the phrase from Sheldon Sacks who explores (in *Fiction and the Shape of Belief* [Berkeley: Univ. of California Press, 1967]) with particular reference to Fielding the notion that "the novelist's beliefs, opinions, and prejudices are expressed in the judgments he conveys of his characters, their actions, and their

still further, they are allowed into his diction, his style, the shape and sound of his language, the form of his presentation. Fielding then turns to another distinction for the new art, one so important to his purpose that he spends three pages working it out:

> In the diction, I think, burlesque itself may be sometimes admitted. . . . But though we have sometimes admitted this in our diction, we have carefully excluded it from our sentiments and characters, for there it is never properly introduced, except in writing of the burlesque kind, which this is not intended to be. Indeed, no two species of writing can differ more widely than the comic and the burlesque, for as the latter is ever the exhibition of what is monstrous and unnatural . . . so in the former we should ever confine ourselves strictly to nature, from the just imitation of which will flow all the pleasure we can ·this way convey to a sensible reader.

It is a very thin line Fielding wants to draw here, imitating not "reality" but nature, allowing himself to distort the detailed "real" in order to achieve nature, but not monstrousness. The novelist's subject, manners, the significant and enduring radicals of human character, are not monstrous and are not to be presented as such, even when the radicals the comic artist is examining are the radicals of folly. And yet "the monstrous" may enter the work—fruitful comic distortion may enter—through diction, through style, through "a certain drollery of style."

It is important when studying Meredith to keep in mind this stylistic latitude that Fielding allows for, and I shall come back to that point at the end of this chapter. But even more important to the question we are now considering—the charge of contempt for his readers that critics

---

thoughts . . . expressed as Hume's formal 'marks'—the signals, which persuade his readers to react to those characters, their acts, and their thoughts in a manner consonant with the artistic end to which all elements in his work are subordinate" (p. 66).

lodge against Meredith—is Fielding's prohibition of the burlesque from the writer's sentiments. The comic novelist's subject is the ridiculous, he says in this same preface, and continues, "The only source of the true ridiculous (as it appears to me) is affectation." The miseries of circumstance, the vagaries of Fate, are not ridiculous, he says; they only become ridiculous when men exposed to them respond unnaturally. The weaknesses of human nature are not the proper game of the comedian; only when those who harbor those weaknesses affect ignorance of them, or play with them, or call them by another name to fondle them, do they become ridiculous. This distinction is crucial for both Fielding and Meredith. Man himself is not legitimately the subject of ridicule, nor is it the object of comedy to awake in the reader the disposition or the skill to ridicule him. Contempt for Fielding is a burlesque, an affectation, of pity; it comes not from a sorrowful understanding of weakness and folly but from a delightedly willful misunderstanding. Fielding does not allow this burlesque into the sentiments of the comic romance, the comic epic poem in prose, that is, the novel.

Meredith's essay "On the Idea of Comedy and the Uses of the Comic Spirit," first delivered in lecture form at the London Institute in 1877, follows Fielding's logic in every particular. He too is aware of the need to rescue comedy from its confusion with the burlesque: "Comedy, we have to admit, was never one of the most honored of the muses. She was in her origin, short of slaughter, the loudest expression of the little civilization of men. The light of Athene over the head of Achilles illuminates the birth of Greek Tragedy. But Comedy rolled in shouting under the divine protection of the Son of the Wine Jar" (p. 12). As Fielding distinguishes comedy from caricature and burlesque, so does Meredith elevate it above Humour, Irony, and Satire, and elevates it mainly according to Fielding's standard that true comedy aims its barbs not at our natural weaknesses and deficiencies, but at our unnatural perversions of our strengths, our affectations, our excrescences:

Incidents of a kind casting ridicule on our unfortunate nature, instead of our conventional life, provoke derisive laughter, which thwarts the Comic Idea. . . . Men's future upon earth does not attract [the Comic Spirit]; their honesty and shapeliness in the present does; and whenever they wax out of proportion, overblown, affected, pretentious, bombastical, hypocritical, pedantic, fantastically delicate . . . the Spirit overhead will look humanely malign and cast an oblique light on them, followed by volleys of silvery laughter. *(Pp. 46-47)*

For Meredith, too, what lives in comedy is manners, not men. Its target is folly, not the foolish *(p. 32)*, and his praise of Molière points clearly to where the comic distortion should be, in character and style: "He did not paint in raw realism. He seized his characters firmly for the central purpose of the play, stamped them in the idea, and by slightly raising and softening the object of study . . . generalized upon it so as to make it permanently human" *(p. 10)*. He points to where comic distortion does *not* belong, in the "idea," the philosophy, the conception, the "sentiment" of the author, his look upon life: "The Comedy of Molière throws no infamous reflection upon life. It is deeply conceived, in the first place, and therefore it cannot be impure. . . . Never did man wield so shrieking a scourge upon vice, but his consummate self mastery is never shaken while administering it" *(p. 17)*. Steady, smiling, its "common aspect" one of "unsolicitous observation . . . without any fluttering eagerness," showing "sunlight of the mind, mental richness rather than noisy enormity" *(p. 44)*, the look of the comic writer upon life is animated above all by the "play of intellect." In such a look, in such eyes, in such a "character," "derision is foiled." And so Meredith comes to the statement by which he is to be judged in this respect, laying out candidly for us the authorial follies of which contempt is the burlesque: "Contempt is a sentiment that cannot be entertained by the comic intelligence. What is it but an excuse to be idly minded, or personally lofty, or comfortably narrow, not perfectly humane?" *(p. 32)*.

So much for theory. Actually to write a comic epic in prose according to this definition of comedy raises problems. In the Fielding tradition, Meredith claimed a freedom of diction and style that led him into more and more presentational distortion—artificial or strained language, eccentric or deliberately oblique construction. At the same time, still in that Fielding tradition, he sought in his readers a singularly chaste, almost ethereal delicacy of stance, of look upon life. He called his reader to a civilization of pure, unruffled, and genial Spirits. But it is one thing to note enthusiastically, as he does in the essay, that Molière's characters "Tartuffe and Harpagon, are, in fact made each to whip himself and his class, the false pietists and the insanely covetous. Molière has only set them in motion" *(p. 17)*. The stage fosters the illusion of the disappearance of the author for the master dramatist. Narrative denies it even to the master novelist. In narrative the author performs; the primary rhetorical gestures are inescapably his. If there is "whipping" taking place, an act inevitably expressive of contempt, the novel fosters the impression that the author is doing that whipping. The comic novel, with its liberal allowance for distortion in the primary rhetorical gestures of style, confirms this impression. So the storyteller in narrative faces this dilemma: the more penetrating and fundamental the indictment, the exposure of folly, the more severe the whipping, the more difficult it is to hide whose is the chastizing hand. "Consummate self mastery" in the wielding of whips and the hunting of folly is a difficult thing to manage under any circumstances, especially within the confines of prose narrative.

One of three things may happen in actual practice, as Meredith sees it. You may give way to sheer brutal egoism, from which comes the contempt of the subject that allows you to enjoy the act of whipping the foolish. Those who do are the cynics, and Meredith works out his own attraction-repulsion to this stance by creating a gallery of cynical characters not unlike Fielding's Parson-baiting Squire and his colleagues, characters who are "allowed" to destroy themselves, in Meredith's and the reader's eyes, because they are shown in the act of lecturing the world while failing to teach it, to make a difference to it. In Meredith's value world that capacity of men to teach and to learn is the supreme value. In his novels, his confidence that he is teaching, while his cynical-characters, sorrowfully observed, are not, makes for self-mastery even while the whip is being applied. But confidence in self-mastery may be misplaced. For an open and severe attention to the follies of cynicism may draw the reader to search out similarities in the author's stance. The space between what an author's cynic-characters, especially his cynic-"authors," are doing and what he is doing, may be very slim indeed, as we shall see in examinations of *The Egoist* and *One of Our Conquerors.*

Second, if, on the other hand, you strive against egoism through an annihilation of self, mistrusting all your own impulses or detaching them from yourself and affecting to receive them as messages from a supersubtle realm of ideas, you may affect to wield a whip without feeling responsible for the hand or arm. Those who do are sentimentalists in Meredith's term, living in a state of holy dislocation from human impulses, a state of Alpine disconnection from human cause and consequence. Meredith works out his ambivalence about this stance by creating a gallery of sentimentalists peculiarly his own[6]—Cornelia Pole, Clara Middleton, Neville Beauchamp, even Diana Warwick—who have, they think, detached themselves from the grossly sensual and the openly selfish only to fall into spiritual sensuality, the chaste eroticism of the worship of ideas, especially that most erotic and intoxicating idea, freedom. Here again an attack on the stance draws the reader's eye

[6] "The combination of sensualism and sentimentalism—of a tyrannous delicacy of imagination with the grossness of developing appetites, has not yet, so far as I know, been attempted; and no one in England has given me credit for it," Meredith complained to William Hardman in 1865. He was talking specifically about *Emilia in England,* later called *Sandra Belloni* (*Letters,* I, 306).

to a comparison with the author's stance, and often, as the author returns in page after chapter after novel to assume and act upon his freedom to scold, shock, or implore on behalf of his own ideas, the difference seems small.

There is a third way out of the dilemma: one may decline to use the whip at all. Other tools are less evident to the reader's eye and less tempting to the author's sense of control. He may use a feather instead of a whip, in which case Meredith would call him a humourist. Or he may seek not to chastize at all, but to draw in, to assemble and count off aspects of life, including folly, to eschew teaching in order to give simply "a convincing impression of life." Such an author is a realist in Meredith's sense of the word, not a teacher but a describer, glued as Meredith's narrator in *The Egoist* phrases it to "the small circular glow of the watchmaker's eye-glass," caught like a child by the detail of life, and therefore, details being what they are, by the imperfect, the pitiful, the unlovely. If such realists are characters, they do not change—the doctors, lawyers, clergymen, merchants, the predatory mothers, the blind and fearful fathers, the satisfied spinsters Meredith paints in his novels. If they are readers, they do not learn—the phlegmatic, the amiably curious, the thoughtlessly worldly of Meredith's imagined prose audience. And if they are authors, they do not teach—the colleagues and critics in that imagined audience in his novels whose aim is portrayed as being too low, whose demands of their readers are too puny.

Meredith, like Fielding, *will* have comedy, that is, to use another of Ian Watt's terms, "realism of assessment," the deadly serious, "deeply conceived," utterly controlled pursuit of folly. To attempt this in narrative is to draw increasingly aggressive attention to the pursuer, especially if, as is inevitable in this Fielding-Meredith tradition of comedy, the reader feels the thing pursued is himself. What reader can easily separate himself from his follies, especially if the follies being pursued are exactly those that characterize readers; that is, which are affectations arising from an attempt to "read" life!

II. Novelist and Audiences: *Diana of the Crossways*

Meredith addresses several varieties of audiences in his novels; the readers personified there are in no sense a "lumpish entity," and if he imagines many of them as hostile he still takes care to distinguish different sources for different hostilities. This notion of a varied audience seems to me most clearly dramatized in the several novels he wrote in which artists are protagonists or "deuteragonists," to use one of his own typically convoluted terms. These novels give him opportunity to be acute and compassionate both about his own audiences and about himself as a novelist. In *Diana of the Crossways*, Diana Merion Warwick, perhaps his most famous novelist-heroine, is seen as having to cope with several kinds of audiences reflecting several kinds of imperfect readership, not the least imperfect of which is the well-meant but unintelligent puffery of her friends.

The first audience that this novelist-heroine has to meet are the critics, a group characterized by Meredith, as they were by Fielding, as essentially shallow, caring for superficial effect, reading by the rules of former novels. The critics are her first readers, literally, for in the mid-nineteenth-century time of Diana's authorship many a book panned by the critics of the leading journals had no further readers at all. Diana needs the critics to enlarge her circle of readers; she is driven to write novels for a living after the fatal mistake of an unloving marriage and a consequent separation from her husband have thrown her both financially and emotionally upon her own resources. She is a person of rebellious spirit and wit, not so much from principle but because she is an original and needs more room, and more forbearance, than the conventional heroine. The same goes for her novels, which reflect, as they must,

65

Diana's flair for brilliant and eccentric language and her attachment to characters of more than ordinary complexity and to events of seeming insignificance. Fear of rejection by this audience works strange permutations in her writing moods; watching her at work on her novel, *The Cantatrice*, Meredith's narrator observes dispassionately: "No longer perversely, of necessity she wrote her best, convinced that the work was doomed to unpopularity, resolved that it should at least be a victory in style. A fit of angry cynicism now and then set her composing phrases as bait for the critics to quote, condemnatory of the attractiveness of the work. Her mood was bad" *(Diana of the Crossways, p. 314)*.

Meredith on Meredith? Exactly. There is a Meredith who revels in his ability to outrage the formal critics, who openly challenges his civilized reader to follow him through the labyrinths of a dense personal style, participating in an intellectual and "civilizing" exercise which is designed to leave the critic with his formulas well in the rear. The critic looks for a work to be "attractive," its language, theme, and construction smooth and easy on the mind's eye, following the rules, offering no challenges in shape or subject. For Diana, or Meredith, this kind of writing would be utterly false to the personal self, and Meredith and his novelist-heroine both believe that this kind of conventional easy writing is false to the potential of the general reader as well, that it underestimates his willingness and his ability to rise to the understanding and enjoyment of new modes. Yet there is also a Meredith who can say of Diana and of himself that this angry anticritic attitude in its more extreme reaches is sheer egoistic moodiness, pardonable, maybe inevitable considering the times, but aesthetically flawed nevertheless. This imagined audience of critics, who snag themselves above all on Meredithian style and its so-called lack of attractiveness, is one of the most important influences on Meredith's prose, and it forms a "character" in his fiction as it does in Fielding's. The critic personifies a reading attitude that the implied reader is rhetorically urged to abandon. But on the other hand the simple anticritic position is not urged as adequate either: "Her mood was bad."

A second audience, often including the critic, is the one Meredith most often calls "the world," a body of readers whose central characteristic is a hypocritically egoistic desire to see art explore and exalt-by-condemning the base and impure, the guilty and shallow, the malicious and stupid side of human nature. This is the audience that calls forth and supports a covey of tame artist-flagellators— "realists" Meredith calls them sarcastically. Theirs is the voice that Diana hears, like that of the tempter in the desert, when she sits down to write under the personally galling burden of her foolish marriage:

> "Exhibit humanity as it is, wallowing, sensual, wicked, behind the mask," a voice called to her; she was allured by the contemplation of the wide-mouthed old dragon Ego, whose portrait, decently painted, establishes an instant touch of exchange between author and public, the latter detected and confessing. Next to the pantomime of Humour and Pathos, a cynical surgical knife at the human bosom seems the surest talisman for this agreeable exchange; and she could cut.
>
> *(Diana of the Crossways, p. 275)*

Here again Meredith is getting very close to his own rhetorical difficulties. He sees the wide-mouthed old dragon Ego in its disguises perhaps better than any novelist of his time. He too can cut. Like Diana, he has been personally wounded by the sensuality, the selfishness and callousness of others; transforming personal injury into a savage contempt for the mixed nature of humanity is a major temptation for authors. Yet the temptation must be rejected, for excessive or compulsive acts of surgery on human nature indicate cynicism and egoism on the author's part, and they breed complacent acceptance of vice or hopeless capitulation to chaos in the reader. As such, the cynical surgical knife, satire, is anti-growth, anti-humor, anti-art, and in fact, to one who believes that, rightly grasped, human nature is "wholesome, bearable, fructifying, finally a delight" *(p. 15)* this attitude is not realistic but anti-real.

A third audience, seemingly much easier for a civilized author and reader to reject, is the largest, most difficult audience of all, the public, Sartre's virtual public, men and women in the most "primitive" stage of readerhood who respond intensely to the tale and its romance trappings and are blind to the attractions of anything but the fiction that is most "moving," in all senses of the word. Meredith's authoress worries about this audience too, and her worries bring her to a perverse originality:

> considering the theme, she had reasonable apprehensions that her Cantatrice would not repay her for the time and labour bestowed on it. No clever transcripts of the dialogue of the day occurred; no hair-breadth 'scapes, perils by sea and land, heroisms of the hero, fine shrieks of the heroine; no set scenes of catching pathos and humour. . . . She did not appeal to the senses, nor to a superficial discernment. So she had the anticipatory sense of its failure, and she wrote her best, in perverseness. *(P. 263)*

Meredith's own construction, his choices of when to dramatize and when to narrate, are heavily influenced by his antipathy to the romantic conventions his heroine muses upon here. But while like Diana he may eject many of the conventions of romance from his novels, the spirit of romance, like the child who is the father of the man, dominates his outlook all through his career until it emerges as Dame Gossip, one of his most arresting narrative dramatis personae, in his last published novel, *The Amazing Marriage*. When we come to examine this novel we will see that what he seems to propose confidently as the smooth process of attaining reading and living adulthood by "rising out of" the childhood attachment to romance is still an open question to the sixty-five-year-old Meredith wrestling with Dame Gossip. In a sense, Meredith obliquely honors this spirit of romance more than all others, more than the philosophic, more than the evolutionary-aesthetic, more even than the comic spirit; and he cares more for, scolds more desperately, this romance audience, this public hooked on the action tale, than the others. For those who love the action, the tale of romance, are at least close to life, close to feeling; if they are children, at least they have not drifted into the phony and destructive maturity of the worldly or the shallowly critical. For the critic or the cynic to reach real reading adulthood, civilized readerhood, he must unlearn bad reading habits. But the public, with its quite promising attachment to "intensity," action, bold happenings, great deeds, strong feelings, need only be brought to see a wider field for action, a subtler domain of happenings, need only turn its attention inward to the landscape of mind, to find there finer but no less intense heroisms, perils, and escapes.

Meredith plays constantly and devotedly to this audience, and my sense of Meredith criticism over the past century is that he did succeed in winning it. At least it is this spirit of amplified and subtilized romance that holds his most appreciative readers to him. The philosophers and stylists abandon him soonest; we of the romance audience remain.[7]

Also condemned, but more mildly, are the reading attitudes not of shallow hostility to authors and subjects but of shallow acceptance, the attitude of an audience of persons reading kindly, blandly, uncritically, swallowing novels like gumdrops, whose main boast is not of reading but of *having read*. Diana Warwick's friend and fellow Irishman Sullivan Smith is like this: "*The Princess Egeria* appeared, with the reviews at her heels, a pack of clappers,

[7] One has only to compare the responses to Meredith of stylists like Henry James, Virginia Woolf, and E. M. Forster, or of "philosophers" like D. H. Lawrence, George Bernard Shaw, and G. K. Chesterton, with those of Richard LeGallienne, J. B. Priestley, and Gillian Beer to see how a special appreciation for the uses of romance will keep a critic longer in charity with Meredith than anything else.

causing her to fly over editions clean as a doe the gates and hedges. To quote Mr. Sullivan Smith, who knew not a sentence of the work save what he gathered of it from Redworth, and then immediately he knew enough to blow his huntsman's horn in honor of the sale" *(p. 200)*.

All these audiences in Meredith are most clearly distinguished with the aid of novelist and reader characters in the plot, where a work and its reception are studied. In addition to Diana's novels, there is the reception of Austin Feverel's book of Aphorisms in *Richard Feverel*, of the panicky newspaper reports in *Beauchamp's Career*, of Colney Durance's satire, *The Rival Tongues*, in *One of Our Conquerors*. Authors and their readers are characters in the plots of many of Meredith's novels and they are made to whip themselves and their writing or reading affectations just like, in their different ways, the supereducated Pole sisters of *Sandra Belloni* and the autodidact philosopher, Gower Woodseer, in *The Amazing Marriage*.

But there is another reader, not a character but "characterized," active not in the plot but in the subplot of the novel, a reader not of Diana Warwick's novels but of Meredith's novel about Diana, a reader imagined and addressed as a person in the audience of the work he is writing. This is the reader who is to become the civilized reader in the course of the book. He is the most important member of the audience, the one shaped to share the values of the heroine and the author. That reader will surely accept Meredith's invitation to move out of the public audience or the worldly audience to identify with Diana and her will to be free of schemes, plots, conventions—even a novelist's: "The woman of flesh refuses pliancy when we want it of her, and will not, until it is her good pleasure, be bent to the development called a climax, as the puppet-woman, mother of fiction and darling of the multitude, ever amiably does, at a hint of the Nuptial Chapter" *(p. 448)*.

The civilized reader whom Meredith has raised from "the multitude" by this kind of rhetoric, the one who identifies with Diana in her quest for freedom, will not rush to the Nuptial Chapter either, and many readers of the novel have taken Meredith to mean that the Nuptial Chapter itself, where Diana accepts the faithful Thomas Redworth, is inconsistent with Diana's character, and that therefore the ending of the novel is a betrayal of his own principles. But what these discontented readers fail to see, I think, is the half-turn away from the civilized stance, the reading-with-the-head, the free philosophic distance, that Meredith is constantly making in the final chapters of his novels. I will be discussing this at length in later chapters, but this half-turn in Diana is one of the most interesting, most "natural," and hence easiest to miss, of all of Meredith's retreats from the ideal of the civilized reader.

To see this we must examine the character of Diana as Meredith created her, to see whether or not his nuptial ending was inconsistent with her development. Here, as in so many of Meredith's characterizations, the key word is "read." His heroine's stance toward her world has always been that of a "reader." The key paragraph that lets the reader of the novel into Meredith's structural problem about the free woman and the puppet woman turns in mid flow to suggest that a woman may be a puppet to a fear *masquerading* as a freedom, that the best "reader" alive is no less a mark for the Comic Spirit:

> [Diana] read both [Redworth] and Emma, whose inner bosom was revealed to her without an effort to see. But her characteristic chasteness of mind,—not coldness of the blood,—which had supported an arduous conflict, past all existing rights closely to depict, and which barbed her to pierce to the wishes threatening her freedom, deceived her now to think her flaming blushes came of her relentless divination on behalf of her recovered treasure: whereby the clear reading of others distracted the view of herself. *(P. 449)*

Here we have the truth of Diana's character: she is deceived in her reading of herself. The real secret Diana has carried all through the novel had nothing to do with politics; it was that she carried heat in her blood, flaming

71

blushes, to the measure of her "brainstuff" and beyond. She won her fame by her exercise of brain, wit, subtlety, analytic power, linguistic brilliance. A society shocked to find these qualities in a woman mirrored them back to her, and she formed her image of herself in that glass. The image was but a partial one that hid from her and the reader—and to stretch the thought almost but not quite to fantasy, the author—the plain truth that all the events of her life were shaped by a desire of the blood, by intense feeling more than keen insight. She first articulated this truth in reference to political life: "Oh, for a despot!" Uttered in an ardent youth when, as the novelist describes, "Romance affected politics, transformed economy, irradiated philosophy" *(p. 46)*, this Carlylean cry stands out starkly at the other pole to Diana's treasuring of her freedom. Though the desire for intensely devoted servitude was moderated under an increasingly perceptive vision of its essential selfishness—"The cry was for a benevolent despot, naturally, a large-minded benevolent despot. In short a despot to obey their bidding"—though the heat of that cry was cooled by dint of reading solid writers and "using the brains they possessed," nevertheless, of the two brainy women who were feeling that heat, it was the friend, Lady Dunstane, who took the lead in the cooling, Diana who "had to be tugged." It was Diana's life that revealed, under its patina of passive victimizations, through the ambiguity of its huntress-hunted imagery, a ceaseless quest for a despot to do her bidding. Each of her lovers Diana rules, then frees, in a search for that peculiarly romantic brand of freedom which is passionate subjection. Hers was "a nature capable of accepting subjection only by burning," and she does not yet know this of herself. She accepts Thomas Redworth's offer as she accepted Warwick's long before, because she thinks she is screening herself off from passion, because it is "the wisest thing a waif can do" *(pp. 64-65)*. But wisdom is not the whole of Diana; she marries to burn, too. In this Nuptial Chapter, thinking she is accepting a cool older man to protect her from heat, she has in fact cornered herself into doing precisely what she wants, burning into love again. One kiss from the surprisingly passionate Redworth is enough to "whirl her out of every sensibility but the swimming one of her loss of self in the man . . . her thoughts one blush, her brain a fire-fount" *(p. 483)*. She has found her despot again, and her reading of herself is somewhat advanced: "All that I have had to endure, or so it seems to me: it may be my way of excusing myself:—I know my cunning in that particular art" *(p. 484)*. But her reading of herself is not yet perfect. Her editor says:

> She was not enamoured: she could say it to herself. She had, however, been surprised, both by the man and her unprotesting submission, surprised and warmed, unaccountably warmed. Clearness of mind in the woman chaste by nature, however little ignorant it allowed her to be in the general review of herself, could not compass the immediately personal, with its acknowledgement of her subserviency to touch and pressure—and more, stranger, her readiness to kindle. *(P. 487)*

Diana's "readiness to kindle," a still unread aspect and foundation girder of her character, has received less attention from her society, her reader, even her author, than her "clearness of mind." Meredith, encompassing part if not all of the romance that moves in him, has prepared a shock for the civilized reader, I think, in the final section of *Diana of the Crossways*, which he slyly opens with the part-chapter title, "An Adventure into Anti-Climax." The shock is that the clearness of mind which characterizes the heroine, with which the civilized reader has identified himself, which he is seeking to make his own in that complex act of perception and judgment which is reading, is adequate only to prevent ignorance "in the general review": it is not alone enough to grasp that wisdom which partakes of the immediately personal. It is as though, operating on that sense of an ending by which the reader requires that

73

he be brought to the expected ending by means of an un-expected route,[8] Meredith were using the exploration, the exploitation, the arduous demonstration and working out of the state of clarity of mind to vindicate romance in the end, as we always had hoped. He means to say that he has read through the layers of Diana's very modern and free-dom-loving character with all the insight and clarity of which he is capable finally to discern that she wants a Nuptial Chapter, that it is in fact her chosen ending. He means to tell the civilized reader, who will have nothing to do with puppet people in life or in art, that the best that clear-mindedness or philosophical analysis can do (and it is a signal service) is to bring the reader face to face with the mysterious and the intensely personal, which, after analysis has shaken all the foam it can to the top, still and always *is* the wine in the bottle of the fiction.

III. Style as Exercise

Meredith is using style, too, I think, to create this careful and exhausting construction of the state of clear-minded-ness, which in the end he must call not fully adequate. Style, it is widely argued, is what "ruined" Meredith. Liberal, even pioneering, in his thought, earnest, not triv-ial or selfish in the service of art, gifted with mind, song, and courage, he missed his place in the pantheon of the truly great, the story goes, because he could not rid him-self of the damaging mannerisms in his style.

Meredith's letters reveal no more than the usual number of confessions about his failures in style. He knew that he sometimes labored, sometimes overhastily shot forth on his

[8] "Peripateia, which has been called the equivalent in narrative of irony in rhetoric, is present in every story of the least structural sophistication. Now peripateia depends on our confidence of the end; it is a disconfirmation followed by a consonance; the interest of having our expectations falsified is obviously related to our wish to reach the discovery or recognition by an unexpected and instruc-tive route" (Frank Kermode, *The Sense of an Ending* [London: Oxford Univ. Press, 1966], p. 18).

course, that he ought to have revised, more and better. Writing as he did for the most part under the guns of magazine deadlines and even sometimes the bill collectors, he had a habit, especially in his first decades of writing, of finishing projects hastily, half-satisfied and looking forward to correcting one novel's errors in the next. He had a very sound reader's dissatisfaction with much of his work, and much of that dissatisfaction in fact had to do with style, if we take style in its broadest sense to mean all those choices in the handling of words to present ideas, from semistructural decisions like when to dramatize and when to narrate to the deployment of diction, all those conscious arrangements in the rhythm of events, of voices, of syllables that constitute the personal mark of a literary craftsman. He worried about the presentation of action in ways I will discuss later; and, despite his faith in the comic ideal of manners not men, he agonized about his people's truthfulness to life in fruitful ways that he dramatized in his plots as well as his subplots. Presenting people largely through the motions of their minds, he also worried about his ability to handle clearly and with coherence the flash and dazzle and disappearance of ideas in the minds of his characters.

But none of these dissatisfactions ever tempted him even to moderate the most typical and most maligned of his stylistic habits, his deliberate effort to suggest, demonstrate, insist upon, the fantastic effort and energy, the complex rhythms of focus and diffusion, in the motion of mind. Indeed it is not an exaggeration to say that Meredith's style was in many ways a straining toward that "stream-of-consciousness" technique by which his immediate descendants in the history of fiction sought to communicate and reproduce the peculiar devious coherence with which the consciousness takes in, plays with, organizes, its perceptions.

In the effort to reproduce the eddies and ripples and rushes of consciousness, an effort that was largely the attempt to reproduce the movement of his own mind among the options, the fears, the intuitions his characters were experiencing, Meredith drew constantly upon half-a-dozen eccentric habits of expression that together form the general critical notion of "Meredithian" style. Perhaps the most immediately noticeable eccentricity is the paragraph-sentence, with its Teutonic splinter of grammatical form and its mannered disregard of clause subordination.

Another basic aspect of Meredithian style is the spacious and sometimes eccentric vocabulary he employs, mixing concepts from nineteenth-century science, philosophy, religion, politics, and even street-lore with fragments of French and German literature, Celtic locutions, and Latin epigram. Meredith's education was spasmodic, part of it received on the Continent. For the most part he was an autodidact. He drew from wide, enthusiastic, but not always precise reading; everything from Juvenal to the *Arabian Nights* to Ferraday to popular melodrama was grist to the mill of his insatiable need for unusual imagery, and he hopped among the mixed contents of his mind with a facility and audacity at times equally irritating to the man in the street and the graduate of Oxford.

Still more irritating both to purists in style and to simple advocates of plain speaking is Meredith's indifference to the first rules of grammar. Indeed it sometimes seems as though he is not merely indifferent but positively perverse in his supposition that a noun might be a verb, an adjective an adverb, and the ill-subordinated clauses may go on forever.

Another distinctive habit of Meredithian style is the tendency to go to the active verb and the characterized abstraction in expressing mental events. This habit is, as we shall see, connected with Meredith's attempt to dramatize the realm of inner history as a place where human qualities act upon one another rather than a realm in which the person may only have things "happen to" him.

These examples all point to verbal habits connected with Meredith's passion for originality and for freedom of expression; he is vulnerable to criticism on these points and he knows it, but he considers that kind of criticism by and large a matter of taste and does not concern himself much with it. There are two other areas of his style, though, where he knows he is vulnerable and at the same time is concerned to affirm both his right to work in this manner and the reader's need to have him work thus. The first of these two very important aspects of Meredithian style is the habit of constructing the narrative so as to focus increasingly on the inner response to events in the world of behavior instead of on the action itself, a habit that plays havoc with conventional notions of good novel construction. The second is the perpetual, dazzling, in a sense desperate dependence upon metaphor to convey not only theme and philosophy, but character, concrete perception, and even the simplest passing observations.

These last two aspects of style are intimately connected with the theme of this study, for Meredith's case to the readers of his novel is simply this: if you will not be made to focus on the movements of mind which are the well-springs of action you have no right to call yourself a reader, and you cannot begin to be an adept in this crucial activity of reading unless you can train your own mind to move with facility and clarity between surface and depth, appearance and reality, suggestion and inference, metaphor and the difficult-to-name reality to which metaphor points. This argument is implicit in all Meredith's novels and is an open and important part of *One of Our Conquerors* and *The Amazing Marriage*. It is in these two areas of style that the charge, or the description really, of "stylization" applies to Meredith. One of the provocative, and I think true, things that Susan Sontag has said about art is that "stylization, as distinct from style, reflects an ambivalence (affection contradicted by contempt, obsession contradicted by irony) towards the subject matter."[9] This remark has particular pertinence to those stylists, like Meredith, whose subject matter was partly the reader. In the tradition of the

[9] *Against Interpretation and Other Essays* (New York: Farrar, Straus and Giroux, Inc., 1969), p. 28.

civilized reader, contempt for the powers and talents of the general audience always hovers around the affection an author demonstrates for his own fictional reader, and an author may well be driven to a heightened argumentativeness about his acceptability to readers by this conflict. For those deeply concerned about the teaching properties of fiction and at the same time aware of their own flaws and of the divided concerns of the reading audience, irony is a tempting defense against obsession. The extravagance and tenacity with which Meredith argued and demonstrated in his novels his position that metaphor and mind could put man together again, and put him in touch with the mystery of creation, can be taken as an indication that his position contained a strong element of *willed* conviction, of faith.

This element of willed conviction is what gives the tension to the paradox that the often craggy and murky Meredithian style offers to the reader, that if he will only work hard enough at the reading, the state of clarity will reward him. Critical readers from his day to ours have unerringly caught that message; where they begin their criticism complaining about technical matters of grammar and construction and mixture of methods they invariably wind up complaining most heartily and convincingly about fatigue. Here for instance is Walter Allen, dismissing Meredith in his respected history of the English novel: "His prose, besides, is as far removed as it can be from our present ideas of what constitutes good style. At its worst it is rebarbatively Teutonic and vulgar, and at its best, except when it fuses into poetry, it is too brilliant, fatiguing because of excess of epigram and metaphor; it dazzles, and because it dazzles, tires the mind."[10] Meredith, arguing back, does indeed find thinking, writing, and reading as fatiguing a composite action as the mountain climbing he prided himself on, and he prides himself on fatiguing, and being fatigued, for much the same reason: not only is

[10] Rebarbatively Teutonic? (*The English Novel* [New York: Dutton, 1954], p. 276).

there a rewarding view at the top of the mountain, but the state of exercise is healthier than the state of idleness. Meredith preached and practiced a sort of Muscular Readerhood that he did not hesitate to invite and create in his reader. If anyone *were* able to estimate the nonfatiguing per-page rate of epigrams and metaphors in "our present ideas of what constitutes good style," it seems likely that Meredith would set out to exceed it. Still, the deliberate play to the reader's reach instead of his grasp has a moral-aesthetic content to it as well as an athletic one. Paradoxically that taking of risks in language is Meredith's way of reaching to the reader's widest capacity for ultimate states of clear-mindedness. The reader is stretched by the effort of filling compressed images, holding together extended metaphors, and following subtle analytic demonstrations of the process of mind, stretched tensely to take in and view coherently more perhaps than he ever has before. Vernon Lee calls attention to this aspect of Meredith's prose, a quality she calls "activity of the rapidly spotting, twigging kind," where the reader "is told a number of things at whose meaning he must make a rapid guess."[11] "Fatigue!" one can sometimes hear Meredith shout scornfully from the next precipice. That is for the world, and the critic, not for the civilized reader.

Yet fatigue figures as one of Meredith's underlying worries, too, or rather not fatigue but paralysis of the muscles stretched to take in so much. So bulked and tensed with complex and contradictory thought, can a man move to take any action? So teased and stuffed with implication, can language flow at all? Meredith takes the risk because he must; like his language he is naturally burdened with (and unthinkable without) ideas, poetry, and conflict. But when he is true to his truest form, he saves a little comic light too for the philosopher, the heartily exercised, clear-thinking man who is at bottom either disconnected from the mysteries of feeling and hence something of a fool or

[11] *The Handling of Words and Other Studies in Literary Psychology* (London: The Bodley Head, 1923), pp. 197, 199.

a scoundrel or else still helplessly rolled in the current of feeling and hence not yet completely "read" by himself.

The clear-thinking person is the characterized reader as well as the character. "This," thinks Lady Dunstane of one of Diana's witty, brainy letters, "was always her secret pride of fancy—the belief in her possession of a disengaged intellect" *(p. 167)*. The disengaged intellect—pride above all of the civilized reader, seeming necessity for the Comic Spirit, identifying mark of the philosopher—is often a fancy and a falsehood in Meredith's world, however paradoxically he insists on exercising and goading his characters and his readers into the heights of clear-mindedness. The very attitude of comedy is compromised if it remains for long as disengaged intellect. Of the varieties of nineteenth-century audience that Meredith dramatized in his novels it often seems as if the romantic public, which favors the cruder expressions of intensity and feeling, runs less risk of falling into serious errors in reading than the worldly, who pretend to an intellectual disdain of the world, or the critics, who pretend to an intellectual control of the rules of art and life, or even the civilized reader himself, who may have achieved his eminence, his intellectual comprehension of all the aspects of life, at the cost of severing himself from his feelings as well as from his fellows. He may have achieved his wise understanding of universals, of Fielding's nature, by the loss of the intensely personal. Even the most courageous and humane of disengaged intellects run this risk; even the most sincere devotees of philosophy may fall, and use their philosophy, their "disengaged intellects," as a mask for some unadmitted human fear or lack or lust. If this is so, then into what fear or lust or lack is the novelist inviting the civilized reader?

3. The Ordeal of Philosophy

> To satisfy his appetites without rashly staking his
> character was the Wise Youth's problem. He had no
> intimates save Gibbon and Horace, and the society
> of these fine aristocrats of literature helped him
> to accept humanity as it had been, and was:
> a Supreme Ironic Procession, with Laughter of
> Gods in the background. Why not laughter of
> Mortals also? Adrian had his laugh in his
> comfortable corner. . . . He lived in eminent
> self-content, as one lying on soft clouds, lapt in
> sunshine. Nor Jove, nor Apollo, cast eye upon the
> maids of earth with cooler fire of selection, or
> pursued them in the covert with more sacred
> impunity. (*The Ordeal of Richard Feverel*, p. 32)

LIKE ST. PAUL'S CHARITY, MEREDITH'S "PHILOSO-
phy" is scarcely definable in its essence, but unmistakable in its acts. It is a slippery term, but because it
recurs so often in Meredith, and is the Grail in the Ordeal
of Richard Feverel, some attempt to grasp what it was to
Meredith must be made. Philosophy is essentially the
integrating factor that keeps blood, brain, and spirit[1] in

---

[1] This so-called Meredithian triad has its most formal expression in the long philosophical pastoral allegory, "The Woods of
Westermain," published in the 1883 volume, *Poems and Lyrics
of the Joy of Earth* (Memorial Edition, *Poems*, II, 43).

> Each of each in sequent birth,
> Blood and brain and spirit, three
> (Say the deepest gnomes of Earth),
> Join for true felicity.
> Are they parted, then expect
> Someone sailing will be wrecked:

touch with each other, that knits feeling, thought, and upward or outward aspiration together. Philosophy is the instinct to "shapeliness" in being, and comedy is the perception of unshapeliness; the two work in tandem. In experience, however, it seems that comedy is the primary act, for by the time consciousness dawns in a young man or woman in Meredith's world he or she is already unshapely —usually with a superfluity of "blood," feeling—and the comic perception of imbalance rightly triggers the effort toward shapeliness. This dynamic reminds one of the old Doctrine of Humours; and yet for Meredith health is far from being a matter of purging blood to restore the balance to the brain. It is much more a matter of developing brain to equal blood, or, as we shall see in the case of Victor Radnor in *One of Our Conquerors*, of connecting a well-developed mind, a strong devoted heart, and a driving progressive spirit, which have somehow become separated and are pulling in different directions. Ideally for Meredith "philosophic" does not mean "detached"; it is not the concentration of consciousness in the brain but the arousal and dispersal of consciousness all through being. In his theory Meredith is surprisingly close to Lawrence.

Still, Meredith saw in man a different, perhaps more Victorian, sort of unshapeliness than did Lawrence, and he chose philosophy with all its connotations of mental keenness, as the word to describe his ideal pitch of human integration because he saw diseases of the brain, cancers of thought, as the central human problem in much the same way as Lawrence saw diseases of the will (perhaps corresponding to spirit in Meredith's triad) at the fountainhead of modern misery.

Separate hunting are they sped,
Scan the morsel coveted.
Earth that Triad is: she hides
Joy from him who that divides,
Showers it when the three are one
Glassing her in union.

Meredith uses the word "philosophy" essentially to indicate three activities of mind. (Indeed one can often substitute the word "psychology" in the modern sense for Meredith's "philosophy," or even, less frequently, the word "psychoanalysis." Philosophy is an action, a process of shaping being.) First, philosophy is simply self-mastery, the treatment of fevers, the control of appetite. This philosophy has two possible perversions: the establishment of a disintegrative tyranny of mind, of "sense," over personality, or worse, the re-establishment of appetite under the cloak of a specious dedication to mind. Such is the sin, one of the sins, of Adrian Harley in *Richard Feverel*. Second, philosophy is simply an educated understanding, a widely broadened appreciation of complexity, mystery, and diversity. This philosophy likewise has perversions, the establishment of a disintegrative tyranny of "sensibility," or worse, the re-establishment of selfishness in the guise of sensibility. Such, we shall see in the next chapter, is the sin of *Sandra Belloni*'s Wilfrid Pole. Thirdly and pre-eminently for Meredith, philosophy is the active integrator of powers inside and outside the person, the integrator of temperament with circumstance, the agent of a man's wholeness, oneness, with nature, of his being-in-the-world, to borrow a phrase from contemporary philosophy. Both internal and external history are present in thought, mingled there, and that mind is "philosophic" which, in a natural rhythm of waiting for, then seizing upon, that mingled presence, can show man to himself as a whole being in a whole nature. "Mind" is a man's look upon himself, an important concept also explored in the "Essay on Comedy." What the philosophic mind sees, the mind that has waited for and seized upon all that is given to and accomplished by thought, is neither "rose-pink nor dirty drab . . . but wholesome, bearable, fructifying, finally a delight." This active element of philosophy in mind, that which waits for and seizes integrity out of the chaos of consciousness, has an inherent paradox in it: philosophy freely creates and invents *a* philosophy, a philosophical look

83

upon life, out of the malleable materials of thought, but what it creates *is* the Real.

It is important to point out here that this philosophy is by no means limited to the mentally exceptional or reserved to the "poet." Philosophy for Meredith is a natural power of the human mind; to exercise philosophy it is not necessary to have a thought-stream full of exalted rational categories or even of manifold and striking experiences; it is merely necessary to integrate fully all the information you do have, from inside and outside, from the look upon self and upon life. Thus, for instance, Mrs. Berry in *Richard Feverel*, or Frank Skepsey in *One of Our Conquerors*, or Madge Winch in *The Amazing Marriage* are shown at the same philosophical activities as their masters, trying to align in their minds the broken human situations around them. While their efforts are often amusing, and meant to be, they usually allow these minor characters to win through to the truths, to image the realities, to see wholly or philosophically, before the central characters in the book do.

Imperfections of sight, narrowness, rashness, childishness, exaggerations or diminishments caused by ill-directed or badly controlled feeling, these are the concerns of Meredith's plots, these are the follies of those without philosophy. For the philosopher the danger is not blindness; quite the opposite. Watching the disasters accumulate around the head of Richard Feverel, old Bessie Berry pins it down in conversation with Lady Blandish: "My lady, if I may speak so bold, I'd say the sin that's bein' done is the sin o' the lookers on" *(p. 472)*.

Lookers-on abound during the education of Richard Feverel: maids, servants, neighbors, indeed the whole world can be said to be looking on as Sir Austin, Richard's father, brings up the boy according to a "scientific" system precisely calibrated to anticipate, control, and often foil each natural urge as it blossoms. For Sir Austin wrote a book about his philosophy, *The Pilgrim's Scrip*, and many of the aphorisms of that book form The Notebook, the curriculum for Richard's education. The philosophy is a Manichean one that seeks to expunge the "devil" in the boy and promote the "angel"—the devil more or less corresponding to woman, or the love of woman, and the angel, it is obvious to almost all except the philosopher, corresponding to Sir Austin himself, or the boy's love and reverence for him. "There are fathers," says Richard's father, "who are content to be simply obeyed. Now I would require not only that my son should obey; I would have him guiltless of the impulse to gainsay my wishes, feeling me in him stronger than his undeveloped nature, up to a certain period, where my responsibility ends and his commences" *(p. 162)*. This sort of talk, as first Adrian Harley and then the narrator confirm for the reader, hides from the philosophic Sir Austin his very personal and damnable intention, the temptation of all philosophers, to be the God of that systematized machine forever—"Man," he orates a moment later, "is a self-acting machine." This distanced view also hides from Sir Austin the very unphilosophic repression/compensation neurosis that the System and the boy represent for the father. Meredith points directly to this neurosis in the first chapter: the Baronet's wife had left him for another man just after Richard's birth and the System is largely a move to protect that mortal psychic wound in himself. Publication of his book has brought numerous fair women to court the philosopher and his intellect, and the narrator reports their failure thus: "He must have been ultimately betrayed by his softness, but as often happens, he was fully armed at his weakest point, namely, the heart. He had a son, and his heart was filled by him. He had a son, and he was incubating a System" *(p. 10)*. Much of the Baronet's subsequent incomprehensible behavior is explained when we remember that in some mysterious dimension of mind his son is his betraying wife and his System is his son. No wonder Richard is capable of experiencing (but not understanding) sudden wild inexplicable rages. He cannot connect them directly with his much-loved father, so he transfers their source to the outside, just as Sir Austin had earlier transferred to the universe the personal betrayal he had suffered, and the seeds of that subservience to the idea of fate that in Meredith's world is sure to destroy a man sprout in the son as in the father. A hysterical partly erotic surrender to this idea makes one a looker-on at one's own life and being, and Richard, killed in spirit in the duel he byronically sought as his fate, his own personal meeting with the "Ordeal of the Feverels," is in this state at the end of the book.

Lady Blandish, Sir Austin's neighbor, is another looker-on at the ordeal of Richard Feverel. She has for years been engaged in a sentimental dalliance with the Baronet, and, although the System outrages her common sense from time to time, she has half-deceitfully applauded it while pursuing Sir Austin's heart and toying with her own. As the dalliance turns to love, however, she begins to see him more clearly (contrary to popular adage, for Meredith real love *lends* perception), and as he senses both her growing love and her growing perceptiveness, the lonely and desperate Sir Austin involuntarily retreats from her toward the novel's most graceful, most garrulous, guiltiest looker-on, Adrian Harley:

> He wished it had been Adrian who had come to him. He had an extraordinary longing for Adrian's society. He knew that the Wise Youth would divine how to treat him, and he mentally confessed to just enough weakness to demand a certain kind of management. Besides, Adrian, he had not a doubt, would accept him entirely as he seemed, and not pester him in any way by trying to unlock his heart. . . . *(P. 393)*

I. Adrian Harley: The Reader's Friend

Let us stop for a moment and consider Adrian Harley as a ficelle. The term is of course James's, and his concept is elaborated in the prefaces to *Portrait of a Lady* and *The Ambassadors*. In the former preface he refers to the reader's sense that some characters belong intimately to the subject or theme of the narrative and others to the treatment of the theme. In the preface to *The Ambassadors*, describing Maria Gostrey as the touchstone ficelle, "the reader's friend," he goes on to say that the ficelle is "an enrolled, a direct aid to lucidity," and calls him a true artist who can maintain in his creation of ficelles "a deep dissimulation of his dependence on them" for that lucidity.[2] Now, Adrian Harley is Richard Feverel's cousin, nephew to Sir Austin Feverel and one of the "inmates" of Raynham Abbey by virtue of his uncle's appointment of him as tutor to the young boy. He is thus enlisted as an administrative aid to the System of education by which Sir Austin, the scientific humanist, intends to raise his son. Adrian has profound doubts about the System—so does Lady Blandish, the novel's other major ficelle. But Adrian has with genial cynicism sold himself to Sir Austin for the meals, the maids, and the library of Raynham, and Lady Blandish is sentimentally in love with the philosopher-king she thinks she sees in the baronet, so the System receives no essential challenge from them in Sir Austin's hearing, only in the reader's. Adrian is the really culpable offender in this:

> "See," he thought, "This boy has tasted his first scraggy morsel of life to-day, and already he talks like an old-stager, and has, if I mistake not, been acting too. My respected Chief," he apostrophized Sir Austin, "combustibles are only the more dangerous for compression. This boy will be ravenous for Earth when he is let loose, and very soon make his share of it look as foolish as yonder game-pie!"—a prophecy Adrian kept to himself.
>
> *(Richard Feverel, p. 62)*

The System produces a kind of schizophrenia in Richard; the exalted hubristic behavior of Prince and Knight alternates with the most abject surrenders to self-loathing.

---

[2] *The Ambassadors*, I (New York: Charles Scribner's Sons, 1909), xix.

At a hysterical pitch of the former he runs off with Lucy Desborough, the innocent beauty of the neighborhood, Miranda to his shipwrecked Ferdinand. At a hysterical pitch of self-loathing he abandons his wife in their honeymoon cottage to try and restore his credit with his father. In the final chapters four violent swings of his personality bring him to disaster. Thinking to play knight-errant to the worldly Bella Mount, he becomes instead her lover, and self-loathing drives him still further from Lucy. Then in a virtuoso piece of writing, Meredith unites the internal working in Richard's mind of the news of the birth of his son and the external passion of an Alpine storm, and Richard, transfigured and exalted, rushes back to his wife to take up the threads of his life again. Fate puts him in the way of the lecherous Lord Montfalcon, who had had designs on Lucy after Richard had abandoned her, and Richard's schizophrenia, wrought up to the highest pitch of simultaneous knight-errantry and self-abasement, drives him to challenge the lord to a duel and leave Lucy again the very night of his homecoming. He emerges seriously wounded and dead in spirit; Lucy collapses and dies under the shock of progressive abandonments,[3] and nothing is left

[3] Meredith took a severe critical beating for the fact and mode of Lucy's death in this novel, and he is still taking it. Victorian criticism followed the line of Geraldine Jewsbury's complaint, "This is a painful book" (in *The Athenaeum*, July 1859 [rpt. *Critical Heritage*, p. 67]), and later criticism has tended to the aesthetic criticism proposed by Samuel Lucas, "The death of Lucy is unnecessary and in defiance of poetic justice" (in *The Times*, Oct. 1859 [rpt. *Critical Heritage*, p. 82]). Meredith was sufficiently annoyed by the criticism to threaten death to Diana Warwick in letters to friends while working on that novel, and sufficiently affected by it to advise George Gissing to provide the public with upbeat endings. He did not, of course, always follow his own advice, as the sudden death of Neville Beauchamp in the last chapter of *Beauchamp's Career* testifies. My own sense of the heroine's death is that it is quite adequately prepared for in the growing anxiety of Bessy Berry about Lucy's health; in the psychic shocks progressively deepening as her lover leaves her first to the marriage schemes of her relatives, then to the unwholesome atmosphere of

alive but the philosophers and the System—the despairing Lady Blandish is "not quite sure that [Sir Austin] is an altered man even now the blow has struck him" *(Richard Feverel, p. 590).*

In all this Adrian Harley seems essentially a looker-on: his only contribution (but an enormous one for Meredith's real purpose) to the *material* has been to do nothing directly, to entirely refuse to act for the good, to use his insights and doubts for nothing but his own entertainment. It seems that he belongs to the treatment of the material. He sees the life around him as a story, a play, and the people around him as characters, and he reports what he sees to himself, sometimes to the other characters, always to the fictional reader, who is also viewing the action of the story. Yet this is Meredith's very point about Adrian. It is one thing to strive for the comic spirit, the philosophic overview, as one of the tools with which to meet life; it is

---

the Isle of Wight, then alone at the much-feared Raynham Abbey; and especially in the scene of tragicomic hysterics with the baby crying and Richard gone and the mother and the nurse trying to calm baby and themselves and absorb the fact of Richard's departure: " 'It's Mr. Richard have gone, Sir Austin! have gone from his wife and babe! Rum-te-um-te-iddledy—Oh, my goodness! what sorrow's come on us!' and Mrs. Berry wept, and sang to baby, and baby cried vehemently, and Lucy, sobbing, took him and danced him and sang to him with drawn lips and tears dropping over him" (p. 587). In Meredith's last novel we shall see again how he alludes to the powerful and destructive neurotic feelings that may arise in a wife whose child is injured or threatened by some action of the father. The loss of reason Lucy suffers when the father of her child leaves touches delicately and damningly on the situation between Sir Austin and *his* abandoned child, as Lady Blandish's perception that "had [Lucy] not so violently controlled her nature as she did, I believe she might have been saved" (p. 589) touches on the fault of Sir Austin's System. Lucy's death and Richard's trauma, of course, leave the child largely under the aegis of the grandfather, giving a special urgency to Lady Blandish's worry that Sir Austin still may not have learned what his mistake was, as it gives a special quality of victory and hopefulness to the emergence of Lady Blandish as a prime and truly "philosophic" force in the life of grandfather, son, and grandson.

quite another to sit in a box and view life itself as a comedy. It is one thing to serve the author and reader of a book as a ficelle, a repository of information; it is another to serve in life as a mere commentator to oneself on the passing show. Adrian is not simply part of the treatment of Meredith's story here; his own treatment of life is part of the material. The "rounded" character of Adrian as disengaged intellect and unworthy tutor of the boy Richard is not simply an artist's disguise of his ficelle but an intimate and complex encounter with one of the central figures in Meredithian characterization, the philosopher gone wrong.

This encounter is all the more poignant because the novel in its whole spirit, not simply in one character or one situation, is a transformation almost literally of Meredith's own internal history, an attempt to integrate fully all that he had seen and felt and understood about the two central traumas of his own life. The struggles to achieve a true and avoid a false philosophy pictured in the book are powerfully linked to his personal struggles.

George Meredith was essentially an orphan: he lived like one, he felt like one, he wrote like one. Critics have seized upon the aloof, ironic, almost historian-curator attitude he often adopts toward England and Englishmen to call his writing that of an exile or an alien. But in fact he wrote like an orphan, out of strong ties established not at the parental but rather at a sort of great-grandparental level—out of relationships one step removed from the guilt and knot of parent-child bonds. His mother died when he was two, and he never established any intimacy with his father. Welsh ancestry, German schooling, French and Latin literature were his grandparents, and they gave him both roots and a point of view, and freedom to criticize from a kind of secure isolation. Insecurity entered with Mary Ellen Peacock Nicolls, whom Meredith married in 1849 when he was twenty-one. She was seven years older than he and strong-willed, and the combination of inadequate income, physical passion, and intellectual rivalry present in the household seems to have made the marriage rocky from the start. The Merediths had a son, Arthur, in 1853, but by 1856 the marriage was in deep trouble. In 1857 Mary met the minor pre-Raphaelite painter Henry Wallis (caricatured as the poet Diaper Sandoe in *Richard Feverel*); she left Meredith to bear Wallis's son the next year. The lovers went abroad for awhile, then Mary returned, alone. Meredith refused to see her again and up to the last week of her life refused to allow Arthur to see her either. She died in 1861.

Such was Meredith's internal history while he conceived and wrote *The Ordeal of Richard Feverel* in 1857-59. Still in the future was Meredith's happy second marriage in 1864 to Marie Vuillamy, but his unforgiving and partly tyrannical behavior to his first wife was already laying the basis for his strangely muted and unsatisfactory relationship with Arthur. He had rashly staked his character on marriage, fatherhood, and authorship, and found himself rejected, broke, cuckolded, and ill at ease in the presence of his son. Without doubt the laughter of gods was audible in the background of his sorely tried mind.

Why not laughter of mortals also? This is the question we can feel Meredith struggling with during this novel of a tyrannical father, a runaway wife, and a son who seems to some philosophic eyes bound to reenact the father's tragedy. As he asks it of himself, Meredith asks the question of the reader too, with the help of the gifted, dangerous, philosopher-artist Adrian Harley.

For he is a sort of artist. As a disengaged intellect and commentator on the tableaux of life, for instance, Adrian names the people around him, reducing them to characters, and further to the status of "walking concept":[4]

---

[4] A term Sheldon Sacks has coined to define "typical" characters who, while not mere indistinguishable dead labels, are animated or slightly rounded by a group of traits relating to a single important trait. One of Sacks's main examples, interestingly for our purposes, is the philosopher Square in *Tom Jones*, whose animating traits—sublimated roaring appetite, concern for reputation,

A venerable lady, known as Great-Aunt Grantley, who had money to bequeath to the Heir, and whom Adrian called The Eighteenth Century, occupied with Hippias the background of the house and shared her caudles with him. . . . Another chief personage of the establishment was Benson, the butler: Heavy Benson, Adrian called him, from the mace-like fashion with which he wielded his respectability, and the fact of a connubial misfortune.

(Pp. 28, 33-34)

Adrian names the relationships between his characters: "Clare had always been blindly obedient to her mother (Adrian called them, Mrs. Doria Battledoria and the fair Shuttlecockiana) and her mother accepted in this blind obedience the entire text of her character" *(p. 341).* He names the very scenery where the actions of the story take place, diminishing all action to the status of tableau: "A little laurel-shaded Temple of white marble looked out on the river from a knoll bordering the Raynham beech-woods, and was dubbed by Adrian 'Daphne's Bower' " *(p. 83).*

More important, he names the actions themselves; he names them comedies, and sees the three major episodes of the book as plays, with himself as onlooker and occasional stage manager. The first and most important naming takes place when the spirited Richard, fourteen and playing outlaw chief in despite of his father, has revenged himself on Farmer Blaize for administering a well-deserved whipping to him during a poaching expedition by firing the farmer's rick, through the handy offices of a disgruntled laborer, Tom Bakewell. Richard's "tool" is apprehended, and the boy is in agonies over the moral choice presented him. His tutor Adrian, no dummy, has guessed the truth immediately, and is making his charge miserable

---

ease of rhetorical analysis, consummate self-deception about his morality—are all bound together to illuminate, negatively, the trait, type, figure, of the philosopher (*Fiction and the Shape of Belief*, ch. 4).

(and a liar into the bargain) by his masterful handling, fisherman to pike, of the dinner table conversations. His cousin Austin, also guessing the truth, proposes action to invite Richard to tell the truth and untangle the wildly confusing situation involving Bakewell, Blaize, Feverel, and the fire. The names alone are too much for a Comic Spirit and Horatian reader to resist: Adrian will not act directly. "I dread the idea of the curtain going down" *(p. 80)* he tells Austin, and again, "Let the wild colt run free. We can't help them, we can only look on. We should spoil the play" *(p. 82).* Meredith's narrator has already adopted all of Adrian's other "names," and he adopts this one, and its vision, for the whole of chapter 14: "In Which the Last Act of the Bakewell Comedy is Closed in a Letter." That letter, one from Richard to his rick-burning fellow outlaw, Rip Thompson, which recounts the safe ending of the incident, truth out, nobody transported, father and son restored to amity, shows Adrian a hilarious observer of the ironic procession: "Well the Bantam was told to state what he had seen and the moment he began Rady who was close by me began to shake, and he was laughing I knew though his face was as grave as Sir Miles. You never heard such a rigmarole but I could not laugh" *(p. 117).* The letter also shows young Richard reacting to his tutor's stance with an emotion the boy might have done well to examine further: "I looked him straight in the face and he said to me he was doing me a service in getting Tom committed and clearing the country of such fellows and Rady began laughing. I hate Rady" *(pp. 116-17).*

Adrian has served as the reader's friend and the narrator's in this episode by giving it the eminently lucid form of a "comedy." The narrator ends the chapter thus: "And so ended the last act of the Bakewell Comedy, on which the curtain closes with Sir Austin's pointing out to his friends the beneficial action of the System in it from beginning to end" *(p. 119).* Has the narrator adopted Adrian's cynical gently superior view, or is he caricaturing it? It is not easy to say. The former, it would seem from an examination of the next major episode in the story, the pivotal ordeal of Richard Feverel, Richard's elopement with Lucy Desborough.

This episode is, from a certain "philosophic" point of view, the New Comedy. As Richard impetuously enlists his new familiar, Bakewell, in a plan to ride off with the lovely niece of the formerly fearsome Farmer Blaize, the narrator remarks: "Tom asked no questions. He saw that he was in for the first Act of the new Comedy" *(p. 254)*. Stopped in this elopement by the Fates and a case of pneumonia and taken home in gentle triumph by his father, Richard veers in his growing schizophrenia to a near catatonic coolness of blood and brain. His trust of his father gone, he plots calmly his escape from Raynham into wicked London. Adrian's eye is on the change in Richard, and he too prepares for a new play:

> Such a lapse from his pupil's heroics to this last verge of Arcadian coolness, Adrian could not believe in. "Hark at this old blackbird!" he cried, in his turn, and pretending to interpret [the bird's] fits of song: "O what a pretty comedy! Don't we wear the mask well, my Fiesco? Genoa will be our own tomorrow! Only wait til the train has started—jolly! jolly! jolly! We'll be winners yet!"
>
> *(P. 279)*

Adrian thinks Richard is plotting to meet Lucy, but Richard is in fact simply fleeing the tutors and the System, thinking Lucy has been hidden away from him in a faraway school. (She had been, earlier, and Adrian was behind the move.) As luck and the Comedy would have it, though, Lucy is returning the same day that Richard arrives in London. One meeting suffices to turn the escape into a second elopement and Richard into a *soi-disant* hero, hiding himself and his fiancée dramatically under assumed names in the home of a guileless old woman named Bessie Berry. The outlaw chief, now turned hero, re-enlists his old crony Rip Thompson, along with Tom, and the narrator records in mock solemnity: "Thus, unaware of his high

destiny, Ripton joined the hero, and accepted his character in the New Comedy" *(p. 292)*. Adrian and other mem-
bers of Richard's family come to town just as the stolen
wedding approaches and Richard, unheroically, loses the
ring under the nose of the Wise Youth, Adrian, who, putting two and two together like a good reader of character,
hints to Richard's aunt that the "right season" for astonish-
ment "will not be long arriving" *(p. 339)*. The narrator
names the marriage chapter in *The Ordeal of Richard
Feverel* one "In which the Last Act of a Comedy takes the
place of the First." There is opportunity in this last/first
act for a felicitous bridal breakfast at the home of Bessie
Berry and an escape to the Isle of Wight for a honeymoon
before chapter 35, "The Philosopher Appears in Person."

The philosopher in this case is Adrian, who has leisurely
worked through his suspicions to their correct conclusion.
Bessie Berry turns out, in one of those unironic Dickensian
plot-connecting mechanisms, to have been Richard's old
nurse, and she has a reminiscence or two about Adrian's
own youthful follies: "Don't you remember his old nurse,
when he was a baby in arms, that went away se [sic] sudden, and no fault of hers, Mr. Harley! The very morning after the night you got into Mr. Benson's cellar, and
got so tipsy on his Madeary" *(p. 364)*. But the philosopher,
naturally, is not fazed by this revelation of his secret
sensuality; it is his job for the reader and his personal
delight to take the confirmed news of Richard's elopement
to the rest of the family so the third and fourth act com-
plications of the comedy may ensue:

> He took the huge quarter of Cake, nodded multitudinous
> promises, and left Mrs. Berry to bless his good heart.
> "So dies the System!" was Adrian's comment in the
> street. "And now let prophets roar! He dies respectably
> in a marriage-bed, which is more than I should have
> foretold of the Monster. Meantime," he gave the Cake a
> dramatic tap, "I'll go sow nightmares." *(P. 367)*

This exquisitely Puck-like journey is recounted in the
next chapter, "The Procession of the Cake," wherein the

reader is, through Adrian's eyes and by his direct in-
tent, granted the privilege of seeing Richard's family, the
foolish, the selfish, and the weak in their different ways,
wince and strike out at the news Adrian brings. A supreme
ironic procession indeed! Adrian loves his work of enlightenment, but he loves even that in philosophic moderation:

> "Adrian," [Mrs. Doria] said, turning upon him in the
> passage, "you mentioned a house where this horrible
> Cake . . . where he was this morning. I desire you to take
> me to that woman immediately."
>
> The Wise Youth had not bargained for personal servi-
> tude. He had hoped he should be in time for the last act
> of the Opera that night, after enjoying the Comedy of
> real life. (P. 384)

The last thing he wants to do is get involved, be responsible for the action. His job is merely to observe, to bring
the cohering light of dispassionate intellect to the mad
jumble of scenes in the Comedy of real life. He withdraws
after the procession is ended. But there is still "the family
muddle" to be smoothed out, and Adrian's sense of an
ending—a comfortable ending, a comic stasis—nags mildly
at him to bring back comfort to his home of Raynham
Abbey in the form of a reconciliation between father and
son. Sighing at the effort, this philosopher takes up the
burden of managing the senior philosopher, Sir Austin, into
seeing his son, and on a bridal visit he manages Lucy into
managing Richard to go to his father:

> "No necessity exists for any hurry, except in the brain
> of that impetuous boy. You must correct it, Mrs. Richard.
> Men are made to be managed and women are born man-
> agers. Now, if you were to let him know that you don't
> want to go tonight, and let him guess, after a day or two,
> that you would very much rather . . . you might affect
> a peculiar repugnance. By taking it on yourself, you see,
> this wild young man will not require such frightful efforts
> of persuasion. Both his father and he are exceedingly
> delicate subjects, and his father unfortunately is not in a

position to be managed directly. It's a strange office to propose to you, but it appears to devolve upon you to manage the father through the son. . . ."

Adrian looked in her face, as much as to say, "Now, are you capable of this piece of heroism?" And it did seem hard to her that she should have to tell Richard she shrank from any trial. But the proposition chimed in with her fears and her wishes. She thought the Wise Youth very wise; the poor child was not insensible to his flattery, and the subtler flattery of making herself in some measure a sacrifice to the home she had disturbed. She agreed to simulate as Adrian had suggested.

(Pp. 410-11)

Thus begins the third comedy on the bill, with Lucy part-willingly playing the actress. The comedy needs still another actress, however, one to send Richard away from the Isle of Wight and one to keep him in London while he waits for a word from his father. *That* baronial philosopher and stage manager, working from a hastily revised script of the System, wants Richard to "learn about life," and Adrian, lazily managing in all directions and indirections at once, is the man to help. He falls in with the Hon. Peter Brayder, whose patron, Lord Montfalcon, has his own lecherous reasons for wishing Lucy's husband kept in London, and the two strike a bargain for another actress to carry the second act of the final comedy:

"I have rather a difficult post. 'Tis mine both to keep [Richard] here and also to find him the opportunity to measure himself with his fellow man. In other words, his father wants him to see something of life before he enters upon housekeeping. Now I am proud to confess that I'm hardly equal to the task. The demi, or damned-monde—if it's that he wants him to observe—is one I have not got the walk to."

"Ha! ha!" laughed the Honourable Peter. "You do the keeping, I offer to parade the demi. I must say, though, it's a queer notion of the old gentleman."

"It's the continuation of a philosophic plan," said Adrian.

97

The Honourable Peter followed the curvings of the whiff of his cigar with his eyes and ejaculated, "Infahnally philosophic! . . . Now there's a woman—you've heard of Mrs. Mount? All the world knows her. . . ."

(Pp. 435-36)

Bella Mount is an actress of considerable talent. For her first part she charms Richard with an invention of a fop-gallant character whom she names Sir Julius, and she disguises herself in breeches to parade the streets with Richard in this character. Her chief role, as the title of chapter 42 makes clear, is "Enchantress": it is a seduction chapter whose feminine parallel to the role of that consummate actor, Shakespeare's Richard III, is pointed up by the narrator's repeated paraphrase of that other Richard's famous lines, "Was ever Hero in this fashion wooed? Was ever Hero in this fashion won?" With this actress Richard breaks his marriage oath, as he later explains to Lucy in real, though picturesque, agony, and once more the indolent Adrian is there to explain what happened next to his cousin Austin, newly returned from what appear to be mild Christian socialist experiences abroad. Adrian reveals to him and to the reader that Richard's child has been born; that Richard, unknowing, has refused all contact and news from home and gone off to the Continent in a fury of self-immolation; and that Sir Austin is still waiting for his son to reconcile himself with him before he accepts the daughter-in-law and grandchild: " 'We're in a tangle,' said the Wise Youth. Time will extricate us, I presume, or what is the venerable Seignor good for?' " *(p. 538)*.

The reader, stuffed with this information and carrying, perhaps fatally, this parting epigram, last sees Adrian in chapter 48, "The Last Scene," making his final effort at lucidity. The family is waiting for what they think is Richard's permanent return, and during the evening Adrian hears from Ripton the news that an unlucky revelation of Lord Montfalcon's earlier passion for Lucy has resulted in his challenging the lord to a duel. "Wearing a composedly amused expression on his dimpled plump face"

98

(p. 568), Adrian spends most of the homecoming scene quietly writing what appears to be an essay, or letter, which he gives to Richard as he leaves home for the last time. We do not see it; we are simply left to read what we can of Adrian's message from the jocular hints he drops:

> "I am engaged on a portion of a Proposal for uniting the Empires and Kingdoms of Europe under one Paternal Head. . . . This treats of the management of Youths and Maids, and of certain magisterial functions connected therewith. 'It is decreed that these officers be all and every men of Science,' etc. . . . And here, oblige me by taking this," he handed Richard the enormous envelope containing what he had written that evening. "Credentials," he exclaimed humorously, slapping Richard on the shoulder. Ripton also heard the words "propagator—species," but had no idea of their import. The Wise Youth looked: "You see we've made matters all right for you here," and quitted the room on that unusual gleam of earnestness. *(Pp. 569, 575-76)*

Let us give our friend Adrian the benefit of the doubt: let us imagine he had written, couched certainly in witty indirection and comic elaboration, the application to Richard's actual case of his profoundly serious last words, "Nature never forgives! A lost dinner can never be replaced" *(p. 575)*. Suppose he had written that the Nature which demands that the father succor his child and his wife in their immediate concrete need will take its calm and unironic[5] vengeance if he abandons himself to the sentimental Byronism of an unnecessary duel. Say he had

[5] Meredith's view of nature, though romantic, was profoundly unsentimental (the distinction between these terms will become clearer, I hope, in the following chapters). Nature takes no joy in deluding or destroying man; for Meredith it is man who often cheapens nature by attributing to it his own perverse cynicism or sentimentality. An aged, ailing Meredith wrote touchingly to the bedridden Leslie Stephen in 1904: "We, who have loved the motion of legs and the sweep of the winds, we come to this. But for myself, I will own that it is the Natural order. There is no irony in Nature" (*Letters*, III, 1491).

99

written truth, as it shows itself to be in the final chapter of the novel: it matters not a bit, for Richard never reads it, and Adrian, thinking his work done and constitutionally unable even to agree that anyone else should take an action, let alone to act himself, goes to bed with his insights locked in his brain, forever unfruitful, having killed Richard Feverel in the manner earlier specified by Bessie Berry to Lady Blandish, by "the sin o' the lookers on."

II. Adrian and the Narrator

Adrian's original sin, the surface dallying with life without risking one's character, one's real blood-brain-spirit, is the occasion for perhaps the most famous Meredithian aphorism on the folly he considered his special quarry: " 'Sentimentalists,' says The Pilgrim's Scrip, 'are they who seek to enjoy Reality without incurring the Immense Debtorship for a thing done' " (p. 266). Like many a crucial "Meredithian" remark, this one has its origin outside the narrator; it comes from the germinating tale, expressed in this novel in the Book, The Pilgrim's Scrip, and it enters the subplot, the action between author and fictional reader, because the author chooses to have the narrator single it out, because the editor wishes to make a point about it, to "explain" it to the reader. This theoretical model of the editor and the book that we saw Sartre arguing about is in Meredith an open, but subtle structural conceit which allows him to duplicate in the subplot the themes and struggles of the plot—in The Ordeal of Richard Feverel the struggle to meet life as a true philosopher. In the plot it is the young Richard Feverel who is to be educated by and toward philosophy; in the subplot it is the reader. The philosophy of The Pilgrim's Scrip and its explanatory textbook, the Notebook, are mediated to Richard by the philosopher-teachers Adrian Harley and Sir Austin Feverel, and to the reader by these two re-mediated through the narrator. By looking at these three characters as readers of The Pilgrim's Scrip we can begin our comparison of

100

Adrian Harley and the narrator of *The Ordeal of Richard Feverel*.

Sir Austin, of course, wrote the Book. But that was just after Richard was born, before he had hardened the Book's insights into a System, and before his son had grown to be a real person to confound and amplify the Book's wisdom. Once out of his brain, the Book has a permanent and almost mystically independent life; its author must read it and use it humbly as an Editor like all other readers, like the narrator of *The Ordeal of Richard Feverel*, who is himself reader-editor of *The Pilgrim's Scrip*, and a rather better reader of it than its author—which is, of course, Meredith's point. It is not Sir Austin who understands Lady Blandish by means of the just-quoted aphorism on sentimentalism, it is the narrator. Worse still, Sir Austin does not read the aphorism by the light of his own conduct. But the narrator does: "And while they sat and talked, 'My wound has healed,' he said. 'How?' she asked. 'At the fountain of your eyes,' he replied, and drew the joy of new life from her blushes, without incurring further debtorship for a thing done" *(p. 267)*.

And yet *The Pilgrim's Scrip* is the product of a real mind alive to real experience. By the last scene, when Lady Blandish has taken the first steps toward becoming a real reader of the Book, not just a sentimental lover of it, she recognizes that "another aphorism seemed closely to apply to him: 'There is no more grievous sight, as there is no greater perversion, than a wise man at the mercy of his feelings.' 'He must have written it' she thought, 'when he had himself for an example—strange man that he is.' " *(p. 572)*. At this point Lady Blandish still loves Sir Austin, is "still inclined to submission, though decidedly insubordinate" *(p. 572)*, but she reads him better, too, and nothing but the sight of a truly reconciled father, son, and daughter-in-law, a truly resolved human situation, will win her now. If the philosopher makes one more mistake, or if any past mistake proves impossible to redeem, he has lost her. Wisdom of a sort is still his, and is still distantly admired, but "Philosophy did not seem to catch her mind, and fine phrases encountered a rueful assent, more flattering to their grandeur than to their influence" *(p. 518)*. Lady Blandish, a most civilized reader of a most complex man, is no longer happy parsing the Book. Having rashly staked her character on the philosophy it contains, she has matured to insist on its bearing good fruit in human happiness. Having rashly staked her character on a love of the philosopher, she is forced to require in him a *man*, and she suffers all his failures. Between the powerful and consistent and confident author of *The Pilgrim's Scrip* and its most willing, most sensible, most devoted reader, "there is something of a contest secretly going on. He was conscious that nothing save perfect success would now hold this self-emancipating mind. She had seen him through" *(p. 569)*.

The author himself has never become a real reader of his Book.[6] He applies its complex paradoxes undiscriminatingly at the simplest level: " 'I expect that Woman will be the last thing civilized by Man. . . .' He conceived that the Wild Cats would some day be actually tamed. At present it was best to know what they were" *(pp. 2-3)*. His is not a self-emancipating mind; he can neither use the aphorisms as a distancing mechanism to free his conscious-

[6] It is primarily this incapacity to *read*, himself or his book, that separates the character from the narrator. Meredith's own identification with the wife-betrayed Sir Austin's situation and his attitudes, noted by many critics and excellently worked out by Gillian Beer in *Meredith: A Change of Masks* (London: The Athlone Press, 1970) is profound and complex. But it is important to recognize that Meredith both as historical man and as implied author identifies most closely with the Sir Austin who suffered the event and wrote the Book, not with the man he has become since. Ms. Beer, with the continuing sensitivity to Meredith's reader-making that distinguishes her work, goes on to comment that "Sir Austin is the reader's chief guide as well as his prey in reading the book. The strain the book imposes on us as readers comes ultimately from the impossibility of setting Sir Austin at a stable distance" (p. 33). I want to suggest that Adrian Harley is in some hidden ways even a more important guide to the reader, and a more difficult one to stabilize because of his tonal identification with the narrator.

ness from the great betrayal that froze it, nor can he use his reading of life to free the aphorisms from the often cramped paradoxicality that hinders their usefulness. Reading is remaking the book as well as remaking oneself, and it is imperfect or egoistic or narrow reading that makes a middling good philosopher an execrable teacher. In this wise the philosopher in Sir Austin has predicted his failure as a teacher of his son: " 'The reason why men and women are mysterious to us, and prove disappointing,' we learn from *The Pilgrim's Scrip*, 'is that we will read them from our own book, just as we are perplexed by reading ourselves from theirs' " *(p. 342)*. Sir Austin was a very flawed reader even of his own Book; Richard's remained forever closed to him.

Adrian Harley is on the other hand in many ways a great reader. He can quote *The Pilgrim's Scrip* obsequiously and comfortingly to its author, but his own reading of the Book has all the necessary discrimination, application to life, and more than the necessary "comedy." When Sir Austin argues to Adrian that the Feverel family is bound to try and get the hapless Tom Bakewell off the hook for Richard's rick-burning by some more sophisticated means than bribing the witness, Adrian sees through the pious aphorism the philosopher offers: " 'Expediency is man's wisdom, Adrian Harley. Doing Right is God's.' Adrian curbed his desire to ask Sir Austin whether an attempt to counteract the just working of the law was Doing Right. The direct application of an Aphorism was unpopular at Raynham" *(p. 108)*. Adrian is in fact the best reader in the story, second only to the narrator. He can read on a face the words being stifled in the heart:

> "What, boy! Is it old Blaize has been putting you up?"
> "Never mind, Uncle!" the boy nodded mysteriously.
> "Look there!" Adrian read on Ripton's face, "he says 'never mind,' and lets it out" *(P. 63)*

He can read hidden messages in the Book of the System:

[Sir Austin] was half disposed to arrest the two conspirators on the spot, and make them confess and absolve themselves, but it seemed to him better to keep an unseen eye over his son. Sir Austin's old System prevailed.

Adrian characterized this System well, in saying that Sir Austin wished to be Providence to his son. *(P. 68)*

It is by way of Adrian's quite keen understanding of the masks and delusions of the people around him that the reader of *The Ordeal of Richard Feverel* recognizes Sir Austin's monomania, Mrs. Doria's hypocrisy, Lady Blandish's soft entangling designs, Richard's schizophrenic impulsiveness, Lucy's fear of confronting Richard's family. Adrian offers us nuggets of philosophic analysis not only of the people around him but of life in general, and we find these often significant, provocative, even brilliant. One of the most quoted Meredithian insights on class is Adrian's:

> I see now that the national love of a lord is less subservience than a form of self-love, putting a gold-lace hat on one's image, as it were, to bow to it. I see too the admirable wisdom of our system. Could there be a finer balance of power than in a community where men intellectually nil have lawful vantage and a gold-lace hat on? How soothing it is to Intellect—that Noble rebel, as the Pilgrim has it—to stand, and bow, and know itself superior! This exquisite compensation maintains the balance. . . . *(P. 420)*

Adrian's power of mind is unrivaled among the characters; so is his capacity for the comic perception of folly. Indeed he is hard put to find a rival in the subplot either, and that is where perhaps the most important clues to Meredith's struggle with the figure of the philosopher are to be found. The narrator in Meredith's subplot here often sounds very like Adrian. We have seen him adopt Adrian's names and comic visions for people and situations, Heavy Benson, The Bakewell Comedy. Often we risk mistaking Adrian's eyes and voice for the narrator's. Again and again we find the narrator picking up the insights, the integrated grasp of a situation, that was Adrian's:

> Throwing banter aside, as much as he could, Adrian spoke to Richard. "You want to reform this woman. Her manner is open—fair and free—the traditional characteristic. We won't stop to canvass how that particular honesty of deportment that wins your approbation has been gained. In her college it is not uncommon. . . . But a woman who speaks like a man, and has all those excellent virtues you admire—where has she learnt the trick? She tells you. You don't surely approve of the school? Well, what is there in it then? Reform her, of course? The task is worthy of your energies. But, if you are appointed to do it, don't do it publicly, and don't attempt it just now. May I ask you whether your wife participates in this undertaking?" *(P. 481)*

Again and again we sense the narrator delighting in the caustic wit, the bright untouchable arrogance, the real, if reductive, wisdom of his character:

> "How has Ricky turned out?" [Austin] asked. "What sort of a character has he?"
> "The poor boy is ruined by his excessive anxiety about it. Character? He has the character of a bullet with a treble charge of powder behind it. Enthusiasm is the powder. . . . He was going to reform the world, after your fashion Austin—you have something to answer for. Unfortunately, he began with the feminine side of it. Cupid proud of Phoebus newly slain, or Pluto wishing to people his kingdom, if you like, put it into the soft head of one of the guileless grateful creatures to kiss him for his good work. Oh; horror! he never expected that."
> *(P. 537)*

Yet of course Adrian Harley is condemned over and over by the narrator.[7] The reader is warned over and over

[7] Frank D. Curtin in an interesting essay called "Adrian Harley: The Limits of Meredith's Comedy" (*Nineteenth-Century Fiction*, VII [Mar. 1953]) points out that Adrian "more than any other character in the book is . . . Meredith's spokesman, his as-

against this fascinating ficelle. Indeed, the narrator's most openly savage attacks are reserved for Adrian. The Wise Youth, the Clever Youth, are appellations that crackle with venom, as the Hero, the Heroine, the Old Dog (for Rip Thompson), the Griffin (for Sir Austin), the Bonnet (for Lady Blandish) do not. The narrator's look upon Sir Austin and Richard is masterfully comic, spanning all humane gradations between the pursuit of folly, the deploring of weakness, the marking of gifts and virtues. Even his look upon the matchmaking mama Mrs. Caroline Grandison, the most burlesque character in the book, has a distance, a control about it: "Mrs. Caroline was a colourless lady of an unequivocal character, living upon drugs, and governing her husband and the world from her sofa. Woolly Negroes blest her name, and whiskered John-Thomases deplored her weight" *(p. 182)*. But it seems that with Adrian the contempt is out of hand, the self-mastery is shaken:

> In a word, Adrian Harley had mastered his philosophy at the early age of one and twenty. Many would be glad to say the same at that age twice-told; they carry in their

---

sistant, in pointing up the comedy." That is, he feels Adrian helps Meredith when he is creating and wielding comedy, and is ignored or attacked by Meredith when he is doing something other than comedy—"his presence is a clue to the limits of comedy . . . when sympathy is called for, or a heartfelt response to beauty or nobility, he sets a limit to his comedy" by attacking Adrian's lack of such response. This is the sort of argument critics are inevitably led into if they will not grant Meredith his all-encompassing definition of comedy and instead try to mark off in his novels the "comic" and "tragic" parts according to traditional definitions. Meredith, again, insisted on including sympathetic response in his idea of comedy—as long as that response was "shapely" and honest. Adrian's sort of "limited comedy" Meredith was to call satire. Far from setting limits to his comedy, Meredith wanted to include in its purifying light all human responses—even the "comic" one which, when it "waxes bombastical or out of proportion" to its subject, man's nature, is equally to be deplored with the selfishness that may corrupt the response to beauty or the sentimentality that may corrupt sympathy.

breasts a burden with which Adrian's was not loaded. Mrs. Doria was nearly right about his heart. A singular mishap (at his birth, possibly, or before it) had unseated that organ and shaken it down to his stomach, where it was a much lighter, nay, an inspiring weight, and encouraged him merrily onward. Throned in that region, it looked on little that did not arrive to gratify it. Already that region was a trifle prominent in the person of the Wise Youth, and carried, as it were, the flag of his philosophical tenets in front of him. A fat Wise Youth, digesting well, charming after dinner, with men or with women; soft-dimpled, succulent looking as a sucking-pig; delightfully sarcastic, perhaps a little too unscrupulous in his moral tone, but that his moral reputation belied him. . . . *(P. 33)*

Adrian's enthrallment by sensual appetite (for food, women, power) is stressed by constant sarcastic and faintly obscene reference to his girth; "succulent" is an adjective that appears more than once. Obviously he is in his element at the dinner party at Richmond among the beaux and demi-reps: "Adrian was jolly and rolled comfortably as he talked" *(p. 449)*. In what seems a gratuitous slam at Adrian, not even the fair Lucy escapes his appetite:

"A nice little woman! a very nice little woman!" Tom Bakewell heard him murmur to himself according to a habit he had; and his air of rather succulent patronage as he walked or sat beside the innocent beauty with his head thrown back and a smile that always seemed to be in secret communion with his marked abdominal prominence, showed that she was gaining part of what she played for. Wise Youths who buy their loves are not unwilling, when opportunity offers, to try and obtain the commodity for nothing. Examinations of her hand, as for some occult purpose, and unctuous pattings of same, were not infrequent. *(P. 418)*

The narrator cannot resist a sneer and an insinuation at the word "parasite" as he links Adrian with the thoroughly disreputable Peter Brayder:

The world said that the Honourable Peter was salaried by his Lordship, and that, in common with that of Parasite, he exercised the ancient companion profession. This the world said, and still smiled at the Honourable Peter. . . . In the voyage back to town, Richard was again selected to sit by Mrs. Mount. Brayder and Adrian started the jokes. The pair of parasites got on extremely well together. *(Pp. 434-51)*

It is this obsessive reviling of Adrian, coupled with constant reference to his unmanly habit of buying compliance, from the rick-burning witness to the Blaize maid, that is responsible, I think, for much of the uncomfortable sexual atmosphere that many Victorian critics called unwholesome. Lucy and Richard are beautiful in their sensuality, Sir Austin and Lady Blandish are complex and serious, Bella Mount's portrait is straightforward and full of real pathos, and Montfalcon merely laughable. But Adrian is dangerous. Combine his appetite, his access to wealth, and his indolent morality with his superb power of analysis and gift of psychological management and you do not have to be that much-maligned abstraction the British Matron to recognize a threat.

It seems to me that Adrian receives this excessively unwholesome and alienating physique and character from his creator exactly because Meredith senses in himself the same mental temptations and tendencies that Adrian surrendered to, and badly needs to separate himself from them. The keenness of sight, the sensitivity to folly, the intellectual detachment from the chaos of ambition and competition, the emotional restraint and chastity in the pursuit of ideas that Meredith promotes as philosophy and wishes to foster in his reader by means of his style, his themes and his medium—all these desirable traits and hard-won skills have somehow reversed themselves in Adrian and become cynicism, solipsism, and, most horrible of all, sterility. Adrian the teacher has no son in Richard Feverel, even intellectually, except insofar as Richard's failure is partly his child because Adrian foresaw the dangers and did nothing. Adrian cannot act at all, so paralyzingly ironic is his attitude, so he leaves all earthly action to time: "Christians as well as Pagans are in the habit of phrasing this excuse for folding their arms, 'forgetful,' says the Pilgrim's Scrip, 'that the Devil's imps enter into no such armistice' " *(p. 409)*. That was one aphorism Adrian did not read. But he is a voluminous reader, the reader is ominously reminded, indeed a voluptuous reader. He goes to bed with Horace after his service to the System is done: "The Wise Youth saw that his Chief was mollified behind his moveless mask, and went to bed and Horace, leaving Sir Austin in his study" *(p. 64)*. When the time comes to join his cousin Austin in aiding Richard honorably to repair his rick-burning peccadillo, the great reader has an ominous alternative to action:

> "Then you leave me to act alone?" said Austin, rising.
> "Without a single curb!" Adrian gesticulated an acquiesced withdrawal. . . . The Wise Youth yawned, and stretched out a hand for any book that might be within his reach. Austin left him, to look about the grounds for Richard. *(Pp. 82, 83)*

Books, it seems, are to hide in. Adrian, in the company of Horace and Gibbon, the aristocrats of literature, the satirical rogues, is in fact a Hamlet unhaunted. He has solved the problem of action, and is in a comfortable state of not-to-be. "What have you been doing at home, Cousin Rady?" asks Richard. "Playing Hamlet, in the absence of the Prince of Denmark," he answers *(p. 61)*. Indeed he is playing a first act philosophical Hamlet to the world of the novel. He quotes a satirical poem on the flaws of the age to the Muscular Christian, Austin Wentworth:

> An Age of Quaker hue and cut,
> By Mammon misbegotten;
> See the mad Hamlet mouth and strut!
> And mark the Kings of Cotton!

109

From this unrest, lo, early wreck'd,
A future staggers crazy,
Ophelia of the ages, deck'd
With woful weed and daisy! *(P. 81)*

And Meredith shows the activist and the philosopher at battle over the image:

Murmuring "get your parson Brawnley to answer that!" Adrian changed the resting place of a leg, and smiled. . . .

"My Parson Brawnley, as you call him, has answered it," said Austin, "not by hoping his best, which would probably leave the Age to go mad to your satisfaction, but by doing it. And he has and will answer your Diaper Sandoe in better verse, as he confutes him in a better life."

"You don't see Sandoe's depth," Adrian replied. "Consider that phrase, 'Ophelia of the Ages!' Is not Brawnley, like a dozen other leading spirits—I think that's your term—just the metaphysical Hamlet to drive her mad? She, poor maid! asks for Marriage and smiling babes, while my lord lover stands questioning the Infinite and rants to the Impalpable."

Austin laughed. "Marriage and smiling babes she would have in abundance, if Brawnley legislated. Wait till you know him."[8]

There is a real and thorny issue here, and Meredith is anxious to answer it. He has tried to answer it partly in

[8] Diaper Sandoe is of course the pseudonym adopted by the poet Denzil Somers, who betrayed Sir Austin with his wife. Both Adrian and Richard are adept at quoting Sandoe, which indicates that Adrian considered it part of his tutor's job to introduce Richard to the philosophical verse of the man who had cuckolded his father. Richard was evidently conceived during the liaison between his mother and the poet, and, while there is no real evidence in the book that Sir Austin might not have been his father, it is nevertheless a real jolt to hear Richard quote the lines of his mother's lover, "And O your dear blue eyes, that heavenward glance/With kindred beauty! banished humbleness!/Past weeping for mortality's distress" (p. 319), while summoning to his mind's eye the picture of his own secret love, Lucy, on the eve of their not-strictly-legal marriage.

the character of Austin Wentworth himself, the first of a line of Meredithian heroes distinguished by a capacity for laughter and philosophy and for an acceptance of their responsibility to act for the good in their worlds. Thus Austin is a disciple of Kingsley, Parson Brawnley, a Republican and a reformer, but a cautious, humane, and flexible one. He is the figure that Richard vaguely identifies with, and whom the fictional reader of the novel is brought to admire. But Austin is absent from the middle two-thirds of the book, and his influence remains vague, because Meredith seemed not to be able to imagine him as intensely as he imagined his other characters. The reason for Austin's absence is given as an unspecified kind of socialist living experiment in South America, but essentially he is a reformer on a personal scale, active in the lives of his immediate friends. The largeness of principle and the smallness of the scale of action make this active hero look ludicrous in the eyes of the wanton philosopher-cynic: on his homecoming Adrian twits Austin on his "drive to reform the world" and the sorry mess that his disciple Richard has made of such a principle. Although it is to Austin that Lady Blandish appeals in her letter after Lucy's death to come and pick up the pieces of the broken family, he remains in the end what he always was, slightly out of focus, a good man but a quiet hero, able to act directly on a small scale, but strangely without power on the large scale.[9]

[9] The other heroes in this category, among them Merthyr Powys of *Sandra Belloni*, Vernon Whitford of *The Egoist*, Maytey Weyburn of *Lord Ormont and His Aminta*, Dartry Fenellen of *One of Our Conquerors*, are also quiet heroes on a very small scale, gentle reformers. Meredith, it sometimes seems, shares with Adrian the view that reform must be a little comic in practice, although he desperately hopes for it. The one man he creates who is a man-of-action on a large scale, Victor Radnor in *One of Our Conquerors*, has let the principle of action, of will, of Meredithian "spirit," run away with him entirely, to his eventual mental destruction. The man-of-action who emerges in Victor's place at the end of the novel, Dartry Fenellen, is much more vaguely conceived in his reforming

111

Not being able to imagine the actively good reformer in this character, Meredith clearly attempts to imagine his narrator in that role. The narrator is not simply an observer, like Adrian, of the passing show; he is a man with a teaching mission. He, like Austin Wentworth or Richard Feverel, is driven by a need to redeem the past and perfect the future, facing the natural and stark truth that there are more things in heaven and earth than are dreamed of in any philosophy. Adrian has philosophy. But he is not haunted, he has no ghost at his back demanding action; enviably, we can feel the narrator sigh now and then. Adrian has not even the manly love that keeps Horatio, and Sir Austin, from being mere philosophers. Adrian is Hamlet reconciled to, battening on, a rotten Denmark; Hamlet sweetly undermining the throne instead of cleansing it; Hamlet answering Claudius in his own coin, demonstrating that a nephew as well as an uncle can smile and smile and be a villain. Adrian is Hamlet stuck forever in act II, unable to go beyond philosophy to the readiness to receive divinity, to hope in Providence, unable to go beyond satire to comedy; Hamlet forever striding up and down corridors reading books by satirical rogues and parading his antic disposition as sanity:

> "Ay," meditates the recumbent cynic, "more or less mad is not every mother's son? Favourable circumstances— good air, good company, two or three good rules rigidly adhered to—keep the world out of Bedlam. But let the world fly into a passion and is not Bedlam its safest abode? What seemed inviolable barriers are burst asunder in a trice: men, God's likeness, are at one another's throats, and the Angels may well be weeping. In youth, 'tis love, or lust, makes the world go mad; in age, 'tis prejudice. Superstition holds a province; Pride an empire. Tinker's right! There's a battle raging above us. One can't wonder at Ploughman's contrary opinion, as to which

activities, a muted hero indeed compared to the powerful potential we sensed in Victor Radnor.

is getting the upper hand. If we were not mad, we should
fight it for ourselves, and end it. We are; and we make
Life the disease and death the cure. Good night, my
worthy Uncle! Can I deem the man mad who holdeth
me much?" And Adrian buried a sleepy smile in his
pillow and slept, knowing himself wise in a mad world.
(Pp. 64-65)

Philosophy can all too easily bring a man to this. Reading can all too easily bring a man to this; an author presenting the truth can hardly picture a fully sane world, and a
reader, absorbing the organized madness on the printed
page, knows himself wiser at the end or the author has
written to no purpose. Yet the dark side of wisdom is the
false separation from the world it suggests, a separation
which, carried far enough, becomes a chain:

Adrian really bore the news he had heard with creditable
disinterestedness and admirable repression of anything beneath the dignity of a philosopher. . . . On this intellectual eminence the Wise Youth had built his Castle, and
he had lived in it from an early period. . . . Jugglers he
saw running up ladders that overtopped him, and air-
balloons scaling the empyrean, but the former came pre-
cipitately down again, and the latter were at the mercy
of the winds; while he remained tranquil on his solid
unambitious ground. . . . Not that voluntarily he cut
himself off from his fellows; on the contrary, his sole
amusement was their society. Alone he was rather dull,
as a man who beholds but one thing must naturally be.
Study of the animated varieties of that one thing excited
him sufficiently to think life a pleasant play, and the
faculties he had forfeited to hold his elevated position
he could serenely enjoy by contemplation of them in
others. *(Pp. 367-68)*

This is the folly of philosophers—to think all men fools
or madmen who have retained those faculties of passion
and idealism, blood and spirit, that cause so much of the
chaos of the world or society. It is a folly to which reading
panders. Yet thinkers and teachers are in the business of

making philosophers as authors are in the business of making readers. It is necessary then to make the right kind of reader, the reader who is invited to lose none of his troublesome human faculties while being elevated to philosophic vision.

Meredith's narrator thus saves himself from Adrian's sin by an act of teaching through the kind of book he is writing, an act of teaching designed not to elevate the author but to make radical contact between him and his audience, the kind of contact that changes the readers in the very act of reading. The narrator speaks directly to this purpose in the subplot of this novel:

> At present, I am aware, an audience impatient for Blood and Glory scorns the stress I am putting on incidents so minute, a picture so little imposing. One will come to whom it will be given to see the elementary machinery at work, who as it were from some slight hint of the straws, will feel the winds of March when they do not blow. To them nothing will be trivial, seeing that they will have in their eyes the invisible conflict going on around us, whose features a nod, a smile, a laugh of ours perpetually changes. And they will perceive, moreover, that in real life all hangs together: the train is laid in the lifting of an eyebrow that bursts upon the field of thousands. They will see the links of things as they pass, and wonder not, as foolish people now do, that this great matter came out of that small one. *(P. 280)*

"One will come." But as we read this passage and mentally separate ourselves from that audience of readers impatient for blood and glory we realize it has come. We are it. We have been elevated above those "foolish people." Here, on our eminence, our enemy is not the deluded Austin Feverel or the passionate Richard or the salacious Mrs. Mount. Our enemy is our friend and fellow philosopher, Adrian Harley. It is child's play for the reader to separate himself from that audience of blood and glory, the romantic public; it is a desperate thing to give up or modify the Adrian Harley in us. The narrator has given the reader more help than is quite fair artistically; he has made Adrian dishonest, perverse, sexually unsavory, and fat into the bargain. Still Adrian is hard to give up. When he goes about with the wedding cake giving ironic enlightenment and comeuppance to all the fools whose self-centeredness has contributed to the runaway marriage, it is a virtuous reader indeed who will not be drawn in to cheer:

> Another message was brought to Adrian that Mrs. Doria Forey *very* particularly wished to speak with him.
>
> "What can be the matter?" he exclaimed, pleased to have his faith in Woman strengthened. The Cake had exploded, no doubt.
>
> So it proved, when the gentlemen joined the fair society. . . .
>
> "Here! Adrian!" Mrs. Doria cried. "Where is Adrian? Pray come here. Tell me! Where did this Cake come from? Whose is it? What does it do here? You know all about it, for you brought it. Clare saw you bring it into the room. What does it mean? I insist upon a direct answer. Now do not make me impatient, Adrian. . . ."
>
> "What is it, Aunt?" asked the Wise Youth. "You want them followed and torn asunder by wild policemen?"
>
> "Tomorrow!" Brandon queerly interposed.
>
> "Won't that be—just too late?" Adrian suggested.
>
> Mrs. Doria sighed out her last spark of hope.
>
> "You see," said Adrian. . . .
>
> "Yes, yes!" Mrs. Doria did not require any of his elucidations. . . .
>
> [Adrian] found it necessary at the same time to duck and turn his head for concealment. Mrs. Doria surpassed his expectations. *(Pp. 378-82)*

Yet this comedy is the most selfish cruelty on Adrian's part. Mrs. Forey does not deserve to have the consequences of her folly modified, perhaps, but neither does Adrian deserve to enjoy the reality of her folly without incurring debtorship for a thing done, without coming down from his castle. This the reader learns in a struggle with the sheer delight of being "invited up" to a wit so sharp, an insight so prophetic. Richard Feverel, the hero of the

115

plot, grows up and away from his teacher, Adrian, quite naturally. Richard sits with him at dinner, can feel the cold fish touch of Adrian's mind through the dazzling quips and undoubtedly wise commentary.

Meredith's narrator, however, is locked in combat with the voice and the attitude of Adrian Harley all through the subplot, and the hero of the subplot, the reader, remains subtly confused by this combat of his teachers. He is confused because the battle is hidden, because the narrator talks *as if he had purged Adrian Harley from his attitude already*. But he protests too much; he has not purged him, and never does, until he purges *himself* from the narrative and leaves the reader to the summing-up of Lady Blandish, an imperfect fledgling philosopher, but one who at least knows she ought to seek charity if she has it not.

In Meredith's other novels, as we shall see, this conflict continues, deepens, gains allies. But it always has this same basic form. Two voices, one the true tone of philosophy and the other its flaw, its vice, its shadow of cynicism, sentimentalism, egoism, fatalism, struggle for control of the narrative. They struggle to control both the material of the plot, the story, and the material of the subplot, the reader's allegiance. It is this shadow, these false uses of brain and fake alignments of blood, brain, and spirit, that Meredith studies in all his works of fiction. In his plots, when he deals with "the world," he makes it clear that no final and pristine purging of that shadow is possible, or even quite imaginable yet. In his subplots, though, when he deals with the reader he anticipates/creates, he struggles to maintain a faith that the reader may come to whom ideal reading adulthood is possible, who has no need at all of the reader-vices of blood and glory, sentiment or satire, who has shed these shadows. In the end, however, he is irresistibly and painfully and admirably true to his faith that "all hangs together" in the activity of fiction as well as in "this life," that philosophy, in fiction as in life, is a blending, an integrity, of blood, brain, spirit—and shadow.

4. The Mask of Sentimentalism

> The Philosopher here peremptorily demands the
> pulpit. We are subject, he says, to fantastic
> moods, and shall dry ready-minted phrases
> picture them forth? As for example, can the
> words "delirium" or "frenzy" convey an image
> of Wilfrid's state when his heart began to
> covet Emilia again . . . ? To be in this state,
> says the Philosopher, is to be ON THE HIPPOGRIFF:
> and to this, as he explains, the persons who
> travel to Love by the road of sentiment mill
> come. *(Sandra Belloni,* II, *184)*

SANDRA BELLONI IS THE FIRST OF MEREDITH'S
novels in which the narrative is handled—battled for,
that is—by two different characterized narrators. The
major voice, the central attitude, is that of the Novelist, a
self-conscious writer of works designed to be sold to a
divided and obstreperous public. The Novelist is a sort of
theatrical promoter-cum-Mudie's-librarian, alive to the difficulties of pleasing the mass audience, aware that he himself has a tendency to pander to the simple and primitive
demands of this audience more than he ought. For this
reason, and some others, he has gone into storytelling
partnership with the Philosopher, a character who has all
the elevated virtues of insight, wit, and prophetic vision
we saw Meredith claiming for philosophy in the last chapter and several of the vices of this attitude—garrulousness,
disengagement from the world, aversion to action. Essentially the Philosopher's role in the subplot of *Sandra Belloni* is to harass the Novelist into stopping the action of the

tale long enough to allow (and demand from the fictional reader) some meditation on character, motive, development, and the implications of events. As the two characterized authors wrangle about proper treatment of the story, they also create two responses in the reader. Just as each of the authorial characters has a shadow, which is somehow cancelled out or balanced by the virtues of the other, so the several kinds of reader responses the authors argue about and work for in the prose audience are seen as flawed and shadowed, and the reader of the novel must shift back and forth among these responses, note their inadequacies, and finally step back from the inadequate reader roles, these shadow selves, to become a much more balanced and complex person himself.

The reader's task is complicated for him not only by the direct attack on readers' habits by two very intrusive authors, but also by the fact that the thing to be read, the story itself, is a mixture of three modes—farce, tragedy, comedy—each of which calls for a particular kind of reading attitude. The aspect of the story involving Samuel Pole partakes of all the elements of farce. Pole is an overextended British merchant trying to support the cultural pretensions of his supereducated three daughters on a dwindling income which he ekes out with embezzled funds from the trust of an amorous Irish widow, Martha Chump. The sentimental and ultimately disastrous love affair between Cornelia Pole and a poor but once noble organist named Purcell Barrett has many of the elements of tragedy, and is indeed named "A Tragedy of Sentiment" by Meredith's Novelist. The romance, education, and final maturing and breaking apart of Wilfrid Pole and the young singer Emilia Alessandra Belloni is Meredithian comedy of the first order. All of these modes co-exist somewhat uneasily in *Sandra Belloni*, a very long and not fully integrated Meredithian experiment.

At this early stage of his career Meredith was still hopeful of gaining a mass audience and a good income from his work. But this novel is heavy going for readers used to simple stories. *Sandra Belloni* is not a simple story; it is several complicated ones all generated out of the Novelist's and the Philosopher's quarrel over the primary material of the novel, which turns out once more to be a Book. Toward the end of the novel we discover that the original material, the germ Book, was written by the Philosopher and given over to the Novelist to treat in his familiar and open role as editor. As we make our way through the farce, the tragedy, finally the comedy of sentiment that the characterized authors have produced out of the Book, we will see how the anatomy of the vice of sentimentalism that these three aspects of the novel invite us to make is turned increasingly from plot to subplot, from characters to the readers and writers of the novel and to the particular kinds of sentimentalism of which *they* may be guilty.

Meredith's dearest subjects for anatomy are always virtues, virtues sick or swollen or fevered, and the virtue he examines in *Sandra Belloni* is the capacity to feel deeply. Feeling, "blood," passion, is the *sine qua non* of character for Meredith, and his profound respect for feeling as the binding element of the self underlies his whole analysis. But his particular attention in this novel is on feeling gone awry, a condition of unhealth that he regards as probably inevitable, especially in the young, but certainly not incurable. He is interested in what can cure the disease, what can kill the patient, what provokes to fever and madness, what swells feeling to unnatural proportions and what reduces swelling, how to wait out disease until health comes, and how this waiting may turn artificial and destructive. In *Sandra Belloni* he greatly expands the analysis of "fevers of the blood" begun in *Richard Feverel*, continuing, in a sense, his reading of the famous phrase in *The Pilgrim's Scrip*: "Sentimentalists are they who seek to enjoy Reality without incurring the Immense Debtorship for a thing done." The phrase, we shall see, applies to authors and readers too.

119

I. Farce and Tragedy

The merchant Samuel Pole is perhaps the guiltiest party in this particular matter of debit in the sense that his failure to tell his daughters the truth generates most of the novel's action. The truth is that commercial misfortunes have sharply reduced his finances and made it impossible for Adela, Arabella, and Cornelia to continue that mounting from city to gentry circles that they have been practicing all their lives. The sisters have disguised their naked social ambition from themselves by seeing their leaps from circle to circle not in social but in cultural terms; what they are after, they think, is not the circle where rank and position guarantee power, but the one where the fine spirits gather, the spirits capable of the subtlest and most civilized feeling for art, culture, nature, humanity. Taking the young singer Emilia Alessandra Belloni into their home gives them an extra counter in those circles.

Even with this added financial strain, however, Pole cannot tell his daughters the truth about money—and not simply because he knows the truth will break the hearts of the daughters whom he genuinely loves. Pole more than loves them; he is in positive awe of them, of their cleverness, their fastidiousness of speech and delicacy of understanding; and, most important of all, he is intimidated by their asserted claim to a mysterious and superior realm of civilized and gentle feeling about life. Where such exalted feeling rules, money has no business, no reality even: so the daughters, not directly of course, but by the smothering, ego-shattering indirection of Fine Shades, have convinced the father. Meredith's point is that although Pole's love for his children and fears for their future are genuine at bottom, sentimentalism has inflamed them, exaggerated and twisted them, until the feeling expresses itself in such grotesque tendernesses as his commands to his son Wilfrid and to Cornelia to marry moneyed mates they do not love. This is an alien something, some outside force that has

120

swollen the natural feeling to ludicrous proportions. Like the Novelist, Pole is inhabited by a shadow self, a shadow *un*businessman unconcerned about money, delighting in the gentility around him, properly respectful of, while unable to share in, Fine Shades and Nice Feelings. Meredith's Novelist creates him and calls him a figure of farce and pathos, and at the end, his health broken by the constant psychic pressure, Pole is well nigh taken over by this unself he has received from his daughters, ludicrously courting the broadly Irish widow Martha Chump in the language of gentility.

His daughter Adela has begun even that courtship for him, forging bits of conversation from Martha to Pole during a time when the widow was in fact deep in a hearty quarrel with him. Much of the farce of the novel proceeds through letters, language detached from persons being much more genteel (and safe) than the messy physical contact that produces such misunderstandings. But indeed the Pole sisters' letters are so genteel, so nicely shaded, so delicately conveyed, that they can mean almost anything. One such letter to their brother closes coyly, "Adieu! Such is my dulnes, I doubt whether I have made my meaning clear." Meredith's hero, Wilfrid, has two responses, one to the medium—"Why doesn't she write plain to the sense?"—and one to the message—"And now he saw meanings in the simple passages, and none at all in the intricate ones; and the double-meanings were monsters that ate one another up till nothing remained of them" *(*i, *135).*

Letters are a staple of that Meredithian habit panned by James as "the evasion of climax" but hailed by one contemporary critic as "the refracted experience."[1] By this

---

[1] "The fragmented chronology, the refracted experience, the dense flux of symbol and metaphor in his novels, all link him with later writers," says Gillian Beer in her treatment of Meredith's style in *Meredith: A Change of Masks* (London: The Athlone Press, 1970), p. 5. She defines this habit of refracting experience later on: "Meredith records the diffused eddying of feeling and action; he insists on the protracted growth of relationships; he

method the artist presents his material, especially his action scenes, not directly in narrative but by shifting to second- and third-hand report on some scene or action already accomplished in time but not dramatized in the narrative. The emphasis is on response instead of event, incidents are known not in their "objective" truth, if there is one, but through the nervous perspectives of several observers. My contention is that this shifting away from action, this "evasion" as James terms it, is not to be viewed negatively as a failure of craftsmanship or of nerve, or even neutrally, as an amusing idiosyncrasy that can be ignored; it should rather be viewed as providing important clues about Meredith's sense of *how* things come to be known and what *can* be known. The refracted experience, with all the strategies that realize it and all the implications it contains, is in a large sense the action of a Meredith novel: he works deliberately not so much with events as with the mind's action upon events as a way of forcibly educating his reader into philosophy. The ubiquitous presence of the ordinary letter throughout Meredith's novels shows us on a literal level what I believe is a major action of a Meredith novel, and, as I have tried to suggest in chapter I, what is a hidden action of many novels in this comic tradition—that is, the action of man-reading-language as a metaphor for man-reading-life. It is important to note that we see all Meredith's letters with the readers of them, not the writers of them.[2]

---

eschews the heightened scene; he rejects novel conventions which tighten and simplify the deviousness of human feeling" (p. 164).

[2] In this sense, Richardson as well as Fielding belongs in this tradition of the novelist-editor wrestling with a text. We see all the letters Richardson edited with the readers of them too, rather than with the writers, which is one reason why I have never been bothered by the supposed impossibility of all those letters being written in the elapsed time of the novel. It may be impossible to write them in that space of time; but it is possible to read them, and the reading, not the writing of letters, seems to me the major action of that book, as it is a major part of the action in several Meredith novels, including this one and *The Amazing Marriage*.

A different and more dangerous sentimentality destroys Cornelia Pole and Purcell Barrett. Despite the super-subtlety, the sexual frigidity, and the social self-distancing that have caused her to accept the sobriquet of "North" Pole, Cornelia comes to love Barrett; and despite the grandly Byronic doom-figure of disinherited son and fortuneless prince that Barrett has made for himself, he returns her feeling. Yet such is their acquired refinement, and at bottom their self-love, that they cannot even name their feeling "love," but must call it the friendship of a poor lover for a glorious creature out of his star. Under the mask of friendship, they cannot call upon each other for a lover's courage to meet their situation. Because their refinement, like Richard Feverel's, makes it impossible for them really to feel and deal with hostility from (and their own hostility to) the fathers who in one way or the other failed them, they transfer that hostility, as he did, to "the Fates," and commit that ultimate sin of the looker-on in becoming lookers-on at their own destruction. Barrett's suicide, when it inevitably comes, seems somehow not done by him but witnessed by him: "On both sides of him, 'yes' and 'no' seemed pressing like two hostile powers that battled for his body. They shrieked in his ears, plucked at his fingers. He heard them hushing deeply as he went to his pistol-case and drew forth one—he knew not which" (II, 275). Cornelia's psychic suttee, a barren widowhood for the rest of her life, also seems not to be her own act, but something seen sleepwalking, as Barrett saw it in a kind of voluptuous daydream before he pulled the trigger: "A woman throwing up the veil from her face knelt to a corpse that she lifted without effort, and weeping, laid it in a grave, where it rested and was at peace, though multitudes hurried over it and new stars came and went, and the winds were strange with new tongues" (II, 271-72). So tenaciously held a sentimentalism, so destructive a human flaw, has a certain majesty that Meredith's Novelist grants, not without some irony, by calling her and Barrett's final chapter "The Tragedy of Sentiment."

II. Emilia and Wilfrid: The Comedy of Sentiment

The method by which Cornelia and Barrett sought sentimental annihilation of responsibility for self was first the
disconnection of feeling and knowing through the denial
or perversion of verbal communication and then the setting
up of ideals of feeling disconnected from the person who
was the true source of the feeling. Meredith is explicit
about this:

> The two were in a dramatic tangle of the Nice Feelings.
> . . . She wished to say to him, "You are unjust to my per-
> plexities"; and he to her, "You fail in your dilemma
> through cowardice." Instead of uttering which, they chid
> themselves severally for entertaining such coarse ideas
> of their idol. Doubtless they were silent from considera-
> tion for one another: but I must add, out of extreme ten-
> derness for themselves, likewise. (ii, *168*)

If we turn from the farce and the tragedy to the comedy
of sentiment, we can see how Emilia Belloni conspicuously
rejects the denial of language that symbolizes separation
of feeling and knowing. We shall see how this capacity for
direct knowledge and expression of her feelings enables
her finally to overcome the sentimental idealization of Wilfrid Pole that she mistook for love. When we come to look
at the dramatic tangle of Nice Feelings in Wilfrid, who is
from the point of view of the subplot the most important
character in the novel, we will see why it is the separation,
not the marriage, of these two "lovers" that marks this
aspect of the novel as a comedy.

Emilia's directness of language is her most startling
and infuriating characteristic; her first words on being
caught singing in the moonlight sound the clear note of
nonsentimentalism: "Oh stay, do stay, if I please you." She
recognizes that she has caused deep feeling in her listeners,
she thinks it natural that she should do so, and she is willing to accept the responsibility for it. The watching Novelist-narrator, diffused momentarily in the consciousness of

"Brookfield," reacts: "A singular form of speech, it was thought by the ladies" *(*i, *12).* Cornelia tries twice in as many pages to melt Emilia into their own rosy atmospheric bemusement, to detach her from her knowledge that *she* is the source of beauty and feeling: "You find the presence of people while you are singing more sympathetic? . . . You feel the place inspires you?" Emilia answers in both cases with a pure ego-statement: "I like having people near me. . . . I love the place."

The point is clear, I think. Emilia borrows feeling from no outside or artificial source; above all, not for her art. She recognizes herself as the source of her art, her feeling, her life. That is the center of her health and of the others' weakness. The Pole family, listening to her, look to the moonlight, the atmosphere, the audience, partly to account for their feeling, not wishing to acknowledge their real indebtedness to its human source. They prefer to see Emilia as the accidental reflector of beauty rather than the source of it; in this way they can both patronize her and sentimentally idealize her, mold her as a sort of diffused phantom image with the trees and the moon.

With this opening scene in the moonlight Meredith sets up his dominant pattern: the sentimentalist is he who will receive or give feeling, passion, love, only through the distancing reflecting medium of a phantom ideal, thus by-passing real persons, real responsibility, reality itself. His sign is the moon, pale reflector of light not its own, and his language is the civilized one of Fine Shades and Nice Feeling. The natural person is she who expresses and acts upon direct contact with her feelings, who does not need to bank off or diffuse her feelings through some outside ideal or reflector in order to accept them. Her sign is the sun and her language is the primitive one of direct utterance healthily dotted with the first person pronoun.

Meredith starts building this pattern of images and attitudes during this encounter in chapter 2 between the Poles and Emilia. They have heard a voice singing in the forest and have gone out, with attendant cavaliers, to investigate, striking romantic attitudes along the way:

> "Does there not seem a soul in the moonlight?" Arabella, after a rapturous glance at the rosy orb, put it to Mr. Pericles, in subdued impressive tones. She had to repeat her phrase; Mr. Pericles then echoing, with provoking monotony of tone, "Sol?"—whereupon "Soul!" was reiterated, somewhat sharply: and Mr. Pericles, peering over the collar of the bear, with half an eye, continued the sentence, in the manner of one sent thereby farther from its meaning:—"Ze moonlight?" Despairing and exasperated, Arabella commenced afresh: "I said there seems a *soul* in it"; and Mr. Pericles assented bluntly: "In ze light!"—which sounded so little satisfactory that Arabella explained, "I meant the *aspect*"; and having said three times distinctly what she meant, in answer to a terrific glare from the unsubmerged whites of the eyes of Mr. Pericles, this was his comment, almost roared forth:
> "Sol! you say so-whole—in ze moonlight—Luna? Hein? Ze aspect is of Sol! Yes!" And Mr. Pericles sank into his bear again. . . . *(1, 8)*

Much of the comedy of this passage lies in the fact that while Arabella thinks that Mr. Pericles is being simply obtuse and unappreciative of Nice Feelings, in a manly way, the reader senses the Greek's willful mockery of her and her attitude, punning in three languages before retiring into his bear. But to look at the passage seriously for a moment, we note that technically the sun *is* the soul of the moon, and that the moon at full (as now) does have the aspect of the sun, so-whole. But it turns out to be false, indeed a lunacy, to confuse the stability and *sui generis* soul of the one heavenly body with the changeability and borrowed soul of the other.

From this point the mutual spellbinding of Wilfrid and Emilia takes place under the auspices of the moon. The earliest romantic encounter takes place in a chapter beginning "The night was warm under a slowly floating moon"

126

*(*i, *29)*. The important chapter where Wilfrid falls in love with the girl his sisters have adopted to help their social ambitions begins, "A pillar of dim silver rain fronted the moon on the hills" *(*i, *101)*. The moon presides over their first kiss: "She lifted a clear full face, to which he bent his mouth. Over the flowering hawthorn the moon stood like a windblown white rose of the heavens" *(*i, *105)*. Over the chapter "By Wilming Weir" where Emilia pledges her life, her career, herself, her "Italy" to Wilfrid's happiness, thinking him as deeply committed to her as she is to him, the moon broods in aspects ranging from "soft" to "sinister" to spiritual:

> Emilia leaned to him more, and the pair fixed their eyes on the moon, that had now topped the cedar, and was pure silver: silver on the grass, on the leafage, on the waters. And in the west, facing it, was an arch of twilight and tremulous rose; as if a spirit hung there over the shrouded sun.
> "At least," thought Wilfrid, "heaven and the beauty of the world approve my choice." *(*i, *199)*

The "shrouded sun" is disturbing, and Wilfrid's pathetic fallacy here takes on ominous overtones of the sentimental distancing of responsibility. Even more ominous for the lovers' future is his imaginative idealization of her right at the beginning: "He reflected with a loving rapture that her manner at that moment was equal to any lady's; and the phantom of her with her hand out and her frank look and trustful footing, while she spoke those words, kept on advancing to him all the way to Brookfield, at the same time that the sober reality murmured at his elbow" *(*i, *107)*. Already the real Emilia has receded and the phantom ideal image of the natural child, the innocent romantic heroine, has become fixed in her place, and Wilfrid is never quite able to unite them again.

Emilia's own lunar madness is the more emphatic here because she has just mused that in giving up her artistic greatness by giving up her chance of study in Italy to remain with Wilfrid she may be giving him a love that does not spring fully from her potential real self: "But I seem to give [my love] to you in tatters: it's like a beggar; like a day without any sun." If this does not make clear enough the fact that in Wilfrid Emilia too is worshiping a phantom image, the image of her own capacity for passion, Meredith repeats the sign of the shrouded sun a few chapters later when Emilia is staggered by Samuel Pole's frantic refusal to listen to her explanation of the love between her and Wilfrid:

> The sun of her world was threatened with extinction. She felt herself already a wanderer in a land of tombs, where none could say whether morning had come or gone. Intensely she looked her misery in the face; and it was as a voice that said, "No sun: never sun any more," to her. But a blue-hued moon slipped from among the clouds, and hung in the black outstretched fingers of the tree of darkness, fronting troubled waters. "This is thy light forever! Thou shalt live in thy dream." So, as in a prison house, did her soul now recall the blissful hours by Wilming Weir. (I, 265)

Emilia does not herself yet see that *she* owns the sun, but she does see now that Wilming Weir is a moon dream. Her temptation here, her sickness, is the wish to inhabit that dream, to take the moon for the sun. It is this sickness, the sentiment of idol worship fed by fires not inherent in the idol, lit by reflected light, driven by artificial means (in this case her will to see in Wilfrid her own passionate response to the idea of love) that Emilia contracts in the moonlight meetings with Wilfrid. Sentiment is responsible for the partly incredible reconciliations she makes with his falseness to her throughout the two volumes of *Sandra Belloni*. The reader cannot be sure she will not relapse into sentimental reconciliation again until the shock of the pistol image ending the "Tragedy of Sentiment" is followed immediately by the new chapter opening, "On a wild April morning, Emilia rose from her bed" (II, 275-76).

This suggests the beginning of the end of the comedy. Emilia has given her promise to Wilfrid that she will not leave England if he will not become an Austrian soldier, and in this chapter we see her reading Wilfrid's letters reminding her of that promise and refusing to release her—"he painted such a superstitious halo around 'the sacredness of her pledged word' that Emilia could not resist a superstitious notion about it" (II, 277). Finally, on that "wild April morning" Emilia decides to break her promise, to go to Italy where her "sun," her self-as-musician, really waits. Wilfrid naturally writes to confront her with her faithlessness. He asks for a final meeting and Meredith pictures Emilia leaning out of her window the evening before it to drink in the old seductive sentimental moon dream:

> April was leaning close upon May and she had not to wait long before a dusky flutter of low [nightingale] notes, appearing to issue from the great rhododendron bush across the lawn, surprised her. She listened, and another little beginning was heard, timorous, shy, and full of mystery for her. The moon hung over branches, some that showed young buds, some still bare. Presently the long, rich, single notes cut the air, and melted to their glad delicious chuckle. The singer was answered from a farther bough, and again from one. It grew to be a circle of melody round Emilia at the open window. Was it the same as last year's? The last year's lay in her memory faint and well-nigh unawakened. And yet the song was sweet. Emilia clasped her arms, shut her eyes, and drank it in. Not to think at all, or even to brood on her sensations, but to rest half animate and let those divine sounds find a way through her blood, was medicine to her.
>
> (II, 281-82)

Although the song of the past is sweet, Emilia does not choose it, nor does she meet Wilfrid, and we do not see the moon again until the next to last chapter—a characteristic Meredithian set piece that burlesques the comedy of chapter 2 by returning all the characters to the moonlit grove to hear Emilia sing and to watch her, whom they adopted as a sentimental pet exactly a year before, move forever out of their reach. The scene is pure midsummer night's dream: "A sharp breath of air had passed along the dews, and all the young green of the fresh season shone in white jewels. The sky, set with very dim distant stars, was in grey light round a small brilliant moon. Every space of earth lifted clear to her; the woodland listened; and in the bright silence the nightingales sang loud" (II, 295). Under that moon Emilia reveals her last and seemingly most stunning act of sentiment: she has bound herself to Pericles to study music in Italy for three years, away from her new hero, the shadowy Merthyr Powys, in return for Pericles' promise to succor the Pole fortunes. Yet the actual taint of sentimentality in this is small, almost nonexistent. A conservatory in Italy is where she *should* be; that commitment violates no part of her natural character as did her promise to Wilfrid to give up her music. Even the delay of her meeting with Merthyr is good; she recognizes herself that she is not ready for him, not fully herself, still able to give only "the tatters" of love: " 'What am I? I am a raw girl. I command nothing but raw and flighty hearts of men. Are they worth anything? Let me study three years, without any talk of hearts at all. . . . I will not have what I do not deserve' " (II, 310). Merthyr himself had given Emilia the key to an escape from sentimentality: "He says that I should not follow an impulse that is not the impulse of *all* my nature— myself together" (II, 278).

Emilia's symbolic drama poses the question that Meredith asks of all his people: Where is the source of feeling? The source of feeling is not Mont Blanc, the moon, or the nightingale, but the self, with all other things ancillary or "medicinal," as Meredith allows in the Keatsian passage quoted a page ago. The soul a man is responsible for seeing is in himself. The more clearly outside the real self the source of feeling resides, the more ridiculous and caricaturable is the resulting sentiment, as witness Samuel Pole's attempt to pretend he values fine feeling more than good business. When the source of feeling is lost somewhere in the anarchy of disconnected selves, the sentiment is no longer just ridiculous but powerful and dangerously destructive, as witness Cornelia Pole and Purcell Barrett and, as we shall see, Wilfrid Pole. But when it is firmly located in a solid self, which is changing by organic enlargement and discarding of irrelevant parts, then the sentiment is simply an excrescence, a youthful aberration. Such is Emilia's passionate idealization of Wilfrid Pole, an ordeal that shows her that the locus of her feeling is in the form of her self, essentially an artist-self, generating feeling spontaneously and, at maturity, generating a control effortlessly with the feeling. The power to feel harmoniously, Meredith says, is the maturity of art, as it is the maturity of the self as well. The power of feeling in Beethoven fascinates Emilia, as Byronism lures Purcell Barrett, and, somewhat less destructively, Wilfrid. But even in the puberty of her art-self Emilia holds Beethovian passion at a distance.[3] Harmony, the resolution of feeling with feeling, feeling with control, spontaneous self with organizing self, tragic self with comic self, is perhaps the Meredithian ideal. Of course, harmonic natures, like other harmonic compositions, are distinguished not by the elimi-

---

[3] Emilia's struggle to tame the Beethovian soul in her, the passionate soul, is mentioned several times both in terms of her art and her life. Beethoven is "like a black angel" to Emilia; she feels particularly "at his mercy" whenever Wilfrid's inexplicable behavior is making her desperate. At one point she bursts out to Wilfrid, "I dreamed about him . . . every night after talking with my father about Italy and this man came over my pillow and made me call him Master, Master. And he is. He seems as if he were the master of my soul mocking me, making me worship him in spite of my hate. I came here to think of you. I heard the water like a great symphony. I fell into dreaming of my music. That's when I am at his mercy. There's no one like him. I must detest music to get free of him. How can I? He is like the God of music" (ch. 20).

131

nation of one line, or even by the blend of two lines into a wholly different third, but by the simultaneous and mutually fruitful presence of both lines.

I have called the affair of Wilfrid and Emilia the comedy of sentiment partly because it fits in so neatly with Meredith's own characterization of other parts of the story as farce and tragedy. For the Meredithian comedy is always resolved in the marriage of the divided self, the reshaping of the individual's character by the connection of blood, brain, and spirit. The marriage of lovers follows only sometimes as a result, or a symbol, of the real marriage. The typical Meredithian situation, especially in his early novels, is the achievement of harmony by one partner while the other partner, already unselfconsciously harmonized, waits by. Interestingly, in most of the early novels, the focus is on the masculine ordeal of achieving harmony. It is as though Meredith believes that women, while no less variously structured, find or are given harmony more easily than men, and that their ordeal is not so much to achieve harmony as to find the considerable strength and insight to await the self-coherence of their mates. It is this presence of the double marriage that I think accounts for the pervasive tragicomedy, in form and in feeling, in the early novels. For while he almost invariably brings off the first marriage—the intrapersonal one governed by moral principle, Fielding's old marriage of prudence and feeling— he seldom brings off the second marriage, the interpersonal one governed by Time and Chance. Thus by the time Edward Blancove in *Rhoda Fleming*, Wilfrid Pole in *Sandra Belloni*, Richard Feverel in *The Ordeal*, and Lord Fleetwood in *The Amazing Marriage* become themselves, win through their ordeal, love is dead in their mates (or in Richard's case, his love herself is dead). Curiously enough, when it is men who are obliged to winter through the waiting ordeal while their women make the journey to harmony, the harmony seems more easily achieved. Thus does Robert Eccles wait out his Rhoda Fleming, Vernon

Whitford his Clara Middleton, and Redworth his Diana Warwick.

If we can call Emilia the hero of her own book, then, the comedy is resolved when she regains at maturity the harmony of her nature.[4] But in fact it is clearly Wilfrid Pole who most fascinates the narrators and that is why I have waited until now to discuss him. His ordeal is central in the hierarchy of ordeals that make up this novel, and his manipulation by sentimental feeling is the most clearly and carefully worked out of all the sentimentalisms. Wilfrid's sentimentalism is that of an eminently worthy youth, English and half-civilized. What is special is the intensity and particularity of the analysis of motive-emotive process in the history of that archetypal ordeal, an analysis the more intensely interesting because it occurs somewhere on the interface between the character of Wilfrid and that of the narrators—that is, Wilfrid's fight with and surrender to sentimentalism is thematically and structurally close to the drama of sentimentalism taking place in the subplot.

Wilfrid is a military man, a young cornet temporarily (and temperamentally) at home in the gardens of England. We first meet him laughing soundlessly at Arabella's "soul in the moonlight" statement, and we know immediately that he is above the salt in that ubiquitous Meredithian conceit dividing the world into "little people" and "higher people." His sisters, in the pursuit of their ideal, the social generalship of Lady Gosstre, are below the salt:

[4] It would be neat to try and see the three names that the heroine receives from Meredith (one in the sequel book, *Vittoria*) as a well-wrought structure of harmonized aspects of her: Sandra the spontaneously self-loving primitive Italian self; Emilia the adolescent, harassed, and self-doubting English self; and Vittoria the harmonized lover-diva-revolutionary self. But the device lies somewhere between the truly operative and the contrived, and (if device it is) must be put down to that "d—d, d—d, d—d uncertain workmanship" that Meredith mourned in himself (*Letters*, I, 302). The same notion suggests itself about another Meredith heroine, Diana Antonia Merion Warwick.

The ladies of Brookfield allowed themselves to bow to her with the greater humility, owing to that secret sense they nursed of overtopping her still in that ineffable Something which they alone possessed: a casket little people will be wise in not hurrying our Father Time to open for them, if they would continue to enjoy the jewel they suppose it to contain. *(1, 34)*

Thus Wilfrid is differentiated from the sisters in the first general reaction to Emilia's singing:

Then the ladies stood together and talked of her, not with absolute enthusiasm. . . . And then it was discovered how their common observation had fastened on the [loose] boot-lace; and this vagrant article became the key to certain speculations on her condition and character.

"I wish I'd had a dozen bouquets, that's all!" cried Wilfrid. *(1, 15)*

Both responses are outside of, elliptical to, the direct response to the singing, for which Emilia's own "Oh stay, as long as I please you" is the cue. But Wilfrid's idol worshiping is clearly a higher sentimentalism than is the ladies' snobbery on behalf of the dignity of art. Meredith implies here, as he often does, that it is more difficult to loosen or expand a limited, pinched-in nature than to prune back or pull together an energetic, scattered one. Throwing bouquets expresses exactly the nature of the sentiment Wilfrid conceives for Emilia. As an abstract enthusiasm she has none of the claims on him that a real woman does, and is infinitely variable, malleable, in form. The point is that whether Wilfrid's feelings are being exercised by Emilia Child of the Silver Wood, Emilia Child of Feeling, Emilia Dauntless in Devotion, Emilia Tamed Genius, or whatever incarnation he and the night and the music are producing, the hero of all these dramas is Wilfrid Sentiens, man-feeling.

What he seeks from Emilia is the exquisite and entirely sensual flattery of evoking the force of her love, not the fact of it. We have seen how she became more phantom than fact to him: "The phantom of her with her hand out and her frank look, and trustful footing, while she spoke those words, kept on advancing to him all the way to Brookfield, at the same time that the sober reality murmured at his elbow." He, if he can help it, never stays still long enough for the force of her real love to reach him directly, discomforting thing that it is.

> He saw no more than that she could not sing because of what was in her heart towards him; but such a physical revelation was a divine love-confession, coming involuntarily from one whose lips had not formed the name of love; and Wilfrid felt it so deeply, that the exquisite flattery was almost lost, in a certain awed sense of his being in the presence of an absolute fact. *(*i, *109)*

Wilfrid wants the credit for setting the streams of feeling running, his and hers, without knowing, wanting not to know, where the streams are going, submerging everyone and no one in the general stream, with everyone and no one responsible for the feeling, with no one responsible *to* the other person. As Emilia, loving him, sings for the Poles: "Wilfrid knew himself the fountain of it all, and stood fountain-like, in a shower of secret adulation: a really happy fellow. This: that his beloved should be the centre of eyes, and pronounced exquisite by general approbation, besides subjecting him to a personal spell: this was what he wanted" *(*i, *207)*.

Meredith's Philosopher-narrator invents a splendid comic analogue for the willful helplessness, the standing fountain-like, the invoked passivity, of the sentimental youth. Wilfrid becomes a horseman "on Hippogriff." The mythical monster, half-horse, half-eagle, full of lion's blood, a lasher of tail and a rider to the winds, both terrifying and ridiculous, is the very picture of the state Meredith wishes to dramatize. The sentimentalist is quintessentially "a creature bestriding an extraneous power. . . . [who] goes on accumulating images and hiving sensations, till such time as (if the stuff be in him) they assume a form of vitality, and hurry him headlong" (II, *185*).

The key to Wilfrid's sentimentality, then, is what I have called the will to be "happened to." From almost inside Wilfrid's consciousness the Novelist-narrator remarks of Wilfrid's admiration for Lady Charlotte: "She was a note of true music, and he felt himself to be an indecisive chord; capable ultimately of a splendid performance, it might be, but at present crying out to be played upon" (I, *177*). This is the operative element in Wilfrid's double deception of surrender to the cool and meritorious Lady Charlotte and to the naïve, demanding Emilia; he loves too well the music they both make of him as he surrenders. He cannot be false to either lady while with her, nor true to either lady while with the other, because he is in thrall to neither of them, but to Meredithian higher sentimentality, the sensualism of the soul. His need, compassionated by Meredith, is to walk amid furious booms and flashes of feeling, the exhilaration of youth for electrical storms. His task is to make sense out of the storm, passion out of the sentimental feeling, to confine the lightning usefully as a current between the positive and negative poles of himself and another, to become, in a word, Ego, "I" to somebody's "thou." His crime is a species of doublethink designed to relieve him of the responsibility to act, or even to be, designed to keep the feeling as lightning flashes without visible source or destination rather than to develop it into a current. He knows and he does not know that he is the source and target of the feeling he has raised in two other beings to enliven his air with storms. When he is confronted by this feeling in an encounter or a letter and he returns it, he is conscious of the flash of indiscriminate feeling by which it is being returned, but he is not conscious that it is he, a solid being, who acts in response, and that the act carries all the responsibilities of any human act. He is not conscious of this, Meredith makes clear, because he is in youth's anarchy of self—the double man in conflict, "at

THE MASK OF SENTIMENTALISM

throttle" within *(*1, *297)*. The temptation is to see this doubleness as the conventional dilemma between reason and passion, with the aristocratic Englishwoman and the vital Italian girl as its personification. This is suggested, of course. But the neatness of this notion is obscured by the healthy and mostly quite cool egoism of Emilia ("Constantly just to herself, mind! This is the quality of true passion," remarks the Philosopher [ii, *185*]) and the half-unconscious sensuality of Lady Charlotte ("No recollection gave her joy except of the hours on the hunting-field. There she led gallantly; but it was not because of leading that she exulted. There the quick blood struck on her brain like wine, and she seemed for a time to have some one among the crowns of life" [ii, *4*]). The two women do not finally represent two options to Wilfrid; they both represent the same option, to turn from the sheer delight in anarchy to the "embrace of Life" *(*1, *297)*, and the responsibility of cleaving to, of acknowledging, debtorship to the real. Anarchy, Meredith believes, is probably an inevitable but certainly a temporary state for the young man, and woe betide the woman at whose feet he kneels then. But in the natural state of things Life's offer of embrace should become irresistible (not least often in the person of a woman herself refined down to her reality by love). He who holds life at bay, who protects himself from the consequences of his responses by falsely evoking those responses, basely transfers his being to a thing outside the self. He is a sentimentalist and embraces anarchy. Held and practiced past a certain crisis point, sentimentality is the abandonment of the fight to become real oneself and to search out corresponding realness in others and in the world.

The way out of sentimentality, what I have called the transformation of lightning into current,[5] is the embrace of

---

[5] Meredith has already begun to play with this image at the beginning of Book ii: "There were probably a dozen very young men in the room waiting to rise with their partners at a signal for

Life, reaching out for contact, that makes oneself and one's embraced object into visible poles. It carries with it shock to the young sensibility, the sense of participation in and, worse, dependence upon fallible humanity. In book II, chapter 57, Wilfrid, in sentimental retreat from the fact of Emilia's newly healthy and maddeningly simple friendship for him, puts a cigar in his mouth, and completes a complex symbolic pattern involving his first sentimental disgust at the smell of tobacco smoke in Emilia's hair. She had been singing at Ipley Club's beer party, unselfconsciously artist and person, unwittingly interfering with Wilfrid's contrived ideal image of her. During the subsequent scene in the moonlight he did not notice that Emilia's hair had been "redolent of pipe smoke" (I, 112), but the morning after he does; the memory comes, "by an odd transition," after he sees in the mirror the black eye and swollen nose he got in rescuing Emilia from the Ipley brawl. Both those sensual images work upon him, that is, he works them upon himself, until he has decided that they impair his ideal images of her and of himself ("the eloquent big lump would have passed him current as hero . . . in the great days of old," the Novelist-narrator comments acidly, "These are the tea table days"). And so he rejects Emilia and the vitality of the Ipley set-to and the simplicity of Emilia's willingness to sing for the peasantry. Several times more Wilfrid finds the tobacco-smoke Emilia impossible to accept, refining on the difference in class and the differences between that image connected with a woman and with a man. Then, in chapter 57, "A Further Anatomy of Wilfrid," the book's hero takes out another cigar:

> The first taste of the smoke sickened his lips. Then he stood for a moment as a man in a new world. This strange sensation of disgust with familiar comforting

---

dancing; and these could not be calculated upon to take an initiative, or follow one—as ladies, poor slaves! will do when the electric hostess rustles. The men present were non-conductors" (II, 24).

habits fixed him in perplexity, till a rushing of wild thoughts and hopes from brain to heart, heart to brain, gave him insight, and he perceived his state, and that for all he held to in our life he was dependent upon another; which is virtually the curse of love. *(*ii, *291)*

Thus Wilfrid's comic enlightenment comes—too late, as it happens, for the reclaiming of Emilia's phantom love. She has not waited; she is on the point of departing for an Italy, where singing fame and revolutionary action await her. But Wilfrid has made a gain, in any case; heart and brain have made a fledgling connection and something may be built on that.[6]

III. The Philosopher's Exit: The Subplot

Intimately bound up with Wilfrid's enlightenment is a major action in the drama of the novel's subplot, the battle between the Novelist and the Philosopher for control of the reading of the story. The dual narrator's own enlightenment takes place at the same time and over the same circumstance as Wilfrid's. The paragraphs immediately following the one quoted above elucidate Wilfrid's state and modulate into a discussion of the narrator's:

"And he passed along the road," adds the Philosopher, "a weaker man, a stronger lover. Not that love should diminish manliness or gains by so doing; but travelling to love by ways of Sentiment, attaining to the passion bit by bit, does full surely take from us the strength of our nature, as if (which is probable) at every step we paid fee to move forward. Wilfrid had just enough of

[6] Alas, nothing is. The lesson has not sunk deep enough, and when we meet Wilfrid in the sequel to *Emilia in England*, *Emilia in Italy* (later titled *Vittoria*), we find that his desire for romantic glory and social position has led him to take advantage of family connections to acquire a lieutenancy in the Austrian army, which sentimentally fatal step brings him into deadly conflict with an Emilia who is now heart and soul with the Italian revolutionary cause.

the coin to pay his footing. He was verily *fining himself down.* You are tempted to ask what the value of him will be by the time that he turns out pure metal? I reply, something considerable, if by great sacrifice he gets to truth—gets to that oneness of feeling which is the truthful impulse. At last, he will stand high above them that have not suffered. The rejection of his cigar—"

This waxes too absurd. At the risk of breaking our partnership for ever, I intervene. My Philosopher's meaning is plain, and as usual, good; but not even I, who have less reason to laugh at him than anybody, can gravely accept the juxtaposition of suffering and cigars. And, moreover, there is a little piece of action in store.

Here, twenty pages from the end of the novel, the Philosopher exits, thrown out, in fact, by the Novelist, who may be having a sudden rush of wild thoughts and hopes between his own brain and heart, who may be experiencing a rare oneness of feeling in himself rather than the duality that has characterized the narrator of the story as much as the hero of the story. Of course Meredith is never entirely without irony when he offers the fictional reader of his novels some "action"—overattention to action is exactly what he does not want, either in writers or readers. But he has caught the Philosopher in a flaw here, one serious enough to break the partnership for a while, a flaw somehow connected with the juxtaposition of suffering and cigars. To find the nature of this flaw and how it operates upon the alignments of Philosopher, Novelist, and reader that have been going on throughout the novel, it is necessary to go back and trace the terms of the doubleness of the narrative voice of *Sandra Belloni.*

I have said that the distinguishing act of Meredith's narration, the fundamental action of his novels, is the way in which he causes the solitary reader to feel the abrasive aggravation and epistemological terror of the near impossibility of finding and saying the truth. I have also argued that much of the hostility generated among serious readers by Meredith's complex and intrusive prose stance comes from the author's deliberate undercutting of the convention of the civilized fictional reader that is pervasive in prose fiction. Meredith invites the reader to join his narrators in lofty survey of the follies of our fellows, and then implicates both himself and us in those same follies.

In this novel, it seems to me, the civilized reader is drawn out of the general audience largely by Meredith's nudging of him to identify just a little more with the Philosopher-narrator than with the Novelist-narrator in charge. The invitation goes out in the very first pages of the novel. The Pole sisters have been introduced as the stars of the folly of Fine Shades and Nice Feelings, "whereof," remarks the Novelist, "more will be said; but in the meantime it will explain their propensity to mount; it will account for their irritation at the material obstructions surrounding them; and possibly the philosopher will now have his eye on the source of that extraordinary sense of superiority to mankind which was the crown of their complacent brows" (1, 6). The reader immediately steps forward, superior to mere entertainment-loving mankind, to become "the philosopher." The Novelist and he together ironically eye the source of the Poles' folly: "Eclipsed as they may be in the gross appreciation of the world by other people, who excel in this and that accomplishment, persons that nourish Nice Feelings and are intimate with the Fine Shades carry their own test of intrinsic value." The Novelist gently reminds the reader of his philosophic duty to discriminate: "Nor let the philosopher venture hastily to despise them as pipers to dilettante life. Such persons come to us in the order of civilization. In their way they help to civilize us." The reader is, then, to be a worldly, not an otherworldly, philosopher. Still, his superior awareness will keep him from follies, at least for the duration of the book. When the Novelist steps out to address a warning to the sentimentalists listening in—"Take it as an axiom, when you utter a sentimentalism, that more than one pair of ears makes a cynical critic. A sentimentalism requires secrecy. I can enjoy it, and shall treat it respectfully if you will confide it to me alone; but I and my friends must laugh at it oughtright" *(1, 8)*—the reader can smile with him at the audience he has just left. When he bids sentimentalists sardonically follow the Way of the World—"Wouldst thou, O man, amorously inclining! attract to thee superior women, be positive. Be stupidly positive, rather than dubious at all!" *(1, 59)*—the reader can wait out the exaggerations, certain whose side the Novelist really is on: "Waver not. If women could tolerate waverings and weakness, and did not rush to the adoration of decision of mind, we should not behold them turning contemptuously from philosophers in their agony, to find refuge in the arms of smirking orthodoxy." The civilized reader welcomes the Novelist's sympathy for the hard brainwork he as philosopher must be performing.

Secure in his conventional identity, the civilized reader delights in having it played with, stirred up, contradicted and vindicated in the very terms of the contradiction:

> The Philosopher (I would keep him back if I could) bids us mark that the crown and flower of the nervous system, the head, is necessarily sensitive, and to that degree that whatsoever we place on it, does, for a certain period, change and shape us. . . . A girl may put on her brother's boots, and they will not affect her spirit strongly; but as soon as she puts on her brother's hat, she gives him a manly nod. The same philosopher who fathers his dulness on me, asserts that the modern vice of fastness ("Trotting on the Epicene Border," he has it) is bred by apparently harmless practices of this description. He offers to turn the current of a Republican's brain, by resting a coronet on his forehead for just five seconds. *(1, 62)*

The reader can see by this time that a little drama is to be played out. The Philosopher-narrator with whom the reader identifies is the Novelist's good angel, fated to save him from the bogs of the public's demand for action that civilized readers know to be the real dullness. The Philosopher breaks in on the action of the novel to set alight the imaginative truth resident in every object of the world that appears dull. The Philosopher interrupts the Novelist to search out at length motives and meanings that can too easily be overlooked in the swift flight along the endless prose line: "When we are knapsack on back, he says, we come to eminences where a survey of our journey past and in advance is desirable" (II, 185). The Philosopher is constantly "intruding" his moral percepts into the smooth surface of the Novelist's take-things-as-they-are attitude:

> Thus we obtain delicacy; and thus, as you will perceive, our civilisation, by the aid of the sentimentalists, has achieved an effective varnish. There, certainly, to the vulgar mind a tail is visible. The outrageous philosopher declares vehemently that no beast of the field or forest would own such a tail. (His meaning is that he discerns the sign of the animal slinking under the garb of the stately polished creature. I have all the difficulty in the world to keep him back and let me pursue my course.) These philosophers are a bad-mannered body. Either in opposition, or in the support of them, I maintain simply that the blinking sentimentalist helps to make civilisation what it is, and civilisation has a great deal of merit.
>
> (I, 290)

But in fact, in the business of producing these pages, it is the Novelist who is the intruder. It was "this garrulous, super-subtle, so-called Philosopher, who first set me upon the building of The Three Volumes" (II, 185), and the Novelist keeps the originator of the volumes noosed as much as he can: "In his soul [Wilfrid] adored the extreme refinement of woman, even up to the thin edge of inanity (which neighbors what the philosopher could tell him if he would, and would, if it were permitted to him)" (I, 83-84). In this schizophrenia, called partnership, the real energy both of origination and of motion comes from the Philosopher. *Sandra Belloni* is his book. Teufelsdrockh-like he surrenders himself to the Novelist for pruning. Editing

143

is not entirely altruism on the Novelist's part. What he loses at Mudie's, he figures he can gain with "that acute and honorable minority which consents to be thwacked with aphorisms and sentences and a fantastic delivery of the verities" (II, 230).

The convention seems complete: the civilized reader-philosopher (with a small minority audience somewhere slightly behind) is at bay before a world that thinks "a novel is to give us copious sugar and no cane" (I, 230). The reader's superiority lies in his ability, his willingness, to chew the cane to reach the sugar. He loves cane. He chews fiercely—metaphor, aphorism, analysis, fantastical delivery of the verities. He chews to the end of the book, vindicated by the underlying rhetoric of the novel despite the characterized Novelist's jabs at him. Well, almost to the end. Twenty pages from the end the Novelist appears to have choked on a piece of dry cane, spat it out, and ordered the Philosopher off the page. He goes, for good. Is the Novelist right to banish the Philosopher?

Yes, I think so. And I think Meredith means me, the civilized reader, to think so, and to feel myself undercut along with the Philosopher. The clue is in the laughter that operates both in the Novelist's reaction at the end of the book to the Philosopher's juxtaposition of suffering and cigars and in his comment at the beginning when he introduces that touchstone sentimentality from Arabella Pole, "Does there not seem a soul in the moonlight?" The Novelist has just warned her (the reader? himself?) that sentimentalism requires secrecy, intimacy, and suggests that another pair of ears will bring laughter at it. As the Philosopher confides his new metaphor to the reader, he is suddenly made aware of the Novelist as another pair of ears. Meredith's Novelist interrupts his Philosopher (the only time he does that; for the other six hundred pages of dialogue he always waits him out and snipes at him afterwards) not because he is fearful for his "market," and only secondarily because he has "a little piece of action" in store. His reaction to the start of another flight into metaphor is simple spontaneous laughter, the Comic Muse's smile: "Not even I, who have less reason to laugh at him than anybody, can gravely accept the juxtaposition of suffering and cigars."

What is the danger in the juxtaposition of suffering and cigars?[7] The same as makes ridiculous and destructive the juxtaposition of the soul and the moonlight, the displacement of response and responsibility, of potency and being, from man to thing, from the seeing soul to the snow-capped mountain peak, from the actual Wilfrid to the symbolic structure the Philosopher wants to erect around his cigar—in a word, sentimentality. The inflated metaphor is the sentimentality of the imaginative soul, the hippogriff of the artist. True metaphor, like true passion, is "noble strength on fire [that] never violates nature, and offends no law, wild as she may seem" (II, *184-85*). Laughable metaphor, like the sentimentalist, "goes on accumulating images and hiving sensations until . . . they hurry him headlong."

Would the Philosopher's flight into the fancy of suffering and cigars have gone past the mark from sensitivity to sentimentalism? Does such a fancy really shed light on the human situation under discussion, or does it use the human situation to call attention to the cleverness, the subtlety, of the Philosopher? Is there not a stage past which the pursuit of philosophical analysis with the aid of carefully interlocked metaphors approximates the building of a Palace of Fine Shades and Nice Feelings? And did the Philosopher pass that stage in the passage in chapter 57, where the linking of the man-travelling-road image, the man-paying-fee image, the man-as-metal-being-purified

---

[7] As a matter of fact, this very juxtaposition occupies several scenes of great importance in the sequel, *Vittoria*. The provocative insistence of the Austrian conquerors of Milan on smoking cigars in public, where they had been banned to the citizenry, finally ignites the city to riot. History, not imagination, provided that juxtaposition; the Tobacco Riots of Milan were one phase in the 1848 Revolution that *Vittoria* covers.

image finally passes human patience and human usefulness with the suffering and cigars image? The question is one that the civilized reader, suddenly abandoned by the rhetoric of the novel, has to answer for himself. The Novelist has banished the Philosopher, not angrily but with a comic smile, and the reader, lest he also feel himself banished, must move away from the Philosopher, closer to the Novelist on the stage of the subplot.

There is a similarity here in the banishment of the Philosopher from the narrative of *Sandra Belloni* and the dropping of the Wise Youth Adrian Harley from the narrative of *Richard Feverel*. But the difference is more important than the similarity: the drama of the struggle with the Philosopher's virtues and his vices is moved overtly into the subplot here, and the climax of that drama —the repudiation of the dark side of philosophy, the sentimental love of the philosopher for his own rarefied language—is accomplished in a much more comic way, without the bitter black satire Meredith was forced to use on Adrian. From now on this momentary withdrawal and comic repudiation of the philosopher's follies will be a part of many of Meredith's subplots, involving the reader directly as the writer struggles to unite the novelistic, comic, romantic, and philosophic impulses within his voice into that "oneness of feeling" that he says underlies the "truthful impulse."

5. The Hunting of the Egoist

> Comedy is a game played to throw reflections
> upon social life, and it deals with human nature
> in the drawing-room of civilized men and women,
> where we have no dust of the struggling outer
> world, no mire, no violent crashes, to make
> the correctness of the representation convincing.
> *(The Egoist,* I, *1)*

HERE, IT SEEMS, IS MEREDITH'S USUAL WARNING to the reader not to look for much "action" in his novels. This first sentence of *The Egoist* suggests that everything in the novel will be splendidly civilized, a game to divert ladies and gentlemen, a sort of entertainment after an eighteenth-century court dinner. One reader, George Woodcock, takes note of this supposed Augustan air to the novel by calling it "the elaboration of conventions within which the appropriately named Patterne dances his pompous minuet of life."[1]

The Egoist seems indeed to contain the most limited of Meredith's plots. Set mainly on one remote country estate, occupying only a few days of the busy world's time, its one action simply a young woman's change of mind over marrying the county's most eligible bachelor, *The Egoist* seems to promise a dull business. Precisely for this reason we can see here better than in any of Meredith's novels the nature of the new kind of action Meredith wanted to introduce into the novel, the action of mind. There are indeed few "violent crashes" of behavior in the novel, although

[1] George Woodcock, "Introduction" to *The Egoist* (Baltimore: Penguin Books, 1968), p. 20.

when they come—when Willoughby smilingly pinches his young nephew Crossjay, for instance—they have all the stunning impact of climax, like Emma Woodhouse's rebuff to Miss Bates on Box Hill. Meredith, who lived in a cottage on Box Hill for most of his life, fully appreciated the violence in a sharp word, the struggle going on beneath compliments and greetings, the mire in which human relationships stumble and go down. He appreciated even more the Gothic violence that may attend the activity of the fantasy life led by the individual ego under the veneer of civilized man or woman. In *The Egoist* his attention to this egoist's fantasy life, an attention focused by extensive use of metaphor, provides a sense of action, danger, and romance in a novel where almost all the events are mental —and no less violent, horrifying, dangerous, threatening, and thrilling for being so.[2]

[2] C. J. Pitt, in a footnote to his satire on *The Age: A Poem Moral, Political, and Metaphysical, with Illustrative Annotations* (London: 1800), gives his reader a wonderful little do-it-yourself primer on how to recognize the Gothic Romance lurking beneath the prosaic veneer of the novel:

The conduct of the poet in considering romances and novels separately may be thought singular by those who have the penetration to see that a novel may be made of a romance, or a romance of a novel, with the greatest ease by scratching out a few terms, and inserting others. Take the following, which may, like machinery in factories, accelerate the divine art.

Where you find	
A castle	put an house
A cavern	a bower
A groan	a sigh
A giant	a father
A blood-stained dagger	a fan
A knight	a gentleman without whiskers
A lady who is the heroine	need not be changed, being versatile
Assassins	telling glances
A monk	an old steward
Skeletons, skulls, etc.	compliments, sentiments, etc.
A gliding ghost	a usurer, or an attorney
A midnight murder	a marriage

A sharper focus on the metaphors of Gothic Romance which provide the action of *The Egoist* may help to dispel somewhat the false impression left by fifty years of critical pronouncements on the "dazzling intellectuality" of this novel. It was *The Egoist* that prompted Virginia Woolf's remark that "Meredith pays us a supreme compliment to which as novel readers we are little accustomed. We are civilized people, he seems to say, watching the comedy of human relations together . . . . He imagines us capable of disinterested curiosity in the behavior of our kind." I hope I have shown that this sort of compliment is one to which as novel readers we are all too well accustomed, and that there is usually an irony waiting inside any such compliment when it is made by Meredith. My reading of Meredith is intended exactly to suggest that he was radically uneasy with the convention of civilized superiority, disengaged intellect, disinterested curiosity. The reader is warned in the first sentence of the novel that he is engaged in some sort of game, and the invitation is addressed to the philosophic imagination, the civilized reader's intellect. But he soon finds that if he participates in the metaphorical structure that hovers over the drawing rooms, the dinner tables, the flower gardens of Patterne Hall, the game is dangerous: a Mythic game in fact, full of threatened deaths, attempted kidnappings, cruel torments, and monstrous pursuits of which not the least monstrous may be the pursuit of the civilized reader himself by that strange, ambiguous hunter, "humanely malign," the Comic Spirit.

Just as in *Sandra Belloni* Meredith was concerned to build a definition of sentimentalism as one of the major controlling ideas of his fiction, so in this novel he is attempting to build a comprehensive definition of egoism. In both novels, he demonstrates that the capacity for powerful feeling that is a central component of human nature may go awry into sentimentalism or egoism depending upon what the individual makes of himself out of the contacts with the world, the human relationships, that form his primary experience. It is important to notice this in Meredith: society is prior to psyche, existence to essence, world to person, but primary not in value, never in value, only in time, process. One makes oneself out of the materials available when the brain awakes to the task of philosophy, to the task of harmonizing and pulling together out of their subservience to and intermingling with world, other people, convention, the disparate elements of blood, brain, and spirit. But the task is to harmonize them according to one's own individual key, to achieve shapeliness and proportion according to one's own personal configuration. In this context it is interesting to note that the materials available to the characters in *Sandra Belloni* included real death, actual madness, the clash of finance and ambition, the violence of brawls, and travels through several cities and even nations. The materials available to the characters in *The Egoist*, except for a dinner party or two, are almost entirely internal—dreads, loathings, imprisonings, stiflings, the dramas of their own feelings, the figures of their own fantasies. With this material no less than with the earlier materials of action and dramatic event, the characters achieve major victories and suffer major defeats in the task of making healthy and human egos.

George Woodcock has proposed "the triangular grouping of characters" as a way into the structure of the relationships and internal dramas in the novel, and the notion seems to me helpful. As the dramas in *Sandra Belloni* seemed to concern couples, Cornelia and Barrett, Emilia and Wilfrid, so in *The Egoist* several entangled trios of persons seem to dominate the action. The presence of the triangle serves not so much to circumscribe the characters' actions but rather as an index to their freedom—any main character with respect to any action has two choices—and so the network of triangular relationships provides much of the novel's dynamic. The main characters are Willoughby Patterne, chief egoist and the lord of Patterne Hall; Clara Middleton, the girl who first agrees to marry him and then discovers she wants out; Laetitia Dale, the

150

worshipful maiden-next-door whom Willoughby has already dismissed but to whom he desperately turns when Clara grows restive; and Vernon Whitford, Willoughby's cousin, foil, and, finally, successful rival for Clara. Willoughby sees the issue of maintaining his "inviolate self" as a choice between Clara the intruder and Laetitia the reflector; on the other hand, he sees the task of maintaining his personal ascendancy over the county and the world as a choice between Clara the diminisher and Mrs. Mountstuart Jenkinson, the inflator of his ego. Clara, in her search for someone to "give her" her freedom, has before her the voluptuous and selfish refusal of Willoughby and the ascetic and selfless refusal of Vernon Whitford; in her search for a refuge in crisis she has at hand Horace De Craye and his bewitching ideal of heroic flight and Vernon with his distressing counsel to wait, gather her strength, and move directly and honestly against her enemy. There are, once we get started, numerous other triangles that parallel or parody these major relationships. In connection with parody, one thinks of Willoughby facing Hobson's choice of being jilted once by Constantia Durham or twice by Clara Middleton, or of conciliating, and thus belonging to, either Mrs. Mountstuart Jenkinson or her rival for county eminence, Lady Busshe. Parallel triangles can be constructed out of the boy Crossjay's love of Clara over Laetitia, despite her freakishness and those hours of waiting in the rain, and of Vernon over Willoughby, despite his sternness and those hours of lessons.

We can see Meredith set up these choices, applauding those that produce a healthy pride, deploring those that demonstrate an unhealthy selfishness, and condemning those that feed the monster egoism. Distinction-making within *this* triad of healthy pride, selfishness, and egoism constitutes the intellectual content of the novel. The content includes in the subplot all the implications of the relationship between the narrative personae—the Comic Spirit and the Comic Imps—the author and the fictional civilized reader; the subplot takes shape once more around a Book the narrator has found, a Book of which the novel is a sort of edition—the Book of Egoism.

All the main characters in the novel are egoists, Meredith makes clear. Clara and Vernon, hero and heroine, make the distinctions between pride and egoism successfully, after a few near-disastrous slips. Laetitia may be on her way to success. Willoughby fails, but it may appear to some readers that he scarcely had a chance from the day he was born into a role approaching that of sun-god among the country gentry.

I. The Ordeal of Clara Middleton

In her effort to develop a true picture of herself, the world, and her fiancé, Clara Middleton faces a barrier within, which is not unlike Richard Feverel's; in fact, the general situation of the two young people is remarkably similar. Critics have tended to see Clara's father, Dr. Middleton, as a sort of comic card, overawed by his prospective son-in-law's rank and especially by his wine cellar. But in many crucial and somewhat sinister aspects he is Sir Austin Feverel all over again; he too is a philosopher and scholar, in all unconsciousness a perfectly selfish man. Like the baronet, he has raised his child according to a system based on his own philosophy of life and that philosophy, like Sir Austin's, centers around a dangerous tenet that Meredith attacks in novel after novel, the view of woman as devil, the "dread of her sex." Meredith's narrator elaborates: "He loved his daughter and he feared her. However much he liked her character, the dread of her sex and age was constantly present to warn him that he was not tied to perfect sanity while the damsel Clara remained unmarried. . . . Why should she wish to run away from Patterne Hall for a single hour? Simply because she was of the sex born mutable and explosive" (i, 225). To this philosopher, as to the other, woman is literally the spirit of unreason, whose "explosions" are marked all through the classical literature that comes so readily, so significantly readily, to his tongue throughout the novel. To allow Clara to leave Patterne Hall without giving reasons simply on the basis of her intuition that marriage with the egoist would be a horror of self-destruction—this would be to be hag-ridden. The "dread of her sex" is the fear of the Furies, no light matter to a man of piety and learning.

We have seen what such a philosophy can do to a Richard Feverel. When the child is itself a woman, the psychic damage is still more pervasive, and it is clear from the start that Clara has been educated by Dr. Middleton at the fountain of his own poisoning. The dread of her sex is a deep scar on her own heart too: "She had read of the reproach upon women, that they divide the friendships of men. She reproached herself, but she was in action, driven by necessity, between sea and rock. Dreadful to think of! she was one of the creatures who are written about" (i, 180). From her first fibs about illness to her last lies about preferring the single life, Clara is driven by "the silliest of human desires, to preserve her reputation for consistency. She had heard women abused for shallowness and flightiness: she had heard her father denounce them as veering weathervanes, and his oft-repeated *quid femina possit* [what a woman can do—Vergil]: for her sex's sake, and also to appear an exception to her sex, this reasoning creature desired to be thought consistent" (i, 211-12). Her intuition about Willoughby is, of course, absolutely true, but her fear of appearing Woman Destructively Changeful keeps her from revealing her change of mind. Like Richard Feverel, she ran rashly to the beautiful object when the Blossoming Season came to her.[3] Similarly, the

[3] Here is perhaps the place to discuss one of the apparent mysteries of the book, Clara's original choice of Willoughby. Meredith says only that Clara had been "caught by flattery" and that Dr. Middleton's liking for the young baronet had powerfully influenced her. Kate Millett in *Sexual Politics* (Garden City, N.Y.: Doubleday, 1970, p. 132) says that Clara's lack of education, the Victorian channeling of woman toward a mate as her work in life,

effort to bring "brain," thought, to her highly emotional situation results not in an access of cool candor but in a highly colored fantasy life alternating between self-loathing and heroics. Like Richard, she transfers her fears and hostilities from the human plane to the universe and the Fates; her picture of herself at bay before the world is infused with an egoist's humility:

> Young Crossjay, whom she considered the least able of all to act as an ally, was the only one she courted with a real desire to please him, he was the one she affectionately envied; he was the youngest, the freest, he had the world before him, and he did not know how horrible the world was, or could be made to look. . . . With her body straining in the dragon's grasp, with the savour of loathing, unable to contend, unable to speak aloud, she began to speak to herself. . . . (I, 119-20)

This picture leads her to court an egoist's excuse and an egoist's escape:

> And she could vehemently declare that she had not chosen; she was too young, too ignorant to choose. He had wrongly used that word; it sounded malicious; and to call consenting the same in fact as choosing was wilfully unjust. Mr. Whitford meant well: he was conscientious, very conscientious. But he was not the hero descending from heaven bright-sworded to smite a woman's fetters off her limbs and deliver her from the yawning mouth-abyss. (I, 181)

---

made the choice of "prince" Willoughby inevitable. Yet the thrust of the book seems to set up an interesting dichotomy between Willoughby's courting of Clara at Cherribrook as made entirely of words and his courting of her at Patterne Hall as the beginning of personal actions. He seemed to have played prince at a distance, and too speedily and vividly to be thought about. For it is with the very first sign of his control of her physical person—his refusing her permission to leave him to look at the garden—that Clara realizes what she has lost, and it is with the very first sign of his sensual hunger for her, his very first embrace, that she begins the recoil from what she has gained.

Vernon Whitford, falling in love with his cousin's fiancée and holding on to his philosophy with all his might, declines the role, and, instead of Vernon, with the tragical-farcical emphasis of a fairy tale, the world supplies Clara with her "preux chevalier," Horace De Craye, a very noble gentleman and egoist willing to snatch the maiden out of the dragon's grasp in exchange for the privilege of turning dragon himself one day.

Vernon follows the escaping woman to the railroad station and returns to Patterne Hall with Clara in a long and crucial scene in chapters 27 and 28, which demonstrate powerfully Meredith's ability to catch in description the terrifyingly nonrational foundation of our thoughts. His first triumph is the picture of Vernon himself, as he bundles Clara away to dry her wet feet, arranges for a signal when her train arrives, and orders a stiff brandy and water, avuncularly commanding Clara to drink it "as medicine." Unnaturally hearty is Vernon, whose own blood is rapidly heating and cooling, Meredith makes clear, with the thought that she and De Craye might be "in concert." More characteristically, Vernon recognizes that she is doing her self-education a disservice by refusing to stay and face out her choices and her fears. Beneath this philosophical attitude, of course, there is growing in Vernon a lover's passionate wish to see her warm, safe, and sheltered. These are the reasons for Vernon's pursuit, reasons that account for his strange unsettling "I will help you go but you ought to stay" attitude, reasons that neither he nor she sees fully but that both the man and the woman feel at the deepest, most silent centers of their personal conflicts. "He was as full of contradiction today as women are accused of being," is Clara's agitated response. "He had also behaved like a man of honour, taking no personal advantage of her situation; but to reflect on it recalled his astonishing dryness," runs Vernon's restless analysis of his own behavior.

There *is* an astonishing dryness in Vernon for most of the book. Meredith obviously knows what he is doing in

155

creating him so, opposing his bleak and tearless profile to the devouring smile of Willoughby and the gleaming teeth of De Craye, the hunter-chevalier. Meredith also knows what he is doing as he plays off the controlled retreat of will in Vernon against the advance penetration of will in the two egoists Clara and Willoughby; he is building the final, ineffably true observation that the leashing of will makes for a self of substance and flexibility where its unleashing empties the self. So much we may note in applauding *The Egoist* as "the most dazzlingly intellectual of his novels" *(Woodcock, p. 5).* Yet the real interest in this scene is not in our recognition of Meredith's recognition of Vernon's dryness, but in Vernon's recognition of it, and, still further, in Vernon's recognition that he *does* exist in a situation that casts him willy-nilly as the second factor in a woman's understanding of man—that in honor and fidelity to reality and to her he must accept the role, and that in the depths of his personal and slowly kindling soul he is outraged at the limitations of the role and at the inevitability of his choosing to accept it. Meredith's second triumph in this long crisis scene is his picture of the way Clara makes her "choice" to come back to Patterne Hall and try to confront her situation realistically. For amazingly the central operative in the choice is that most ubiquitous and sly Meredithian stirrer of blood and brain, strong drink.[4] A stranger to brandy, Clara gulps down

---

[4] Meredith is full of fine drinking scenes: one thinks of Richard Feverel desperately drowning his ambiguous pursuit of and surrender to Bella Mount in champagne, of the Ipley-Hillford beer brawl in *Sandra Belloni*, of hearty Rob Eccles standing up to the local gaffers in *Rhoda Fleming*'s Pilot Inn, of Cecil Baskelett baiting Dr. Shrapnel while flying on bad wine in *Beauchamp's Career*, of Victor Radnor drinking optimism and Old Veuve in *One of Our Conquerors*. Behind Meredith's continual resort to this prop is undoubtedly the comfortable Victorian assumption that wine makes good fellows better and bad fellows reveal their dishonor. But behind *that* is the antisentimentalism that puts the responsibility for "making" good or bad fellows squarely on the individual. He will attribute mitigation but not essential motivation to the

half a glass in a haste that would make even a hardened drinker's eyes water, and, "panting," finds herself not "fortified" by it but rather rendered "painfully susceptible" to Vernon's remarks. Still planning to take the train with De Craye, she moves out to the platform, where also waits the vehicle that could convey her back to Patterne Hall. But the crucial moment of recognizing that "this thing done would cut the cord" calls up in her not passion or fierce thought but a "sensation of languor." The narrative shifts at this point into simple statement, "referential" language:

> De Craye took a stride. He was accosted by one of the railway-porters. Flitch's fly was in request for a gentleman. A portly old gentleman bothered about luggage appeared on the landing. "The gentleman can have it," said De Craye, handing Flitch his money. "Open the door," Clara said to Flitch. He tugged at the handle with enthusiasm. The door was open: she stepped in. (II, 40)

In this mental blank Clara has made her choice; she does not know how or why she made it, but she knows it was *her* choice: "She had acted of her free will: that she could say. Vernon had not induced her to remain." "Nervous and languid . . . swayed by languor" is Clara's own understanding of her condition during the drive back to the dragon's cave. It is difficult to be clear about what has happened. Meredith certainly does not want to give us a drunken heroine, nor, I think, does he want to call up that sense of the laying asleep of moral consciousness associated, for

---

cluster of outside agencies and events surrounding the individual. This permits Meredith to wield the Dionysian wine-jar aspect of comedy with considerable sophistication. *In vino veritas*, Vernon tells Clara at the station, but wine-truth seems to be the kind of truth of feeling or intuition best conveyed by the metaphoric dramatization of an altered state of consciousness rather than by the meticulous anatomy of our self-justifying moods and the merciless tracking down of the fibs and evasions in our thinking that forms Meredith's basic method of characterization.

instance, with the famous languor experienced by Maggie Tulliver drifting downstream with Stephen Guest. Quite the contrary. Somehow, Clara has reached the source of moral consciousness, her free will. And languor was the condition, the calming of mental activity, the laying asleep of all those desperate imaginings, heated defenses, and reckless fantasies that had kept her bubbling for so many days. Did the brandy do it? "She held the glass as an enemy to be delivered from, gasping, uncertain of her breath" (ii, 29). Did some stirring of Puritan pride do it? "The smell of the glass was odious; it disgraced her" (ii, 38). Did Vernon, who imposed on her the brandy as well as the duty, do it? "She could have accused Vernon of a treacherous cunning for imposing it on her free will to decide her fate." How clearly did Meredith intend us to see? "She could not have said what the something witnessed to. If we by chance know more, we still have no right to make it more prominent than it was with her" (ii, 38), says the narrator.

Meredith deliberately melts his "prominences" into his prose because we are intended simply to grope through the crisis much as Clara does, with the realization that whatever "more" we know of the urgency of Vernon's reasons, or the potency of brandy gulped, or the delicate recoil from the association of brandy and assignation, we do not know all. Clara thinks herself "incomprehensible" because she is a woman. Meredith agrees, partly, but for another reason. Here, as in all his works, as a delicate counterpoint to what is perhaps the densest, most fanatical concentration on the movements of mind in all English fiction, Meredith insists on the essential mysteriousness of persons. It is by no accident that in *The Egoist*, acclaimed the brightest- and steadiest-lit of all his works, the light goes off at the crucial moment of the first major choice we see the heroine make. In his precise study of how the self, the ego, is won or lost or destroyed, the brainy Meredith makes here and there a graceful bow to the incomprehensible.

II. The Ordeal of Willoughby Patterne

At this point exactly in the center of the novel Clara and Vernon's story is well-nigh fixed; she need only strengthen her youthful courage and he need only recognize and relax into his love for her for them both to be free of the "dragon." The second half finds the choices of Willoughby Patterne taking center stage under the eye of the Comic Spirit. Increasingly, as he tries to deal with the ego-shattering sensation of being jilted, Willoughby's social world, the very amniotic fluid that supplies his being, becomes his enemy. Personified by the amiable Mrs. Mountstuart Jenkinson, another looker-on like Adrian Harley with a penchant for coining social code names for people, the world and Willoughby exist in a symbiotic relationship. The world needs a prince to keep it excitedly revolving. The prince needs the world to reflect his glory, to create his glory. "The policy of the county is to keep him in love with himself, or Patterne will likely be as dull as it was without a lady enthroned," sighs Mrs. Mountstuart; "When his pride is at ease he is a prince" (ii, 331). But the psychic cost to the prince is incalculable. The following ends the description of Willoughby's twenty-first birthday party in chapter 2; it applies equally to his childhood and to the end of the book: "He had to continue tripping, dancing, exactly balancing himself, head to right, head to left, addressing his idolators in phrases of perfect choiceness. This is only to say that it is easier to be a wooden idol than one in the flesh; yet Willoughby was equal to his task."

Thus Willoughby's fault is not simply pride, not even the exaggerated sort of mad pride where the self becomes an idol. Pride scorns the pressure of the world and means it. Pride would wait out a Clara Middleton through twenty runaway trips to London, and a truly mad pride, feeling itself to be "in the jaws of the world, on the world's teeth" (ii, 280) would rather renounce twenty Claras, cut dead forty Mrs. Mountstuart Jenkinsons, than play out a scene

159

in such a position, trifle with such a ridiculous beast. Willoughby plays out the scene because he must; he knows his slave status perfectly well at bottom, and in a perverse way maybe he even enjoys it:

> One step there warned him that he was in the jaws of the world. We have the phrase, that a man is himself under certain trying circumstances. There is no need to say it of Sir Willoughby; he was thrice himself when danger menaced, himself inspired him. He could read at a single glance the Polyphemus eye in the general head of a company. Lady Busshe, Lady Culmer, Mrs. Mountstuart, Mr. Dale, had a similarity in the variety of their expressions that made up one giant eye for him perfectly, if awfully, legible. . . . bowing to Lady Busshe and Lady Culmer, gallantly pressing their fingers and responding to their becks and archnesses, he ruminated on his defenses. (II, 279-80)

Willoughby is thus tormented, hunted, and snared because his self is not in fact an idol but an "eidolon," as Meredith phrases it, not a solid, frozen, impenetrable thing but an insubstantial, shivering phantom, a helpless, bloodless, scarce-breathing "tender infant Self swaddled in his name before the world . . . which it was impossible for him to stretch out hands to protect" (II, 50). It is the terrifying instability of the self that makes Willoughby clutch his chains—his name before the world—around him as swaddling bands or rather, to use Dorothy Van Ghent's phrase, as "wearing the world as a custom-made womb."[5]

---

[5] Van Ghent's lucid essay on *The Egoist* (*The English Novel: Form and Function* [New York: Rinehart, 1953], pp. 183-94) makes an important argument against the book—essentially it is an analysis of "our indifference" to the novel. Her argument is that Meredith fails to provide the spiritual context for Willoughby, that he is presented as a "perfectly lonely aberration, a freak," and that "our" failure to respond to him is because as a freak he does not really, in the novel's world, threaten any of the values "we" want to go in and protect there. I would counterargue that it is in *Willoughby's* imagination that he exists as a lonely aberration, a freak, not in Meredith's. The world of the novel is full of egoists;

It is that gap between the brain-directed hands and the spirit-cherished self, that fearful blank gap through which educated feeling should be healthy flowing, connecting brain and spirit, that is the occasion of the central relational choice for Willoughby. Brain he has, without question. Spirit, he has, ambition, nobility, civilization of a sort. But where blood should be, warmth and strength of feeling to feed both shivering self and busily quivering brain, Willoughby has only a frantic, galvanic charge of action, most primitive of animators, blind, roaring brutality. It is as a connoisseur of brutality that he confronts a choice between Clara Middleton and Laetitia Dale.

Brutality is the raw material of action, and for Meredith, here as always, civilization is the necessary condition for the transformation of brutality into human, and humane, vitality. Whatever civilization is, it is clearly not separable from the world, despite the chaotic, amoral aspect the world presents to the eidolon self.[6] Diseases of feeling are perhaps Meredith's main subject, and where I have suggested that sentimentalism is Meredith's term for a sort of fever or cancer of feeling, I think that Egoism, with a

---

Willoughby has such an unusually visible and powerful case of the disease because his world and society created for itself, out of the most ordinary if promising material, the prince of egoism it wanted. And I think the reader is meant to ponder the smallness of the world actually involved in the novel and in the creating of this egoist, and wonder about his own complicity in such creations in his own larger world.

[6] Meredith's intuition of these two qualities, world and self, seems to me very modern, Heideggerian in its sense of the urgent buzz of time and space in the consciousness, Sartrean in its sense of the intolerable fragility and coldness of the isolated self. Between the structures of the world or reality or other, which can be usefully manipulated by the brain, and the structures of volition, or consciousness, or the self, which are traditionally apprehended as spirit, there seems to be no philosophically discoverable connecting structure, only this aether, this nourishing, indispensable, barely controllable, difficult element of sentient nature called feeling, emotion, or, by Meredith, blood.

161

capital E, becomes for him here a referent for a sort of anemia or dwarfism. Sentimentalism is an unchecked growth of the power to feel, accompanied by a tendency to throw onto the world or the fates or circumstances the origin of and responsibility for that growth. Egoism is a stunting and checking of that growth, also accompanied by a tendency to blame the world, providence, and the Powers. Willoughby, like Wilfrid Pole, has a need to set the streams of feeling flowing from others toward himself without incurring a reciprocal responsibility. The comment that "his desire was merely to move her without exposure of himself" *(*ii, *89)* indicates Willoughby's relationship to Laetitia as it does Wilfrid's to Emilia. For Willoughby, as for Wilfrid, enjoyment, the sensual, is the foundation of feeling, however refined the sentimentality, however civilized the egoism.

The central symbol of Willoughby's anemia, of his failure to grow in the capacity to feel, of his remaining in the state of primitive brutality rather than maturing into a passionate human creature, is the satyr, which is linked with Willoughby in several scenes but visibly captured in a passage in book i, *130-31.* It is crucial again to note the ambiguous nature of the passage as narrative. This is not one of Willoughby's meditations, but it is not entirely a narrator's commentary either. The introduction to the passage reads: "When we have harpooned a whale and are attached to the rope, down we must go; the miracle is to see us rise again." The image is of Willoughby sounding his own psychic depths with fictional reader and narrator attached, and the fact that the diving is Willoughby's (maybe involuntary) act and not the narrator's is plain from the image in the preceding passage, where Willoughby, having told Clara complacently that he has shown her "the worst of him," is also seen as a whale: "It was on the full river of love that Sir Willoughby supposed the whole floating bulk of his personality to be securely sustained; and therefore it was that, believing himself swimming at his ease, he discoursed of himself." It is the "touchstone" of passion that in this psychic dive reveals Willoughby as "requiring to be dealt with by his betrothed as an original savage. She was required to play incessantly on the first reclaiming chord which led our ancestral satyr to the measures of the dance"—the reclaiming first chord being the worship of the virgin for the sensual satyr. Meredith goes on:

> Strange and awful though it be to hear, women perceive this requirement of them in the spirit of the man; they perceive, too, and it may be gratefully, that they address their performances less to the taming of the green and prankish monsieur of the forest than to the pacification of a voracious aesthetic gluttony, craving them insatiably, through all the tenses, with shrieks of the lamentable letter "I" for their purity. Whether they see that it has its foundation in the sensual, and distinguish the ultra-refined but lineally great grandson of the Hoof in this vast and dainty exacting appetite is uncertain.

Of the connection between the satyr and the eidolon, the primitive state of feeling and the infant self, it is difficult to say which is causal, which way the equation goes. Certainly at this point in Willoughby's life the equation is reversible. The primitive brutality of his search for warmth and nourishment for the infant self drives away the sources of warmth, and the weakness of the tiny self makes any control of his brutality impossible. Despite his quite deliberate game with words like "self," "selfishness," "I," and "Egoism," Meredith's dramatic attention is more consistently and intensely on the satyr than on the eidolon. Willoughby's brutality to the two women whose passion he seeks as his nourishment, having none of his own, is pronounced—only the more so when it takes the form of sadistic fantasy and Gothic imagination. The egoist, we are told, is himself "fiercely imaginative in whatsoever concerned *him*" (italics mine), although he is the snuffing out, literally the "death" of the imagination in others (II, *183*).

163

But we hardly needed the reminder. For it has been suggested all along that almost the whole fiercely Gothic, animistic structure of metaphor that provides the action of the novel is a product of the egoist imagination. The narrator indeed contributes his share in the opening chapter with his images of the hunting Comic Spirit taking us all for a breathless "run at his heels," of the pack of Comic Imps watching the development of Willoughby's character "with the sympathetic eagerness of the eyes of caged monkeys for the hand about to feed them" (I, 10). The narrator, as we shall see, has something of an egoist's imagination. Vernon Whitford has something of it too. Electrified by the half-dream contact with Clara under the double blossom cherry tree, he treats himself briefly to a vision of himself as Endymion, "cruelly kissed." But the vision is soon under control: "He was aware of the fantastical element in him and soon had it under. Which of us who is of any worth is without it? He had not much vanity to trouble him, and passion was quiet, so his task was not gigantic" (I, 137). I have already pointed out how Clara's imagination, in its primitive egoist stages, produced the maiden-straining-in-the-dragon's-grasp structure of images. But right from the start the foremost imagination pouring out those Gothic images of self and world is Willoughby's. Here is the supreme egoist in the third chapter, for instance, musing on Laetitia's devotion to his memory:

> She might have buried it, after the way of woman, whose bosoms can be tombs, if we and the world allow them to be; absolutely sepulchres, where you lie dead, ghastly. Even if not dead and horrible to think of, you may be lying cold, somewhere in a corner. Even if embalmed, you may not be much visited. And how is the world to know you are embalmed? You are no better than a rotting wretch to the world that does not have peeps of you in the woman's breast, and see lights burning, and an occasional service of worship. (I, 38)

164

As we focus on the choice confronting Willoughby between Laetitia Dale and Clara Middleton, we will see the roused imagination of a true and powerful egoist at work, fixedly and elementally brutal in all his dealings.

In point of fact Willoughby commits only one act of direct physical brutality in the book, but it is splendidly placed and dramatized to show the civilized satyr. It happens just after Clara returns with De Craye from the railroad station, just as the book begins to sharpen its focus on Willoughby. Clara has sent Crossjay to retrieve the letter she had left explaining her flight. Poor Crossjay, ever the touchstone of the character of others, is caught by Willoughby and dragged back to be present at the lover's confrontation of his fiancée, "held fast, that [Willoughby] might have an object to trifle with to give himself countenance" (ii, 47). During the exchange that follows, Willoughby is seen "still clutching Crossjay and treating his tugs to get loose as an invitation to caresses." The climax comes as the party enters the house:

> She turned to the colonel as they stepped into the hall: "I have not thanked you, Colonel De Craye." She dropped her voice to its lowest: "A letter in my handwriting in the laboratory."
> Crossjay cried aloud with pain.
> "I have you!" Willoughby rallied him with a laugh not unlike the squeak of his victim.
> "You squeeze awfully hard, sir."
> "Why, you milksop!" (ii, 47-48)

The incident shocks, as it is meant to, because it reveals the satyr near the surface, defending its own pain with spontaneous cruelty. But Willoughby's painful caress of Crossjay is a mere bagatelle in comparison to the fantasy acts of sadism that he commits. The very first chapter points to Willoughby's "Hereditary Aptitude in the use of the Knife" and makes clear that the "Cutting" of people who threaten the egoist, even by mere presence, is an in-

165

stinctual operation likely to show itself in such civilized cruelty as the refusing of shelter in the rain to Crossjay's father. The man Flitch, failed seeker after independence in London who was refused return to the Hall, is only a puny representation, he and his starving wife and children, of the formidable fantasy act of "extinction" Willoughby performs on those who leave his feudal service. One of the most interesting of the smoke screens Willoughby throws up for the world, the humble hauteur with which he confesses to his "pride," is the source of a particularly vivid and satisfyingly brutal fantasy life of himself as a second Lucifer, "glorifying in the black flames demoniacal wherewith he crowned himself" (I, *106*). After Clara's first rattling of her chains in chapter 13, Willoughby, "wrapped in meditation," conjures up for his delectation the "soft cherishable Parsee . . . she supplying spirit to your matter, while at the same time supplying matter to your spirit, verily a comfortable apposition" (I, *157*). Verily the relationship of a man to his dinner! As Willoughby meditates through the book on various "throwings-away" of Laetitia, images of cruelty—"casting her over a hedge" (I, *159*), "[tossing] her away, vexed to the very soul by an ostentatious decay" (I, *196*)—reveal a satyr's delight. The first prolonged fantasy of Willoughby's, the coveted scene of Clara's bitter regret because she forfeited his love from silly jealousy (I, *269-72*), is packed with images of brutality and vengeance: "Ten thousand Furies thickened about him at a thought of her lying by the roadside without his having crushed all bloom and odour out of her which might tempt even the curiosity of the fiend, man." The voluptuously imagined repentant Clara lends herself to "one last—one holy kiss," and Willoughby's satyr leaps: "Ay, she had the kiss, and no mean one. It was intended to swallow every vestige of dwindling attractiveness out of her."

The problem with this fantasy, as with every other fantasy of Clara crushed and swallowed that Willoughby makes for himself, is that she is real, and lovely, and the groveling sensualist in him adores her: "Unhappily, the fancied salute of her lips encircled him with the breathing Clara. She rushed up from vacancy like a wind summoned to wreck a stately vessel." All of his sadistic fantasies about her, then, are essentially masochistic. Nourishing himself on pictures of a Clara "fast bound, soul and body . . . in a good roasting fire," Willoughby himself becomes the fire —"he was flame, flaming verdigris"—and in the end consumes only himself, burning "himself out with verdigris flame having the savour of bad metal, till the hollow of his breast was not unlike to a corroded old cuirass, found, we will assume, by criminal lantern-beams in a digging beside green-mantled pools of the sullen soil, lumped with a strange adhesive concrete" (I, 278).

We are constantly sent back by these frequent self-destructive fantasies of Willoughby's to the last paragraph of the prelude to *The Egoist*, titled "Of Which the Last Page Only is of any Importance." There, we recall, we are introduced to the "comic drama of the suicide" and warned to keep in mind the verse line, "Through very love of self himself he slew." The progress of the egoist is toward discovery of himself as a suicide. Brooding in the laboratory, alone after his spectacular verbal ropewalking among an enlightened Clara, a spying Lady Busshe and Mrs. Mountstuart Jenkinson, an elegantly befuddled Dr. Middleton and Mr. Dale, Willoughby realizes that he is condemned to marry Laetitia by his own appetite for a victim outside himself: "The discovery he made was, that in the gratification of the egoistic instinct we may so beset ourselves as to deal a slaughtering wound upon Self to whatsoever quarter we turn" (II, 293).

How is his choice of Laetitia a slaughtering blow to self? Clara has divined the reason, supplied the operative image for Willoughby, and predicted the outcome, all in an early outburst to Laetitia:

"Here is the difference I see; I see it; I am certain of it: women who are called coquettes make their conquests not of the best of men; but men who are Egoists have *good*

167

women for their victims; women on whose devoted con-
stancy they feed; they drink it like blood. I am sure I am
not taking the merely feminine view. They punish themselves too by passing over the one suitable to them, who
could really give them what they crave to have, and they
go where they. . . ." Clara stopped. "I have not your
power to express ideas," she said. *(*I, *191)*

Willoughby is like a vampire suicidally mated to his
first, only, and already drained victim; and it was by choice,
it is important to state. A vampire cannot reject the world
and live. It was by good instinct of his nature that Willoughby sought Clara—"Oh, she was healthy!" *(*I, *278)*.
References to Laetitia's growing anemia are numerous,
and most of them come, with a curious kind of attracted-
repulsed fascination, from Willoughby: "An examination
of Laetitia's faded complexion braced him very cordially.
His Clara jealous of this poor leaf!" *(*I, *p. 160).*[7] Yet Willoughby, having no real feeling, real blood, of his own, but
only primitive howling satyr appetite—"Nor had he al-
together yet got over the passion of greed for the whole
group of the well-favoured of the fair sex. . . . He was of
a vast embrace" *(*I, *162)*—cannot loose his clutches on
Laetitia: "Of his power upon one woman he was now perfectly sure: Clara had agonized him with a doubt of his
personal mastery of any. One was a poor feast, but the
pangs of his flesh during the last few days and the latest
hours caused him to snatch at it, hungrily if contemptuously. A poor feast, she was yet a fortress, a point of
succour, both shield and lance; a cover and an impetus"
*(*II, *92)*. And so he wins her, as he chooses and deserves.
Laetitia has little blood left, as she warns him, and the
connection between her declining health and her increasing lovelessness is made many times throughout the book.
She makes it herself in the end. Aware now that her

---

[7] We are not, of course, to take Willoughby's strictures on
Laetitia's "decay" at face value. Willoughby's requirements are
special.

original feverish adulation of Willoughby was sentimentalism, she has seen that fever subside in herself, not into
warm health but into cold gray indifference. Nothing is left
but curiosity—"Wealth enables us to see the world"—and
duty—"Wealth gives us the power to do good on earth"
(ii, 320). "A sentimental attachment," she muses (incor-
rectly) on the same page, "would have been serviceless to
him. Not so the woman allied by a purely rational bond:
and he wanted guiding. Happily, she had told him too
much of her feeble health and her lovelessness to be
reduced to submit to another attack." "Wanted guiding":
Meredith gives us new speculations with this picture of
a Laetitia with the channels of feeling dry and the channels of mind beginning to thirst. "He had the lady with
brains!" Willoughby rejoices, and the narrator adds aus-
terely (perhaps with Mary Peacock Meredith in mind),
"He had; and he was to learn the nature of that possession
in the woman who is our wife" *(ii, 327)*. Brains without
feeling in the woman who is our wife could provide not
simply diminishment and criticism for the egoist, but real
hell for him, or indeed for any of "us." The nature of the
change in Laetitia's character is only sketched here, and
we are left to decide whether the diminishment of feeling
and the animation of critical brainpower in her has re-
balanced her, or whether it may simply be unbalancing her
in a new direction. In the latter case, the Comic Imps who
watch over Patterne Hall may be welcoming in the Hall's
new mistress not an ally but another victim.

III. The Reader and the Comic Spirit

That "game" of comedy the reader agreed to play with the
writer in the first sentence of *The Egoist* includes not only
the intellectual spotting of types and the dispassionate
participation in the fantastical verities of the inner life; it
also includes the positioning of himself somewhere between
the character whose folly is being hunted so mercilessly
and the narrative characters doing the hunting. In this

context, it is important to note at the outset that the novel affords the reader several kinds of opportunities to identify with Willoughby, more perhaps than one would think.

In the first place, although Willoughby is clearly at grievous fault in his paranoia about "world," Meredith has dramatized the world with a healthy respect for society's power, even half-conspiratorily, to force roles on the individual, to narrow his choices and cloud his perceptions. The novel's picture of poor Willoughby growing up as a prince, receiving and painfully playing that role to satisfy society's insatiable need of princes, starving on the pseudo-love that Mrs. Mountstuart Jenkinson feeds him— "When his pride is at ease he is a prince"—is informed with compassion. But Meredith's pity has no tincture of sentimentality in it, and he warns the reader right at the start against too deep an identification with the individual-at-bay-before-the-world: "The Egoist surely inspires pity. Only he is not allowed to rush at you, roll you over and squeeze your body for the briny drops. There is the innovation" (1, 5). If readers fail to avoid the briny handkerchief, being warned once in plain words and several times by example, they may look for themselves in the Book of Egoism. The emotion of pity almost always translates into self-pity in Meredith's fiction.

In the second place, although Willoughby is one shivering mass of psychosis within, he remains pretty much the prince on the outside, capable of brilliant, if desperate, improvisations on the social scene. Civilized people watching that brilliance cannot help but enjoy it. But Meredith makes clear to the reader the essential hollowness of that display of social generalship even while he admires it, especially in a virtuoso piece of drama that takes place in the afternoon following Willoughby's unsuccessful proposal to Laetitia. Here Willoughby, run to earth at last by the world, the fates, and the Comic Imps, fronts all his enemies at once in his own drawing room, seemingly defeated in every maneuver. The technical problem in the scene is to keep Dr. Middleton and the Patterne ladies, his aunts, thinking that Willoughby has proposed to Laetitia on behalf of Vernon, while Mr. Dale and the other outsiders are to be kept thinking that Willoughby has proposed *himself* to her, successfully. The truth, of course, is that he has proposed unsuccessfully to Laetitia, lost Clara, and may have to stand before the world as a thrice-jilted prince. When Willoughby arrives on the scene he must first deduce under which misapprehension each person labors, then support each in that misapprehension, if he is not to be revealed as a laughingstock. When Laetitia arrives she must be kept from enlightening anyone, and the campaign to make her change her mind and marry him must be forwarded.

All of this Willoughby achieves in a splendid manipulation of ambiguous dialogue that demonstrates a kind of grace under pressure, Willoughby being "three times himself." Since this scene is the formal climax to the metaphoric structure of Willoughby as a fox being harrowed by the Comic Spirit and attendant pack of Imps, the sheer exhilaration of the hunt suggests that the acme of civilized feeling may be with the fox when he turns to fight, and that brilliance on the fox's part will draw bravos from the very huntsmen, including the reader-hunter. But at the same time as he is picturing Willoughby's prowess, Meredith is exposing the blasted roots of that success by interspersing the dialogue with a running internal monologue from Willoughby:

> Mr. Dale sank into a chair, unable to resist the hand forcing him.
> "No, Sir Willoughby, no. I have not; I have not seen [Laetitia] since she came home this morning from Patterne."
> "Indeed? She is unwell?"
> "I cannot say. She secludes herself."
> "Has locked herself in," said Lady Busshe.
> Willoughby threw her a smile. It made them intimate. This was an advantage against the world, but an exposure of himself to the abominable woman. . . .

"You will regard Patterne as your home, Mr. Dale," Willoughby repeated for the world to hear.

"Unconditionally?" Dr. Middleton inquired, with a humorous air of dissenting.

Willoughby gave him a look that was coldly courteous, and then he looked at Lady Busshe. She nodded imperceptibly. Her eyebrows rose, and Willoughby returned a similar nod. Translated, the signs ran thus: "—Pestered by the Rev. gentleman:—I see you are. Is the story I have heard correct? Possibly it may err in a few details."

This was fettering himself in loose manacles. . . .

"Which is the father of the fortunate creature? I don't know how to behave to him."

No time was afforded him to be disgusted with her vulgarity and audacity. He replied, feeling her rivet his gyves: "The house will be empty tomorrow."

"I see. A decent withdrawal, and very well cloaked. We had a tale here of her running off to decline the honour, afraid, or on her dignity, or something."

How was it that the woman was ready to accept the altered posture of affairs in his house—if she had received a hint of them? He forgot that he had prepared her in self-defense.

"From whom did you have that?" he asked.

"Her father. And the lady aunts declare it was the cousin she refused."

Willoughby's brain turned over. He righted it for action, and crossed the room to the ladies Eleanor and Isabel. . . . (II, *280-82*)

This tension between our sight of the outside Willoughby and of the inside is a dramatic evocation of the attraction-repulsion Meredith sets up for his reader as the very condition of his exploration. The spiritual exhaustion of Willoughby when he realizes what an empty victory this spectacular action has won is the reader's too. I have said that Meredith's most characteristic way of alluding to his metaphysical doubt of the importance, in a sense even the reality, of actions, is to refuse to dramatize "climactic" experiences in themselves but rather to refract those events through the memories and reports of those who are dealing mentally with the events. Here we see him doing the opposite but gaining the same effect, dramatizing the emptiness of the event while holding the reader strictly to account for every one of those bravos.

It is when we come to examine this posture of the reader as hunter that we begin to approach the complexity of Meredith's narrative strategy in *The Egoist*. For the hunting figure here is the Comic Spirit, a creature of indeterminate sex and quite ambiguous humanity. If Meredith has left us plenty of clues to retard any simple or sentimental identification with Willoughby the hunted, he has also proposed some that should make us hesitate to identify easily with the hunter.

I have suggested as a thesis for dealing with Meredith's difficult, antagonistic, and ambiguous narrative stance the notion that after *Richard Feverel* the figure of the Wise Youth—the uninvolved observer, the philosopher of human conduct—escaped from the field of narrative action alone to enter as well the field of narrative strategy. I have said that if we look to the superior figure or stance in the narrative attitude, the philosophic, we will find him ambiguously or qualifiedly approved at best, and we will see and be made to experience Meredith's own difficulties with this superhuman view of humanity. Since the Comic Spirit clearly serves that function in *The Egoist*, it is here we should look for the heart of Meredith's strategy, as well as for the reader's most direct brush with the problem of the book, egoism.

Meredith conceived the character of the Comic Spirit in a lecture on "The Idea of Comedy and the Uses of the Comic Spirit" written in early 1877, at least a year before he wrote the prelude to *The Egoist*, and delivered publicly at the London Institute, Finsbury Circus. The hero of this essay has features most ungentle: "It has the sage's brows, and the sunny malice of a faun lurks at the corners of the half closed lips, drawn in an idle wariness of half-tension. That slim feasting smile, shaped like the long bow, was once a big round satyr's laugh, that flung up the brows like a fortress lifted by gunpowder. The laugh will come again, but it will be of the order of the smile" *(Essay, p. 141).* Note the resemblance to Sir Willoughby Patterne. Note also the maleness of the Spirit here, pitched to hunt down folly as female: "For Folly is the natural prey of the Comic, known to it in all her transformations, in every disguise; and it is with the springing delight of hawk over heron, hound after fox, that it gives her chase, never fretting, never tiring, sure of having her, allowing her no rest" *(Essay, p. 120).*

Male, too, is the Comic Spirit that opens the prelude: "For being a spirit, he hunts the spirit in men; vision and ardour constitute his merit" *(I, 1).* But he soon changes to female: "She it is who proposed the correcting of pretentiousness, of inflation, of dulness, and of the vestiges of rawness and grossness to be found among us. She is the ultimate civilizer, the polisher, a sweet cook" *(I, 4).* The Comic Spirit becomes the Comic Muse, prepared to hunt down egoism as male, and female the philosophical spirit remains, to the last sentence of the book. This feminization of the Comic Spirit represents a softening and humanizing of the essay's original formidable figure, but a closer look at the cast of narrative characters will show us that the original Comic Spirit has not been softened, but rather split. Faced with humans committing folly, the Spirit in the essay "will look humanely malign, and cast an oblique light on them, followed by volleys of silvery laughter" *(Essay, p. 142).* Humane silvery laughter is the portion of the Comic Muse in the novel, but the malignity is concentrated in a whip-bearing, haunches-squatting, monkey-eyed, human-steam-drinking tribe of "very wicked imps."

Now the narrative conceit of this novel, set up in the prelude, is much like that of the other Meredith novels we have considered. There is a Book to start with, the Book of Egoism, compiled by sages and containing, it seems, both aphorisms and stories. It is an enormous work in many volumes, and the narrator, who wants to tell the story

174

suggested in the Book, struggles for a method by which to communicate the meat of the Book briefly and truthfully. He could tell it piece by piece in rigorous and convincing detail, "read it by the watchmaker's eye," he muses. But there are two problems with this method. First, it is possible to get lost in detail, "in a land of foghorns," and lose the broad moral outlines of the story's lesson. But worse, by its very excess of specific case history, it may convince the reader that somebody else, not he, certainly not he, is involved in this story: "such repleteness, obscuring the glass it holds to mankind, renders us inexact in the recognition of our individual countenances, a perilous thing for civilization." It is the old Carlylean editorial situation again: the Book, the original vision, is mad, massive, and alien; how can it be made familiar, accessible, and urgent to the ordinary man? The narrator is fascinated by the possibilities involved in the "broad Alpine survey" of the Comic Spirit. Comedy, cold, pointed, intelligent, attentive to type, yet cruelly accurate in its finding of that type in individuals, "condenses whole sections of the book in a sentence, volumes in a character; so that a fair part of a book outstripping thousands of leagues when unrolled may be compassed in one comic sitting" (1, 3).

Well and good. The narrator opts for these advantages, seized with urgency to get the story told: "For verily . . . we must read what we can of it, at least the page before us, if we would be men." He becomes, with the attendant Imps, servant of the Comic Muse, and the story is to be told in her language and with her Alpine comprehensiveness and impermeability. Yet right from the start of the story proper, we find the narrator being pulled at by his subject-victim. The line between Willoughby's interior monologues and the narrator's commentary is very, very thin:

> Young Sir Willoughby was fond of talking of his "military namesake and distant cousin, young Patterne—the Marine." It was funny; and not less laughable was the description of his namesake's deed of valour; with the

175

rescued British sailor inebriate, and the hauling off to captivity of the three braves of the black dragon on a yellow ground, and the tying of them together back to back by their pigtails, and driving of them into our lines upon a newly devised dying-top style of march that inclined to the oblique, like the astonished six eyes of the celestial prisoners, for straight they could not go. The humour of gentlemen at home is always highly excited by such cool feats. We are a small island, but you see what we do. (1, 8)

There are times when the elevated Spirit telling the story seems to take limiting flesh and blood in the very Patterne drawing room:

Willoughby conducted Mrs. Mountstuart to the supper-table.

"Were I," said she, "twenty years younger, I think I would marry you, to cure my infatuation."

"Then let me tell you in advance, madam," said he, "that I will do everything to obtain a new lease of it, except divorce you."

They were infinitely wittier, but so much was heard and may be reported.

"It makes the business of choosing a wife for him superhumanly difficult!" Mrs. Mountstuart observed, after listening to the praises she had set going again when the ladies were weeded of us, in Lady Patterne's Indian room, and could converse unhampered upon their own ethereal themes. (1, 16)

The narrator is, in fact, telling the story both ways. Willoughby is both a person and a type. We have, in our Comic Spirit mood, exactly harpooned a whale, and when the whale pulls, he pulls us under to learn what we must of our mutual element. The tension of this strategy is obvious: from Willoughby as type—Willoughby Patterne —we can comfortably recoil; Willoughby the person draws us uncomfortably close.

There is no doubt that the fictional reader would sooner identify with the philosophic, comprehensive Comic Spirit than with the narrator, whose position inside the mind of

Willoughby Patterne keeps him so uncomfortably close to, involves him so fascinatedly in, "the heat of his centre," Willoughby's self-love. The Comic Spirit provides a tasty bait indeed for the civilized reader. But the hook beneath that bait is surely the resemblance between Willoughby and the Comic Spirit. Recall the civilized brutality of each, the view of people as types, the contempt expressed in the prelude and by Willoughby for the "dust of the struggling outer world." Watch Willoughby sin against his own quite real acuteness:

> A flying peep at the remorseless might of dulness in compelling us to a concrete performance counter to our inclinations, gave Willoughby for a moment the survey of a sage. His intensity of personal feeling struck so vivid an illumination of mankind at intervals that he would have been individually wise, had he not been moved by the source of his accurate perceptions to a personal feeling of opposition to his own sagacity. *He loathed and he despised the vision, so his mind had no benefit of it, though he himself was whipped along. He chose rather (and the choice is open to us all) to be flattered by the distinction it revealed between himself and mankind.*
>
> (II, *161*)

The choice, the narrator reminds us, is open to us all.

The problem here, as with any analysis of narrative strategy, is how much authorial intentionality to read into the strategy. Was Meredith aware of the ambiguity of his portrait of the Comic Spirit? Did he construct it at all deliberately, or at least assent to it?

Yes, I think so. I think so partly for reasons extrinsic to *The Egoist* and detailed in my readings of Meredith's other novels. But strong evidence for intentionality in the ambiguousness of the power of pure comedy seems to me to be suggested by the opening of chapter 49, in which Willoughby pursues Laetitia through the night trying to persuade her to make an honest man of him to the frightful laughter of his surrounding Imps. On one level, this scene is a skillful rendering of paranoid schizophrenia; we are reminded that the Imps are not supernatural beings, but natural—"Men who, setting their minds upon an object, must have it, breed imps"—and we see Willoughby split in two, a stranger to himself because of his desperate monomania:

Willoughby became aware of them that night. He said to himself, upon one of his dashes into solitude, I believe I am possessed! And if he did not actually believe it, but only suspected it, or framed speech to account for the transformation he had undergone into a desperately beseeching creature, having lost acquaintance with his habitual personality, the operations of an impish host had undoubtedly smitten his consciousness. (ii, 318)

On another level this scene represents a sort of climax in the narrative drama not unlike the "suffering and cigars" passage in *Sandra Belloni*. For the narrator at this point begins to be uneasy about the way of the Spirit whose book this is: "We cannot be abettors of the tribes of imps whose revelry is in the frailties of our poor human constitution." As he comes to dramatize the nadir of Willoughby's distress, he finds that the Imp side of comedy, the brutal, satiric, or satyr side, has slipped its leash and waxes demonic "under the beams of Hecate." And when the satyr Imps "are uncontrollable by the Comic Muse," he asserts, "she will not flatter them with her presence during the course of their insane and impious hilarities, whereof a description would out-Brocken Brockens and make Graymalkin and Paddock too intimately our familiars." Thus the narrator touches only briefly on the scene, though not too briefly for us to imagine the psychic catastrophe the night represented for Willoughby: "Nay, it is in the chronicles of the invisible host around him, that in a fit of supplication, upon a cry of 'Laetitia!' twice repeated, he whimpered" (ii, 319). Then the Imps, like the philosopher upon hippogriff, are dismissed for exceeding their human serviceability: "Let so much suffice."

Lionel Stevenson thinks this is simply Meredith's old trick of refusing to tackle scenes that he does not feel equipped to do. And certainly there is some self-criticism, not to mention criticism of the Victorian audience, in Meredith's final comment on his choice not to describe the scene with the thoroughness of a watchmaker: "What men will do, and amorously minded men will do, is less the question than what it is politic they should be shown to do."

Nevertheless there is a compelling aesthetic-ethical reason for the narrator's behavior here. Asserting Willoughby's personal defeat is essential to the story. Dramatizing it would almost certainly topple reader and narrator into the vice which is the Egoism of pure comedy—contempt, and its literary expression, satire. The Imps in this novel represent the original sin of comedy; they are the Luciferian side of the Comic Spirit. "Contempt," we recall from the *Essay on Comedy*, "is a sentiment that cannot be entertained by comic intelligence. What is it but an excuse to be idly minded, or personally lofty, or comfortably narrow, not perfectly humane?" (*p. 120*). Contempt is the egoism of the philosopher, too, the brutality of the spiritual, the satyr side of the superiorly sensitive or intelligent. Adrian Harley demonstrates that. So does the George Meredith who wrote sardonically to E.W.B. Nicholson that the title he had proposed for his next public lecture, on "The Novel as a Work of Art in Relation to Human Nature and Manners," "would not give an occasion to flatter the English public, as one would distinctly have to show that all the great English novelists delineating modern times have had recourse to Satire, and black Satire."[8] So, Meredith allows himself to propose, does the reader who huffs and puffs disappointedly at being deprived of this scene. Meredith knows his devil. He knows ours too.

[8] Letter of August 22, 1881 (*Letters*, II, 635). Nicholson was superintendent of the London Institution at Finsbury Circus, which had invited Meredith to give the lecture "On the Uses of the Comic Spirit." Meredith declined this invitation, or rather, as I hope to show in the next chapter, declined the medium, and went on to delineate both modern society and black satirists in *One of Our Conquerors*.

6. The Making of Civilization

Colney Durance had his excuses. He could point to the chief creative minds of the country for generations, as beginning their survey genially, ending venomously, because of an exasperating unreason and scum in the bubble of the scenes, called social, around them. *(P. 236)*

IN THE LETTER QUOTED AT THE END OF THE PREVIous chapter we saw the private Meredith mourning that an artist looking at civilization must be driven to satire, and black satire at that, if he is to report on it. In *One of Our Conquerors* it is the character Colney Durance who takes this attitude, and Meredith's narrator, while he understands Colney and compassionates him, emphatically does not side with him. Colney is a brilliant development of the Adrian Harley figure, similarly acute, similarly detached in mind, similarly given to cloaking his insights in metaphorical wit. Colney's satire, *The Rival Tongues*, with its muffled warning to Englishmen that they have overestimated their position as cultural "conquerors," is not unlike Adrian's witty essay on the "Education of Youths and Maidens in the Commonwealth" in that the warnings go unheeded, unread, and so are sterile. Colney's position with regard to the conqueror in the novel, Victor Radnor, is essentially that of Adrian to his novel's hero, Richard Feverel: he is a tutor who cannot teach, a philosopher whose message is discounted by the people who most need it, precisely because the surrender to satire and the emotion of contempt has separated him from his fellow men.

Like Adrian, Colney is on a philosophic eminence which may enable him often to see more clearly and comprehensively than his fellow men, but at the same time prevents him from reaching them.

Meredith has given us the dislocated and satiric philosopher in this novel without any of the handicaps that marred his presentation in *Richard Feverel*. Adrian was selfish, comfort-loving, morally and sexually perverted, and unscrupulous; Colney loves his small circle of friends sincerely, tries to work for their benefit, makes himself active in their affairs without egoistically trying to manage them. He does not consider personal life a comedy to be watched, like Adrian, but he does consider public life, civilization, worthy only of black satire, and says so in all his books and essays. Meredith's ruthless conclusion is that such a split is not acceptable and will not work, however promising a compromise between the personal and the public it may seem.

The novel chronicles the history, both inner and outer, of Victor Radnor, the conqueror of the title. His public life seems one long string of victories. A brilliant and ambitious man, he acquired his first capital by marrying a wealthy widow, went on to entrepreneurship of diamond mines in Africa and at the novel's opening is one of the most powerful men in London. He can afford to purchase an additional magnificent estate in the country; he can virtually count on a marriage alliance for his daughter with a noble house, and he is moving toward a run for Parliament that seems likely to make him a political power as well. His personal life seems cloudless too; he has a beautiful wife, a lovely and gifted daughter, a circle of close friends active in music and literature. He is himself musically gifted, a man of great personal charm and public stature, loved and respected by all. Or almost all. When in the opening incident of the novel the conqueror trips and falls on London Bridge and speaks condescendingly, if genially, to the workingman who helps him up, an anonymous voice in the crowd of passersby speaks with

181

sharp hostility to the merchant prince, and slowly Victor's seemingly serene and mastered world begins to dissolve, as a much larger world than he had recognized appears. In the course of the novel we learn that the woman whom the intimate world of Victor's circle knows as Nataly Radnor is in fact not his wife, that his daughter Nesta is not legitimate, that the mysterious and desperately ill old woman called Mrs. Burman is still his wife and still refuses him the divorce that would sanction his elopement with Nataly twenty years before. By the middle of the novel the reader is aware that Victor's schemes to enter the ranks of the country gentry by purchasing the estate of Lakelands, to enter the nobility by marrying his daughter to Dudley Sowerby, heir to an earldom, and to transform his social and financial power into political power by mounting a public campaign for Parliament rest on a totally inadequate, almost a mad, reading of himself and of his position in the world. He sees that the conqueror is doomed to failure all along the line, in personal and in public life, because he cannot, or will not, see all the implications and ramifications of that fall on London Bridge.

In his astute friend, the essayist Colney Durance, Victor has an aid to the reading of himself and the world; Colney knows the truth about Nataly's status, and while he loves them both he is well able to see and protest against the mistakes they make. But Colney has not the comic look upon life; he is a satirist, and there is something of the brutal satyr and something of the egoist personally embittered toward the universe in his private conversation as well as in his public essays. Victor has therefore become disastrously adept at dismissing Colney's quite perceptive remarks on his situation as sheer "pessimism" or "bile." By the very nature of his identity and habitual activity as a satirist Colney is held at a distance by his friends, and so his insights do them little good. The unfructified relationship between Colney Durance and Victor Radnor, between the satirist and civilization, is at the heart of the novel.

The solution to the crucial difficulty posed by this relationship, that is, how civilization is to be *taught* to know itself and act for its own natural development, is going to have to be an act of faith in the possibility that strength and individual virtue kindled from common sense—the enlightened sense of the Commonality—will finally dismiss the unreason and "scum" from the scenes called social around us. There are in Meredith's view two main sources for this enkindlement. A man may be kindled to a sense of the common responsibility, the common contingency of men by intense contact, blood and brain, with another person who has himself achieved or is achieving this sense. Victor's clerk Daniel Skepsey has the beginning of this sense, and it expresses itself rather farcically in Skepsey's patriotic and sometimes belligerent sense of his nation, class differences understood and allowed for, as a whole nation. Skepsey's fiancée Mathilda Pridden has the germ of this sense, and it also expresses itself farcically in her devotion to the Salvation Army and its tenets of the brotherhood of man. But these two types, the heated patriot and the heated religionist, stand in Meredith's view for two important but essentially unsuccessful tries at a true leap into commonality by an evolving civilization. The paths to brotherhood that they propose are too emotional, too "gross," for supercivilized spirits like Victor Radnor to respond to.

Victor's daughter Nesta, equally subtle, youthfully ardent, is closer to him and might have kindled him to the common sense, for she develops a spirit of sisterhood with the injured and outcast Judith Marsett that symbolizes her commitment to the inspiriting of the whole society. But Victor has idealized his daughter so strongly as a psychic self-defense for the incalculable injury he did her by being responsible for her bastardy and by deceiving her about it that he cannot allow her to be his teacher. That leaves only his friend Colney Durance, who has the insights that might kindle in Victor a more realistic view of himself

183

and his responsibility. But Colney's satirical bent has given Victor the means of distancing him, and so, as we shall see in the last part of this chapter, he fails Victor.

There is another way that a man may come alive to his existential entanglement with all men, and that is by the prompting of his own nature. This inward light is another important expression of Meredithian "optimism," one brought to full light in this novel. Even if a man's attempts at self-disguise and withdrawal from connection have brought him to the point where he can let no other man help him, his own nature, his own consciousness, will prick and goad him everlastingly back toward integrity. Meredith's vehicle for conveying this operation of nature, and for conveying his own central idea of the commonality of man, is the metaphor of "the idea" that pursues and eludes Victor all through the novel. The idea that the world is full of other men who are in some important way connected with him and necessary to him and that he is not really in contact with (by which he means in command over) them as he thought he was, and that this lack of contact is somehow threatening and dangerous, comes to Victor after the fall on London Bridge and the flash of hostility and accusation of punctilio that greets his condescension to the man in the street. The idea starts as an uncapitalized notion, more a feeling than a thought, as Victor ponders whether there might not have been excuse for the workman's hostility:

> But we will try that: on our side, to back a native pugnacity, is morality, humanity, fraternity—nature's rights, aha! and who withstands them? on his, a troup of mercenaries!—And that lands me in Red Republicanism, a hop and a skip from Socialism! said Mr. Radnor, and chuckled ironically at the natural declivity he had come to. Still, there was an idea in it. . . .
>
> A short run or attempt at running after the idea, ended in pain to his head near the spot where the haunting word punctilio caught at any excuse for clamouring.
>
> *(One of Our Conquerors, pp. 9-10)*

But Victor has his own hostility toward the notion that he may be humanly responsible to and for all men, responsible to his abandoned first wife Mrs. Burman, to Nataly, the woman who now bears his name illegally and who has suffered torments for two decades because Victor's social ambitions have constantly made her vulnerable to gossip and scandal, and to Nesta, his secretly scarred child. He is hostile to the notion of responsibility and yet his nature yearns toward it as well, and in the tension of that double impulse the notion grows in Victor's mind into an abstract personification, the Idea. Sometimes the Idea seems hostile and alien to him, when it demands more self-recognition than he is willing to risk; sometimes the Idea seems glorious and golden to him, when it promises him a greater position in the interconnected fabric of mankind than he has really any right to hold. Like a "shrouded figure," like "the flap of wings," like the last whisper of skirts moving around the next corner of the stairs, the Idea passes and pursues Victor and evaporates. The narrator notes at the start of the novel: "She was very feminine; coming when she willed and flying when she wanted. Not until nigh upon the close of his history did she return, full-statured and embraceable, to Victor Radnor" *(p. 10).* And, nearly five hundred pages later:

> His lost Idea drew close to him in sleep: or he thought so, when awakening to the conception of a people solidified, rich and poor, by the common pride of simple manhood. But it was not coloured, not a luminous globe: and the people were in drab, not a shining army on the march to meet the Future. It looked like a paragraph in a newspaper, upon which a Leading Article sits, dutifully arousing the fat worm of sarcastic humour under the ribs of cradled citizens, with an exposure of its excellent folly.
>
> *(P. 493)*

The Idea in words looks dead, or grossly laughable, like Mathilda's Salvation Army. Putting aside the dead thing, bathing for a public meeting, Victor imagines himself leading a rejuvenated England from the Parliament he intends to enter: "Colney's insolent charge, that the English have no imagination—a doomed race, if it be true!—would be confuted. For our English require but the lighted leadership to come into cohesion, and step ranked, and chant harmoniously the song of their benevolent aim." Personal egoism, disguising itself under good intentions, strikes again at civilization through the mind of its benevolent conquerors. And the satirist who is never entirely expunged from Meredith's narrators strikes it down in his turn: "Surely he had here the Idea? He had it so warmly that his bath-water heated. Only the vision was wanted. On London Bridge he had *seen* it—a great thing done to the flash of brilliant results. That was after a fall. . . . His bath-water chilled" *(pp. 493-94)*.

It is important to point out here that this metaphorical Idea that dashes around after and runs away from Victor, whose presence warms and absence chills his bathwater, which is both poignant in its refusal to give happiness and slightly ridiculous in its animated forms, is *Victor's* metaphor, not Meredith's. It is Victor's tool for explaining his world to himself, and by its presence and operation in this novel Meredith is showing the reader first how a man turns instinctively and necessarily to metaphor when trying to account for the shadowy, the difficult, the elusively important in his life, and second that when he does turn to metaphor for enlightenment he may, if his fears or his desires override his sense of proportion, use a metaphor more to darken the shadowy places than to enlighten them or expose them to understanding. I introduce the subject here because there is an abundance of metaphor in this novel, and while a great deal of it derives from the narrator's itch for metaphor, a surprising amount of it is due to the same itch in the characters' minds, and as such is one of Meredith's most effective tools for demonstrating what those characters' minds are like. Many of Meredith's showiest productions in the realm of metaphor, in this novel and in all his novels, are in fact intimately bound

186

up with his description of the mental habits and activities of his characters, who reveal themselves in the metaphors they make or use. The fact that the use of metaphor by his characters and his narrators is so strikingly continuous and pervasive as to constitute practically a definition of his style indicates Meredith's belief that the capacity to use metaphor is as intrinsic to man's nature as play. It is a form of play to him; it is the mind's play with the mysterious correspondences that signal the immense correspondence of nature itself. As such, metaphor in Meredith has a special status that is almost independent of its usefulness in characterization, a special status that points to Meredith's almost childlike awe and confidence that metaphor just *is*, to be played with, before it exists to be used as a tool of adult awareness.

One other point needs to be made about style in this novel. The sympathy is much more confident and natural than in the other novels looked at, the comic look is humane and without malice, the fascination with his attractive and powerful and warped characters, especially Victor Radnor and Colney Durance, is open and unambiguous. There is no need for the warfare of narrative personae here; the mental activity of the narrator is always parallel to and often integrated with the mental processes of his characters. His identification with their story, his validation of their dilemmas, is so complete that the battle they fight with the dark consequences of a wrong use of their gifts is his own battle, and in the end the fictional reader's too. The novel exists largely as a stream of consciousness. The rhetoric of this novel, like that of any stream-of-consciousness novel, does not aim at persuasion by lesson but by the simple and powerful experience of passing through minds, some of which survive as a consequence of their mode of mental activity and some of which do not. That is why this is the most moving of Meredith's novels. For where the complex rhetorical strategy of most of his novels pulls the reader away from some temptation, some dark aspect of his living self, the rhetoric of *One of Our Con-*

querors offers him a more primitive choice. The reader's recoil here is from death, a recoil all the more important and painful because he is held like the narrator in a full and unsatiric sympathy for the dying right to the end. It is a full sympathy for the reason that distinguishes the real stream-of-consciousness technique from simple interior monologue—the full sensual basis and background of thought is conveyed. What Meredith has always striven to do, what he succeeds brilliantly in this novel in doing over and over again, is to testify with passion but without sentimentalism to the organic foundations of spirit, to convey how it *feels* to think, reflect, remember, scheme, debate oneself, organize one's position, to pursue or encompass or hide from those elusive Ideas just forming on the edge of emotion where language is born of the effort of feeling to become thought, or the effort of the brain to contact the blood. Meredith of course uses his famous anatomic triad of brain, blood, and spirit in symbolic, sometimes quite abstract, ways in *One of Our Conquerors* as in all of his novels. But the sensitive reader of his narrative cannot be unaware of the concrete physical existence of this triad in his thinking people. In this novel, especially, the thinking brain is vividly present as an organ, with its pulses, its charges, its flexes and recoils, its distillery of sweet and sour juices, and, most importantly, its poignant, mortal capacity for exhaustion. The diseases of brain and heart that destroy Victor and Nataly and paralyze Colney Durance are intensely "real" with that Meredithian realism that admits no poles between real and ideal, content and form, the idea and its metaphor, but instead asserts a continuum or wholeness that is confirmed in the narrative by the strong pull toward stream of consciousness.

Structurally, Meredith's vision of the interpenetration of personal, social, and civil action within the unity of civilization is developed through the book from a series of images and implications contained in the first sentence, a sentence notorious and memorable for its characteristically complex grammar and its choppy, but somehow compelling, rhythms:

> A gentleman, noteworthy for a lively countenance and a waistcoat to match it, crossing London Bridge at noon on a gusty April day, was almost magically detached from his conflict with the gale by some sly strip of slipperiness, abounding in that conduit of the markets, which had more or less adroitly performed the trick upon preceding passengers, and now laid this one flat amid the shuffle of feet, peaceful for the moment as the uncomplaining who have gone to Sabrina beneath the tides.

As the incident unrolls in Victor's mind, it lays open to the reader more and more areas of meaning in his personal and public life.

I. Victor and Nataly

The truth is that the Victor Radnor we know through most of the novel is mad. The two who know and love him best, his wife and daughter, suspect it, though they shrink from the suspicion. Nataly compounds and collaborates with the madness as she has always done:

> He sang: he never acknowledged a trouble, he dispersed it; and in her present wrestle with the scheme of a large country estate involving new intimacies, anxieties, the courtship of rival magnates, followed by the wretched old cloud, and the imposition upon them to bear it in silence though they knew they could plead a case, at least before charitable and discerning creatures or before heaven, the despondent lady could have asked whether he was perfectly sane. *(P. 50)*

Nesta, his growingly perceptive daughter, slides reluctantly around its edges: "She put a screw on her mind to perceive the rational object there might be for causing her mother to go through tortures in receiving and visiting; and she

189

was arrested by the louder question, whether she could think such a man as her father irrational" *(p. 427)*. The hyperaction of the scheming, the schizoid questioning of the "familiar behind the waistcoat," the paranoid extremities of innocent joviality and nightmarish fear with which he regards mankind, all evidenced in the initial incident on the bridge, suggest a brain sufficiently exhausted and strained to bear close watching.[1] The original fissure probably happened twenty years before, on a night when the husband of Mrs. Burman-Radnor and her young companion Nataly broke through the constraints of prudence, law, family, and good sense to pledge each other love and the mutual living and serving that love entails. We do not see it because it is Meredith's purpose here, as so often, that we should know "events" as we most often really do know them, through the dark glass of memory and reflection. We do not see the escape from Mrs. Burman but we do see clearly that the event impressed itself most deeply on its two participants *as a determinant of Victor's sanity.* Locked into a marriage financially profitable and physically distasteful, forced to live and work in the same house with a beautiful young girl, Victor was on the point of a severe mental crisis before Nataly agreed to rebel with him. Both Victor and Nataly insist that the act of escape resulted in the saving of the conqueror's sanity, and is justified thereby. Victor, in his cups, pleads to Simon Fenellen: "For the sake of my sanity, it was! to preserve my . . . but any word makes nonsense of it" *(p. 32)*. Nataly, at bay before Colney Durance's accusations, pleads the same: "And I do not feel the guilt! I should do the same again, on reflection. I do believe it saved him. I do; oh! I do, I do. . . . It

---

[1] In 1906 Meredith mentioned in a letter to critic John H. Hutchinson that "a doctor of the Insane wrote to my Publishers from Australia that the opening chapter [of *One of Our Conquerors*] showed all the intimations of incipient lesion of the brain, and he wondered whether I had studied the disease." Meredith added rather testily, "Had I done so I would not have written it" (*Letters*, III, 326).

sounds childish; it is true. He had fallen into a terrible black mood" *(p. 115)*. The irony of this situation is that by being used as the justification for the rebel act, the very issue of sanity becomes sacrosanct, locked away from examination. For examination would shake that case. Escaping the intolerable situation in Mrs. Burman's house drew Victor out of his black mood, it is true; but it drove him into a frenzied attempt to be king of the mountain in spite of—because of—the illegitimacy at the heart of his claim.

Victor's drive has elements of the honorable, the admirable, even the quixotic. But Victor's madness is darker and more mortal than the Don's. For in time, the time that the novel explores, it surfaces as an essentially destructive engine of sheer motion, a perversity of the "force in Nature which drives to unresting speed" *(p. 137)*, a flight to achievement, to schemes, an engine in which Victor is more a passenger than a driver: "Observe how fatefully he who has a scheme is the engine of it; he is no longer the man of his tastes or of his principles; he is on a line of rails for a terminous; and he may cast languishing eyes across waysides to right and left, he has doomed himself to proceed" *(p. 199)*. His failure is one that has dogged him all his life, a failure to *reflect*, to relax his mad forward drive long enough to let meaning *come to him*. Instead, he considers reflection the "disease" of the active mind, and pursues his Idea as he has pursued his other schemes. By the end of the novel he has committed the final destructive sin against the brain; he has disconnected half of it, the part that has spent a year chasing and being chased by that important Idea: "His Nesta had knocked Lakelands to pieces. Except for the making of money, the whole year of an erected Lakelands, notwithstanding uninterrupted successes, was a blank" *(p. 494)*. We are not surprised to find him the next moment dickering in mild panic with the Mephistophelian figure who inhabits the runaway active part of him:

191

The scheme departs: payment for the enlisted servants of it is in prospect. A black agent, not willingly enlisted, yet pointing to proofs of service, refuses payment in ordinary coin; and we tell him we owe him nothing, that he is not a man of the world, has no understanding of Nature: and still the fellow thumps and alarums at a midnight door we are astonished to find we have in our daylight house. *(P. 494)*

Having mortgaged his own soul and almost that of his lover to the capacity for sheer Faustian drive, Victor finally meets the devil at the midnight door inside himself. The disease of brain we find to have been more a symptom than a cause of his disintegration; the real cause was a monstrous disproportionment of will, Meredithian "spirit." The inability to act is the risk that comes to philosophers, but the drive to keep on acting, keep on moving, keep on conquering, brings on a different sort of damnation, one that Meredith clearly intimates waits for civilization as well as civilization's prince.

The prince, and the civilization, are in fact paranoid schizophrenics. His friends know it. The reader knows it, and it is part of Meredith's considerable achievement in characterization that we find both Victors somehow credible, that we can watch even so incredible an episode as Victor's disloyal flirtation with Lady Grace Halley take shape alongside his undoubted fidelity to his Nataly and feel pity (and perhaps terror), not contempt.

Victor's satirist, Colney Durance, understands his perversion and can do nothing, finally, to help him, for reasons I want to discuss later. But the really tragic knower and collaborator is Nataly herself: "Oh!—poor soul—how he is perverted since that building of Lakelands! He cannot take soundings of the things he does. . . . He is desperately tempted by his never failing. . . . And it sets me thinking of those who have never had an ailment, up to a certain age, when the killing blow comes. . . . Had I been stronger, I might have saved, or averted. . . . But, you will say, the stronger woman would not have occupied my place" *(p. 360)*. Thus Nataly to her friend Dartry

Fenellen, as the great Lakelands scheme for the conquest of position begins to collapse after she has had the courage to tell Dudley Sowerby the truth about her, and Nesta's, status. Her tragedy is that she has failed the man she loves by failing to challenge *his* obsession with *her* clearer understanding, by failing to support his brain with hers. Thrusting down her doubts, she has let him do the thinking for both of them, while she submitted to play the "woman's part," surrendering to passion, to feeling, to "heart."

Nataly's heart, in both senses of the word, falters and falters all through the novel. It achieves one final burst of strength when Nataly breaks up the final complex of Victor's mad schemes by telling the punctilious Dudley Sowerby the truth about Nesta's birth. Then the heart stops. Victor's hyperactive brain, however, only increases its destructive activity. When one scheme is broken, another proposes itself: "This name for successes, corporate nucleus of the enjoyments, this Victor Montgomery Radnor, intended impressing himself upon the world as a factory of ideas" *(p. 493)*. Out of his factory of ideas comes this contradictory one: "I want to save the existing order. I want Christianity, instead of the Mammonism we're threatened with. Great fortunes now are becoming the giants of old to stalk the land: or medieval Barons. Dispersion of wealth, is the secret. Nataly's of that mind with me. A decent poverty! She's rather wearying, wants a change. I've a steam-yacht in my eye, for next month on the Mediterranean. All our set. She likes quiet. I believe in my political recipe for it" *(p. 498)*. Victor has exactly a steam-yacht in his eye, big enough to blind him not only to the welfare of those in his care but to the flaws in his vision of society too. He does not want a decent poverty, he wants a giantlike eminence, not even, really, for the sake of enjoying it, but rather for the sake of engaging in the action that will bring him to it. Meredith is nicely clear, even stern, about this. Victor is not simply a man in the grip of a social idea, a good scheme, who in the process has corrupted his humanity. Again no real separation of spheres of being is allowed. The flawed humanity has in fact corrupted his social ideas too, the same flaw, the mystique of conquest, the metaphysic of action. It is not old Mrs. Burman as accusing "collective society woman," nor the unknowable community of men in the street, nor the rigidity of divorce laws, nor the pressures of business, nor the stupidity of press and Parliament, nor any outside thing that has made Victor Radnor mad and resulted in this mad "political recipe." There is, it is undeniably true, an "exasperating unreason and scum in the bubble of the scenes, called social," around a man. But it is the unreason within that kills him. And this is no small tragedy. Victor was worthy of being saved. It is in fact necessary to civilization's safety, *our* safety we are urgently made to feel, that he be saved. He offers so much. He needs to be helped to see himself clearly. Comedy does that. He needed a comic poet for a friend, and his tragedy, civilization's tragedy, is that he got a black satirist instead. Colney Durance, Victor's friend, the reader's friend, the "reader" of Victor, has tried in his satiric withdrawal to contribute clarity and sanity to Victor's self-image and has only helped drive him deeper into madness. As Victor dies peacefully in a sanitarium Colney Durance the satirist comforts himself with the hope that Victor's daughter Nesta may more successfully challenge some of the unreason in civilization's scenes. The reader's hope is the same, and we know by then that one of the reasons Nesta is better armed for the fight than Victor was is that when the satirist's rancor gets too black and his diatribes against civilization too self-excusing the much more tough-minded girl, much as she likes and respects Colney Durance, tunes him out.

II. Colney Durance:
"The Failure to Work Amendment"

We come now to the relationship between Victor Radnor and Colney Durance, which seems to me the touchstone of all the novel's concerns as well as the most comprehensive and sophisticated statement Meredith makes of his vision of society, "the world," civilization. Meredith uses these terms in very different ways throughout his novels. Often, as in a very schematic novel like *The Tragic Comedians* or *Diana of the Crossways* or *Lord Ormont and His Aminta*, "society" or "the world" functions as a kind of character in the plot, with a rather definite and limited identity; the "society" that corrupts Clotilde or the "world" that bays after Diana seem that old stock villain, the society page's society. Often, as in *Harry Richmond* or *The Egoist*, the hero is not so much pursued by society as enraptured, enslaved by the world, which is again limited in definition to a specific environment of people. When Meredith uses society or world this way, as an enslaving enemy, he is almost always setting up an ironic relationship between the hero and the enemy that culminates in the demonstration, most subtly presented in *The Egoist*, that the hero is his own enemy, that the villain world "out there" is very largely the mirror of his own worst fears, deepest wishes, most monstrous and perverted desires. Such a hero creates the enemy he deserves. Even Diana, giving all possible emphasis to the ludicrous Sir Luken, bolts before she is really attacked. A novel with the world cast as villain can remain a comedy only so long as somebody else, not the novelist, is doing the casting. The emotions of horror and contempt that create villains are ideally alien to the comic spirit as Meredith conceives it, "showing sunlight of the mind, mental richness rather than noisy enormity" *(Essay on Comedy, p. 141)*. He goes on to say that "its common aspect is one of unsolicitous observation, as if surveying a full field and having leisure to dart on its chosen morsels without any fluttering eagerness." It is this sense of the world, not as a character, nor as a creation of any kind, but as a full field surveyed with mental richness rather than noisy enormity, that marks Meredith's own best comic performances and that makes *One of Our Conquerors* stand out as the most subtle and yet lucid examination, rich and unhurried, of Meredith's idea of civilization.

"Civilized" is a word fraught with irony in Meredith's vocabulary. Sir Austin Feverel announces, "Woman will be the last thing civilized by man." Such persons as the Pole sisters "come to us in the order of civilization. . . . In this way they help civilize us," the narrator of *Sandra Belloni* urges, with a wink. "The ancestry of the tortured man had bequeathed him this condition of high civilization among other bequests," *The Egoist*'s narrator cries a crocodile tear over Willoughby. Clearly to become civilized is not to be freed from any of the vices of the barbarian we all are, except perhaps to be freed by the sort of lobotomy that Austin Feverel's aphorism implies. Civilization may simply make gorgeous the rituals by which man satisfies the appetite to draw all eyes, all feeling, into and around the "small shivering eidolon" of self. Meredith's recurring personification of this kind of civilization is the Turk, or more broadly the Oriental, whose evolution has consisted in sheer embellishment of the most primitive. Or civilization may be a true evolution, transformation, of the primitive to the mature—but the transformation may be uneven, with some facets of the person, some organs of the body politic, stalled at intermediate stages or overwhelmed by the rapid transformation of other facets or organs. It is this unevenness of transformation that Meredith alludes to in his picture of the "unfinished" English nation waiting for its Celtic gifts to contribute shape to the Anglo-Saxon bulk and power. It is this weary waiting period he as a Victorian feels most strongly, and connects, understandably if somewhat provincially, with London, in one of the most important passages in *One of Our Conquerors*:

> For this London, this England, Europe, world, but especially this London, is rather a thing for hospital operations than for poetic rhapsody; in aspect, too, streaked scarlet and pock-pitted under the most cumbrous of jewelled tiaras; a Titanic work of long-tolerated pigmies;

of whom the leaders, until sorely discomforted in body and doubtful in soul, will give gold and labour, will impose restrictions upon activity, to maintain a conservatism of diseases. Mind is absent, or somewhere so low down beneath material accumulations that it is inexpressive, powerless to drive the ponderous bulk to such excisings, purgings, purifyings as might—as may, we will suppose, render it acceptable, for a theme of panegyric, to the Muse of Reason, ultimately, with her consent, to the Spirit of Song. *(P. 40)*

Meredith sees civilization here as a whole, unified, animated being whose health depends upon the internal coherence of all its parts. Incoherence is an outrage to the natural law, and so the images of the fabulous tiara above the pocked face and the peanut brain in the massive bulk are images that go beyond the simple irony of the mask-reality figure to real outrage, ponderous and slightly ludicrous outrage, dogmatic and severe, the outrage of the satirist. Meredith feels this outrage as fiercely as any of the "chief creative minds of the century, beginning their survey genially, ending venomously." But he has before him an ideal of comedy that excludes venom, and an ideal of human personality that tries to exclude it, too, from the author-reader relationship as well as from all other human relationships. There remains, nevertheless, this "exasperating unreason and scum in the bubble of the scenes, called social" that inevitably calls forth venom from a creative mind.

Meredith, then, wants it both ways, wants to be satirist and comedian, and in *One of Our Conquerors*, by the simple device of creating his satirist not as narrator but as character under the control of the comedian, he gets it both ways. His Colney Durance is the philosopher we saw being used and tested and finally, if equivocally, dismissed in *Sandra Belloni*. He is the satiric Imp of egoistic Imperial Britain we saw struggling with the truly comic impulse governing *The Egoist*. He is the worrisome figure of Adrian Harley, maturely and compassionately encom-

197

passed at last by this foremost advocate of philosophy in fiction, who knew that in the cool and disengaged Adrian novelists had met the dark side of that philosophy.

Colney Durance enters the story, like all the novel's major elements, by way of the episode on London Bridge and he enters it strangely, as an accusation lodged half inside, half outside the rocketing brain of Victor Radnor: "Yes, well, and if a tumble distorts our ideas of life, and an odd word engrosses our speculations, we *are* poor creatures, he addressed another friend, from whom he stood constitutionally in dissent, naming him Colney; and under pressure of the name, reviving old wrangles between them" *(p. 5)*. Our conqueror has a mental victory in this encounter with the satirist, though it is pyrrhic as always: "Colney had to be overcome afresh, and he fled, but managed, with two or three of his bitter phrases, to make a cuttle-fish fight of it, that oppressively shadowed his vanquisher:—*The Daniel Lambert of Cities: The Female Annuitant of Nations*:—and such like, wretched stuff, proper to Colney Durance, easily dispersed and out-laughed when we have our vigour" *(p. 6)*. The satirist, squirting his ink at the myriad discernible follies and evils of "a people professing in one street what they confound in the next, and practicing by day a demureness that yells with the cat of the tiles at night" *(p. 41)*, does indeed rout his enemy. But in the process a cloud of mighty indistinction is produced over the whole area of the argument, a cloud that subverts truth and arrests all forward motion. Such is Victor's complaint of his friend Colney. Knowing himself to be one of the activists, the producers, of his time, Victor evades the Colney within himself because of a quite warranted concern for the destructive action of satire upon "vigour," which he knows to be the quintessential part of himself and of his country. Colney is clearly engaged in a struggle for Victor's mind, and is gaining a foothold. Time and again Victor catches himself thinking Colney's thoughts. But he throws off Colney every time he can in a reflex both necessary and tragic. Following up the majestic half-truths of the satirist, surrendering voluptuously to his scourge as he lays bare his guiltiest apprehensions produces no reforms; it produces in the worst of us fanaticism, and in the best, like Victor, "despondency."

It is interesting that Meredith chooses as his first example of Colney's satire a truly malicious, faintly hysterical sketch drawn, as Meredith says sardonically, in "literary sepia," of "the Jew dominant in London City" (p. 6). The sketch plunges Victor into despondency not because it shocks him out of a complacency in Anglo-Saxon superiority, but because it repeats his own secret masochistic nightmare: "Our fishy Saxon originals . . . are shown blacking Ben-Israel's boots and grooming the princely stud of the Jew . . . with our poor hang-neck population uncertain about making a bellrope of the forelock to the Satyr-snouty master; and the Norman Lord de Warenne handing him for a lump sum son and daughter, both to be Hebraized in their different ways." This sort of satiric detail, which a modern reader might condemn as blatantly pornographic and a seedling of Fascism, Meredith would condemn as uncomic, blatantly sentimental, and, worst perversion of philosophy in art, as *abstract*. The abstraction of satire is the sin against philosophy for Meredith, because abstraction renders philosophy infertile. Colney Durance has the last of many hard words on "the shallowness of the abstract Optimist" (p. 514), and so he should. But Meredith, the comedian, is even harder on the abstract pessimist, whose crime against civilization is sterility and whose personal tragedy is the same as his social—he cannot teach.

Meredith builds a surprisingly large part of the actual plot of One of Our Conquerors on the inability of the reflective Colney Durance to communicate his wisdom persuasively to the active people of the story. Colney understands that Victor's Lakelands plan, with Dudley as its cornerstone and Parliament as its crown, would be utterly destructive to his family, his love, and himself. He knows that Nataly is shirking her duty to Victor by falling in so easily with his schemes and her duty to Nesta by shielding her from all "knowledge of the world." His opinions of his friends' actions are evident, and are delivered with considerably less rancour than his sociological pronouncements. Why then can he not avert the disaster?

He cannot do so because by his excess, by his invulnerable certitude, and most of all by the distance his literary abstractness creates between him and others, he has made himself into a tool for the use of the desperate spirits around him. Victor's jocular cry, "But don't let me hear of bachelors moralists" *(p. 225)* rings over the whole Meredith canon and opens up the heart of Colney's (and Meredith's) problems as satirists. Very simply, no one so steeled against the battle of life as to be beyond the careful and vexing task of drawing the utter distinctness of every human situation is ultimately to be trusted. Satire, the morality of bachelors, comes into the engaged human brain with so alien a shape and color, "literary sepia," that the organ spontaneously encysts it in disbelief and neutralizes it. Worse, the brain uses its very alienness to comfort itself. Poor Colney, having chosen to love abstract pessimism, has become an abstraction to his friends, and for every time a Victor muses fruitfully that "Old Colney" may be right, a sore beset Nataly uses satire to teach herself untruth:

> One motive in her consultation with [Colney] came of the knowledge of his capacity to inflict [the lash] and his honesty in the act, and a thirst she had to hear the truth loud-tongued from him; together with a feeling that he was excessive and satiric, not to be read by the letter of his words: and in consequence, she could bear the lash from him, and tell her soul that he overdid it, and have an unjustly-treated self to cherish. *(P. 117)*

The satirist is too easily bested by the human race, in its cunning, desperate, not entirely unhealthy need to love itself. Here is Nataly, contriving an escape from the truth of the satirist's view that knowledge is greater protection than ignorance by striking out an uncomfortable truth about the satirist's motives:

Whatever there was of wisdom in his view, he spoilt it for English hearing, by making use of his dry compressed sentences. Besides he was a bachelor; therefore but a theorist. And his illustrations of his theory were grotesque; meditation on them extracted a corrosive acid to consume, in horrid derision, the sex, the nation, the race of man. The satirist too devotedly loves his lash to be a persuasive teacher. Nataly had excuses to cover her reasons for not listening to him. *(P. 147)*

And here is Victor, taking his satirist like draughts of medicine:

Dudley drove him to Colney for relief. Besides it pleased Nataly that he should be bringing Colney home; it looked to her as if he were subjecting Dudley to critical inspection before he decided a certain question much, and foolishly, dreaded by the dear soul. That quieted her. . . . And she was, in her queer woman's way, always reassured by his endurance of Colney's company:—she read it to mean, that he could bear Colney's perusal of him, and satiric stings. Victor had seen these petty matters among the various which were made to serve his double and treble purposes; now, thanks to the operation of young Dudley within him, he felt them. Preferring Fenellen's easy humour to Colney's acid, he was nevertheless braced by the latter's antidote to Dudley, while reserving his entire opposition in the abstract. *(Pp. 211-12)*

Reserving his entire opposition in the abstract, Victor has gratefully taken the satirist's invitation to abstraction, to the seeing of life at two poles, "rose pink and dirty drab," as Meredith calls them in literary terms in *Diana of the Crossways*. In this novel the poles are emotional attitudes personified as optimist and pessimist, illegitimate children of the nineteenth century, "gosling affirmatives and negatives . . . divorced from harmony and awakened by the slight increase of incubating motion to vitality" *(p. 212)*. Meredith's image of civilization in this passage is important: the "omnibus of the world" is speeding up and the motion is challenging the coherence of the organism, but the task is nevertheless to continue to see creation, nature, man, civilization, as a whole. If the optimist-pessimist in man, the active-reflective, the creative-conservative, all the gosling affirmatives and negatives in man and society do indeed seek their separate wholenesses, the wholeness will be abstract and unreal. The affirmatives will be shallow, and so proceed nowhere; and the negations, heavy, abstract, too smooth and blunt to lodge in the rough texture of received reality, will no longer perform their vital evolutionary function as a spur to the creatively active. Civilization will pass by its negations, or eliminate them, or ignore them, going ahead to spin madly in the circle of its runaway affirmations, its abstract god, Progress. And who can blame it, if negation has sold out to abstraction? Victor could not really take Colney into his confidence, for the abstract pessimist has already warned him by a thousand acid sentences that he has no confidence to return: "He cannot perform his part in return; [Optimy] gets no compensation; Pessimy is invulnerable. You waste your time in hurling a common *tu-quoque* at one who hugs the worst" *(p. 213)*.

This is not to say, of course, that the optimist should be shielded from "the worst." Meredith's Colney may be abstract, may be sepia-toned, may even grow tiresome to the point of dismissal: "A tiresome tirade: and as it was not on his lips but in the stomach of the painful creature, let him grind that hurdy-gurdy for himself" *(p. 236)*. But he gets off many a splendid shot at the nineteenth-century worst, and gives Meredith many a splendid satirio-comic scene. One of the best of these is in the chapters on Colney at Lakelands, a place which always "gripped him with the fell satiric itch" *(p. 84)*. These chapters view the Lakelands scheme, its master, and the English society he courts largely through Colney's eye, but behind that is always the laughter of the comic spirit, "humanely malign," signaling to the reader that the final victim of the satirist is himself. In the foreground, however, is the enjoyable spectacle of the English, led featly by their satirist into exposing the extremest of their follies, vanities, delusions, and hobby-horses. For this purpose Meredith's narrator becomes the cunningly abstract, bemused, superior "we" of civilized England, "the most sheepy of sheep" *(p. 73)*, a satirist's creation for a satirist shepherd to maneuver:

> We are induced temporarily to admire the French people. They are sagacious in fruit gardens. They have not the English Constitution, you think rightly; but in fruit-gardens they grow for fruit, and not, as Victor quotes a friend, for wood, which the valiant English achieve. We hear and we see examples of sagacity; and we are further brought round to the old confession, that we cannot cook —Colney Durance has us there; we have not studied herbs and savours; and so we are shocked backward step by step until we retreat precipitately into the nooks where waxen tapers, carefully tended by writers on the Press, light-up mysterious images of our national selves for admiration. Something surely we do, or we should not be where we are. But what is it we do (excepting cricket of course) which others cannot do? Colney asks; and he excludes cricket and football. *(P. 85)*

Civilization's "we" appears again in the boudoir of the Duvidney ladies, who, we recall, were identified as England itself by Colney Durance, an identification shaken into Victor's consciousness by the falling-down on London Bridge.[2] The ladies represent a civilization not so barbarously worldly as the Lakelands assembly, one nearer to the proper pitch of the evolving natural ideal, but still unbalanced; their spiritual sensitivity is alive but awry, and therefore they are fair game for the comic spirit:

[2] The sage Meredith, as I have been saying, retained a child's delight in fairy tales and the use thereof, and his letters show, especially in the sixties and seventies, a remarkable sensitivity to street songs and music hall ditties, many of which he caricatured in letters to friends. I do not want to make too much of the falling-down on (and of) London Bridge, but it would be unjust to the real shapeliness of this philosopher not to mention the matter.

Possessing, for example, nine thousand pounds per annum in Consols, and not expending the whole of it upon our luxuries, we are, without further privation, near to kindling the world's enthusiasm for whiteness. Yet there, too, we find, that character has its problems to solve; there are shades in salt. We must be charitable, but we should be just; we give to the poor of the land, but we are eminently the friends of our servants; duty to mankind diverts us not from the love we bear to our dog; and with a pathetic sorrow for sin, we discard it from sight and hearing. *We hate dirt. (Pp. 269-70)*

Colney, thinking about Victor's attempt to overcome the ladies' invulnerable gentility, spits sour venom indeed:

They were England herself; the squat old woman she has become by reason of her overlapping numbers of the comfortable fund-holder annuitants: a vast body of passives and negatives, living by precept, according to rules of precedent, and supposing themselves to be righteously guided because of their continuing undisturbed. Them he branded, as hypocritical materialists, and the country for pride in her sweatmeat plethora of them: mixed with an ancient Hebrew fear of offence to an inscrutable Lord, eccentrically appeasable through the dreary iteration of the litany of sinfulness. *(P. 271)*

But the reader, having been introduced comically to the ladies, knows this to be "entertainment" wide of the mark, and has himself as an example when the comedian describes the satirist's doom: "Colney suffered as heavily as he struck. If he had been no more than a mime in the motley of satire, he would have sucked compensation from the acid of his phrases, for the failure to prick and goad, and work amendment" *(p. 271)*.

It is crucial to note here that the satirist is not being satirized. Meredith has drawn not a caricature but a portrait of a man whose saturnine temperament took the early reversals of social circumstance as the final damning proof of civilization's irresponsibility; Colney's mime of satire is the first and last case pled against society by the "briefless barrister disposed for scholarship" *(p. 212)*, the intellectual, the reflecting man for whom there seems no work in late Victorian civilization unless it were the productions in literary sepia whose motley renders them ineffectual. Civilization, developing new barbarisms to accompany the growth of mind, keeps tame satirists by the dozen. Colney is not fully aware that poor Victor and Nataly are taking him like a physic not to gain real health but to "maintain a conservatism of disease." He can see that he has failed to work amendment, but he does not know why. The reader does:

> Colney Durance accused [Victor] of entering into bonds with somebody's grandmother for the simple sake of browsing on her thousands: a picture of himself too abhorrent to Victor to permit any sort of acceptance. Consequently he struck away to the other extreme of those who have a choice in mixed motives: he protested that compassion had been the cause of it. *(P. 46)*

But with respect to the larger concern Meredith has, the larger mass, civilization itself with its sheer mind-burying bulk, Colney is permitted to be more than half-aware of his tame-satirist status. Out of this half-knowledge he produces *The Rival Tongues*, a satire on the English, on Western civilization, and, most essentially, on the notion that there may be "miraculous transformations of a whole people at the stroke of a wand" *(p. 217)*, an idea in which Meredith himself clearly believes—minus the magic. Exaggerated, sour, confusing, provocative, this tale of the Western nations in rivalry to be chosen linguistic and philosophical model for the East is given us only in snatches, hasty summaries from largely hostile readers like Victor. It was concocted out of the acids "ground" in the stomach of Colney Durance as he watched society at the Lakelands assembly. It has a damsel named Delphica whose wit and independence Nesta recognizes as her own and whom she is subtly able to show to her half-affianced nobleman as an earnest of her unsuitability for him. Serialized, it receives the expected harsh reaction from "a dragon-throated public," and a very dubiously superior welcome from the "elect" who expected no better of the dragon:

> The pained Editor deferentially smiled at her cheerful mention of Delphica. "In book form, perhaps!" he remarked, with plaintive resignation; adding: "You read it?" And a lady exclaimed: "We all read it!"
>
> But we are the elect, who see signification, and catch flavour; and we are reminded of an insatiable monster how sometimes capricious is his gorge. "He may happen to be in the humour for a shaking!" Colney's poor consolation it was to say of the prospects of his published book: for the funny monster has been known to like a shaking.
>
> *(P. 437)*

We arrive again at the moment present in nearly all Meredith's novels when he begins the undercutting of the civilized reader, the elect, the philosophers of sophistication, in this case the tame satirist and his court. Here, in a reversal exactly correlated to Victor's sudden alienated response to his fellow man-in-the-street, a response compounded of false joviality, contempt, and fear, we see again the great dissociative act that marks the nineteenth century in Meredith's eyes, that uncoupling of affirmatives and negatives, the projection outward of all that is "incomprehensible," massive, and threatening, into a beast-form Other, the mob, the public—us. Clearly Colney fits his adjective "dragon-throated" better than his readers, just as Victor already inhabits that warm cage, Merrie England, with its "stout menagerie bars" of obsession in which he heartily wishes to enclose "that enormous beast," the mob. Disconnection, polarization, does appear to have its uses in the evolution of persons; civilization, reason itself, and satire, or the satyr, the beast-form, is one of its allies. " 'Yes,' Colney said; 'We unfold the standard of extremes in this country, to get a single step taken: that's how we move: we threaten death to get footway' " *(p. 442)*.

That strategy looks good on paper. The philosophy has

a symmetry and an economy fatally, almost sensually, pleasing to the mind's eye. It has an enormous appeal to a mind like Victor's, aching to run free and stay morally safe at the same time; to a mind like Colney's, seeking both to wound and to heal; to the civilized reader, who would be both human and "elect"; and to Meredith, who would both be himself and be loved—if not now, then later, when civilization will have moved a step. Prophecy is the job, and the cold comfort, of satirists: "Who can tell," says Victor of Colney's proposal for optional marriages, renewable every seven years, "they're donkeys until we know them for prophets. Colney may be hailed for one fifty years hence" *(p. 286)*. But such a prophet furnishes nothing but entertainment, even to posterity. Such notions, pitched deliberately, even "philosophically," to the extremes of outrage rattle harmlessly off the wall of the living man's healthy suspicion of abstractions; and the common man is partly right. Meredith agrees that "the truth" may lie at the extremes of experience, in the intensities of single special moments. But common human perception and human reality, "civilization," keep instinctively to the dense and cloudy domain of the day-by-day. Penetrated and violated as it is by the truths of love, pity, egoism, sentimentalism, of romance and satire, action and philosophy, the day-by-day is the sphere in which the comic is possible, that is, the sphere in which philosophic minds who are not simply egoists, who want to teach, must work. "An incomprehensible world indeed at the bottom and at the top," muses Victor Radnor. "We get on fairly at the centre. Yet it is there that we do the mischief making such a riddle of the bottom and the top." The philosopher, of light or heavy temperament, drifts irresistibly toward the top and bottom of the world, and must fight to stay at the center, where he may have some influence on the mischief that is being made.

Meredith's fight to stay at the center of the world despite both his gifts and his flaws is not always successful. The Colney Durance in him breaks out once or twice even in

207

this novel: the transition he makes from the not-very-successful Dramatic Satire in the fifth chapter, for instance, is repellently Colney-like: "Granting all that, it being a transient novelist's business to please the light-winged hosts which live for the hour, and give him his only chance of half of it, let him identify himself with them, in keeping to the quadrille on the surface and shirking the disagreeable" *(p. 41).* One would feel more confident of Meredith's comic ascendancy over Colney Durance in *One of Our Conquerors* if Colney did not have all the last words. Still, Colney himself is not entirely cut off from the center of the world; he maintains an active and on the whole fruitful friendship with the two beings in the novel closest to the center of the world, Daniel Skepsey and Nesta Radnor. These two, he in his comic way, she in her romantic one, are protected from Colney's more dangerous and debilitating abstractions by literally not being able to understand all he says, as if, when he drifts too far from the center into abstraction he becomes inaudible to them. Skepsey in his busy "water-wagtail" way, Nesta in her dreamy-ideal way, are the counterpoint of action and reflection that civilization needs, that civilization is.[3] These two are blessed with and animated in a comic and noble friendship by common sense—that is, a sensitivity to the commonality of life. "If you believe that our civilization is founded in common sense (and it is the first condition of sanity to

[3] It is not by accident that some of Meredith's best stream-of-consciousness writing takes place within the minds of these two young people, swimming, as in their natural element, in the milieu of reflection upon action that marks the center of the world. Nor is it by accident that two of their most important reflective moments occur on and to the rhythm of the railway train, which is elsewhere a symbol of the thoughtless commitment to action, progress, and achievement that has been the ruination of Victor Radnor and threatens to ruin Meredith's civilization (Skepsey on the train, pp. 103-05; Nesta leaving Dudley and catching from the music of the train a "shudder in the blood" for Dartrey, pp. 412-14). *One of Our Conquerors*, one notes with pleasure, is finally being reprinted, by the University of Queensland Press.

believe it)," says Meredith in the "Essay on Comedy," then you will perceive the comic spirit. Philosophers of abstract action, like Victor, or of abstract pessimism, like Colney, will never see it. The society that succeeds in making all its great minds into black satirists cannot call itself a civilization. For Meredith civilization equals comedy, and the equation is reversible.

7. The Survival of Romance

> It really seems these moderns think [narrative]
> is designed for a frequent arrest of the actors
> in the story, and a searching of the internal
> state of this one or that one of them: who is
> laid out stark naked and probed and expounded,
> like as in the celebrated picture by a great
> painter: and we, thirsting for events as we
> are, are to stop to enjoy a lesson on Anatomy.
> And all the while the windows of the lectureroom
> are rattling, if not the whole fabric shaking,
> with exterior occurrences or impatience for them
> to come to pass. (Dame Gossip, *The Amazing
> Marriage, pp. 132-33*)
>
> Dame Gossip boils. Her one idea of animation is
> to have her dramatis personae in violent motion.
> . . . The fault of the method is, that they do
> not instruct, so the breath is out of them before
> they are put aside, for the uninstructive are
> the humanly deficient. . . . To preserve Romance
> (we exchange a sky for a ceiling if we let it go),
> we must be inside the heads of our people as well
> as the hearts, more than shaking the kaleidoscope
> of hurried spectacles, in days of a growing
> activity of the head. (The Modern Novelist,
> *The Amazing Marriage, p. 209*)

IN DAME GOSSIP THE MODERN NOVELIST IN *THE Amazing Marriage* has a powerful dissenting presence to contend with throughout the narrative. Meredith's Novelist takes as his subject the appearances of reality that men are most familiar with and probes them for the lesson he wishes to share with his fictional reader, but if he stays too long at this detailed inspection of the appearances the reader already knows, or if he becomes fascinated with the process of inventing and classifying detail then Dame Gossip is immediately there to remind the reader that the Novelist is turning lecturer, and to urge the reader to repudiate such dullness.

The Dame is often convincing to the reader, so that from a purely practical standpoint the Novelist cannot afford to alienate her and her audience. This battling pair make a crucial point in Meredith's general theory of fiction too. In his fiction he undertakes the preservation of romance at the same time as he fights for the analytic and philosophic qualities of the "modern" novel, because he believes that psychological realism needs not only to take account of the impulses of romance, not only to use them, but also to heed them, to live in them for a time, according to the actual rhythms of human beings who, if they do live at the center of the world, still hunger for the extremes. For Meredith reality is a mystery, partly known and partly not, and increasing one's knowledge of it is a matter of maintaining contact with all the mysterious impulses, the romantic impulses, that penetrate man's nature, while at the same time trying to penetrate those impulses with the tools of consciousness. Losing contact with romance is not simply exchanging a sky for a ceiling, it is losing contact with reality; by the same token, ignoring or misusing the tools of consciousness is for Meredith aborting the nature of man, which is part of reality. True romance seems to be in this scheme the respectful embrace of all the impulsive energies in our reality that remain present and mysterious even after the most intense and subtle application of the tools of knowing, and false romance, which we have seen before in characters who surrender too willingly, too voluptuously, too egoistically in the last analysis to the "mystery" of themselves or of "fate," is to be eschewed. The abandonment of false romance and the preservation of the true is a major concern in *The Amazing Marriage*. By Meredith's and Fielding's lights a false realism in fiction was to be deplored, because in the multiplication of worldly detail the realistic approach somehow convinced the reader that it was not he but some other reader who was being studied, and thus failed of its teaching purpose. Meredith deplored false romance in the same way because in its frenetic worship of the fatality of things, the helpless energetic rush and flow of things, this writing attitude somehow convinced the reader that self-analysis under the ceilings of modern scientific understanding is not only tedious but useless. The battle of the Dame, romance, and the Novelist represents a serious conflict over the best, the most humane look on life, and in this last novel Meredith proposes the marriage of both looks to us.

The Amazing Marriage is Meredith's picture of the destructiveness of false romance, as *One of Our Conquerors*, with its portrait of the cynical satirist and the merchant conqueror, is a study of the impotence of false realism. But there is an extraordinary difference of effect. Over the characters who preach and practice false romance in *The Amazing Marriage* the novelist has clear and compassionate comic control, as he does over the false realists like Colney Durance in *One of Our Conquerors*. But the main expositor of romance in *The Amazing Marriage* is not a character in the plot but one in the subplot, the characterized narrator called Dame Gossip, and she is much harder to control. Slightly absurd, painted old and garrulous in the same rather suspicious way as Adrian Harley is painted fat and "succulent," the Dame is nevertheless a most convincing and powerful imagination of the impulses of romance. As such it is her nature to resist nit-picking distinctions about true and false romance made by analyzing philosophers who are more interested in dead categories and invisible ideas than in live people and the palpable events that are shaking the windows of the lecture room. She has a point. Meredith's novelist-narrators have been painfully probing the dimensions of true and false philosophy too, as the Modern Novelist does here. But, the Dame finds the whole business repugnant, all this analyzing, distinguishing, chemical distilling, and surgical probing of human nature in antiseptically distanced prose; there is something small and cold, evil-smelling, actually, in the process. She will have none of it, or of philosophers either, heaping open scorn upon the philosopher character Gower Woodseer and prudently reserving for small digs and jabs the scorn she feels for the much more powerful philosopher novelist, the Modern Novelist who is her colleague in telling the story.

Yes, the Dame of romance has a point about the possible smallness, the antiseptic deadness of the philosopher's contribution to humanity or the Novelist's contribution to the tale, the same point Meredith has been playing with all along. What is more, the Dame of romance has the story itself. Nowhere in Meredith is there so clear a demonstration of my earlier speculations about the written sources of story in this tradition of the novel as in *The Amazing Marriage*, whose editor-novelist is shown trying to make sense out of a confusing but powerfully interesting set of books and documents lent to him by the mother of romance, Dame Gossip. There are in fact three stories, three "times" present in this novel, two having to do with the plot and one with the subplot, and in this novel more than any other of Meredith's the story of the subplot, the existential time of the writing-reading of the novel, is in the forefront.

The earliest time, the first story we meet in the novel, is set in the period just after Waterloo at the peak of that public impulse called romantic, where Dame Gossip is most at home, and where she begins the novel: "Everybody has heard of the beautiful Countess of Cressett, who was one of the lights of this country at the time when crowned heads were running over Europe, crying out for charity's sake to be amused after their tiresome work of slaughter: and you know what a dread they have of moping" *(p. 1)*. This time is not within the Dame's living memory. But there are documents. Countess Fanny of Cressett has left a book of *Meditations in Prospect of Approaching Motherhood*, and her hero-abductor Captain John Kirby has left a book of *Maxims for Men*; in addition there are numerous ballads, newspaper articles, a volume of correspondence, and even a playscript in the public domain, which contain in fascinating if inexact detail the story of how the beautiful twenty-three-year-old countess fell in love with the splendid sixty-three-year-old, or maybe sixty-seven-year-old captain fresh from heroic fighting under Bolivar, how they ran away together from her husband and his country and lived in Austria through the birth of a son and a daughter ("both children born in wedlock, as you will hear," interjects the Dame, who has her pockets of prudery [*p. 12*]) and then died within a week of each other, he at ninety-one, unable to sustain life without her. A romantic tale indeed, but verified in several of its essential points by memoirs ("as the young lord tried to relate subsequently, as well as he could recollect the words—here I have it in print. . . ." [*p. 9*]) and letters.

In the Dame's possession also are documents relating to the second time in the novel, the main story shared in the telling with the Modern Novelist. This centers around the marriages of the Kirby children, Carinthia Jane and Chillon John. Carinthia's union with the complex and profligate Lord Fleetwood is the amazing marriage of the title; the marriage comes to be called that by the public when Fleetwood deserts his wife of one day after taking her to a honeymoon prizefight, and it gets more not less amazing as Carinthia first pursues her husband, then bears him a child, surprising all who knew of the quick abandonment, and finally turns her back on him just at the moment he is ready to love her. Another major part of the story is the marriage of Chillon to Henrietta Fakenham, a reigning beauty of the time whose mercurial temperament and love for hectic gaiety and music had tempted her to listen favorably to Fleetwood's Byronic courtship before the Kirbys, brother and sister, appeared on the scene. Some of the documents referring to these events are authentic private ones in the Dame's family—"The letter, lost for many years, turned up in the hands of a Kentish auctioneer . . . our relative on the mother's side had it knocked down to him, in contest with an agent of a London gentleman. . . . Thus it ran, I need not refer to it in Bundle No. 3" *(p. 141).* There is also, presumably in another bundle before the Dame and the Modern Novelist, the notebook of Gower Woodseer, the wandering philosopher whose friendship with the enigmatic Fleetwood involves him in the amazing marriage and eventually in a marriage of his own with Carinthia's maid Madge. This is the time of the 1830's, a period of what has been called *fin de siècle* decadence in society countered by liberal uprisings abroad and the beginnings of Chartism at home; it seems to be the period of the two narrators' youths, and so they have their own dim personal memories to support the story too. But the Dame's memory of that crucial period of transformation in British history is that of the dwindling of romance, while the Novelist clearly relishes the period as the beginning of the modern age, of liberalism, of philosophy.

Touchstone for this sense of metamorphosis is the friendship between the carpenter's son Woodseer and the nobleman Fleetwood. Fleetwood, as we shall see, is in the fell grip of high romantic cynicism; a worship of his own incomprehensibility and that of the universe is the driving energy in his character. Woodseer is a sort of scholar-tramp with a tendency to high-flown abstract thought expressed in lyric asides to his notebook; it is this lyricism that first attracts the Earl to him. But Woodseer, for all those philosophic tendencies to abstractness and dislocation of brain and blood that we have seen Meredith treat comically throughout his novels, has a reasonably strong grasp on his responsibility continually to strive to know himself more fully and to seek more carefully his position in and debtorship to the universal reality.[1] It is this quality of true philosophy in him that also attracts

---

[1] Gower Woodseer, it is agreed by all critics, is a portrait of Meredith's friend and philosophical admirer, Robert Louis Stevenson. Stevenson was proud of his friendship with Meredith and was used, in a philosophical way, to seeing himself in Meredith's novels. He it was who recounted the famous story of an admirer who came to Meredith with the cry that "Willoughby Patterne is me!" "No, my dear fellow," Meredith replied, to Stevenson's delight, "He is all of us."

the restless nobleman. There is a dawning of philosophy in Fleetwood too, and though in the end he fails to metamorphose from false romance into the true balance of philosophy, it is clear that the urge is alive in this period and will make its way to fruition—perhaps, one gathers, sooner in the life-disciplined minds of the lower classes than in the undisciplined hearts of the aristocracy. There is a relationship between Fleetwood and Woodseer that approaches the symbolic in this novel: even the juxtaposition of names suggests that they are in some sense aspects of the same being, man self-damned by the riot of his own energies and man self-integrated by his vision, a kind of seer-vision which for Meredith is always included in the overriding metaphor of "reading" that we have noticed in his novels.

Reading this story is the job of the novelist-editor who has in front of him the documents that attest to the story's existence. This reading-writing of the novel, the present ongoing crucial experience of choosing detail, examining testimony, reflecting upon event, the whole handling of story, is the third time of the novel and the most crucial one for this study. The question of the handling of story is more troublesome, is put more openly and aggressively to the reader here than ever before in Meredith; the actions in the subplot invade all aspects of the novel so that here it will be impossible to confine a discussion of it to a separate section of the chapter. The effort to grasp and shape the story (and the conflicting motives that exist to power that effort) is the action most vividly present, an action even more carefully dramatized than those of the characters in the story. For the main activity studied in the novel is reading in its broadest sense. In a way the personality the reader feels most strongly here is himself as he is shown struggling with the two narrators to make the story come together. The Dame from whose hands the story descends, the romance narrator, has no wish to have the story "read"; she would rather have it told, acted, so that there may be demonstrated "the melancholy, the

216

pathos of it, the heart of all England stirred by it . . . and the panting excitement it was to every listener" *(p. 510)*. Like the philosopher in *Sandra Belloni* the Dame is pictured jostling the Novelist's elbow frequently, and three or four times breaking in to narrate a small portion of the novel in her way. But the difference is more important than the similarity here. In the early novel philosophy sought control of the narrative in order to introduce thoughtfulness, introspection, reflection. In this final novel the Novelist is himself the philosopher; philosophy has won control and the results of "reading" are everywhere, in long passages of analysis of motive, in drastic parings or even eliminations of the major action scenes in favor of letter-narration or other refractions. The hand at his elbow pleads not for thought but for more action, not for analysis but for more receptivity to mystery, not for clearer understanding but for exhilaration. Here as in *Sandra Belloni* the two narrators play to several audiences of readers assumed to favor one or the other kind of narration, and the fictional reader of the novel is obliged to shift between the several kinds of response laid out for him and somehow assimilate in himself what is true in each response. But it is not so simple a matter for Meredith to establish the civilized reader's primary identification with the philosophic figure in this subplot. For Dame Gossip attains an almost irreversible ascendancy in narrating the first thirty pages of the novel, which are some of the most sprightly and intellectually entertaining pages in all Meredith. Moreover, her strictures against the weighing, measuring, and categorizing of life in which philosophers engage, and her distaste for their distance, come right from the heart of Meredith's own doubts about the risks of philosophy, and so she cannot be expunged from the narrative as her minority-voice counterpart in *Sandra Belloni* was. In the battle between romance and the philosophic novel that takes place in the subplot of *The Amazing Marriage*, it is in fact the Novelist who bows out five pages before the end, leaving the Dame to conclude triumphantly upon the very

217

contention that the philosopher—and the Novelist—must fight against for his very life: "My story . . . has been sacrificed in the vain effort to render events as consequent to your understanding as a piece of logic, through an exposure of character! Character must ever be a mystery, only to be explained in some degree by conduct" *(p. 511)*. Meredith's attempt to combat or modify that statement in the name of "a growing activity of the head" through a struggle to control a narrative that treats of many mysterious characters is the third and perhaps most interesting of the stories in this novel, taking up much of the "felt time" of *The Amazing Marriage*.

Lionel Stevenson has compared *The Amazing Marriage* to *The Tempest* for its "rich, sunset glow," calling it Meredith's "tenderest, his least worldly, his most poetic novel" *(p. 332)*. This seems to me a very "rose-pink" view indeed of a novel whose central plot offers one character blowing his brains out with a pistol, another done to death by the gunpowder explosion of half his estate, another permanently scarred on her face by her veil catching fire, another falling halfway down a mountainside, not to mention a bloody prizefight, an encounter with a rabid dog, one kidnapping of a pregnant woman, several private duels, one pitched battle of lower and upper classes in the streets of London, and the First Carlist War. Like the "dazzling intellectuality" of that other unworldly novel, *The Egoist*, the "tenderness" of this one results from Meredith's attempt to confront and humanize a world of extreme violence and chaos both inside and outside the head. All the explosions of the story along the way from Britain to Austria and Spain and back again are carefully linked to the lusts for freedom, power, and pleasure, the fear of love and commitment, the idolization of "fate" and "fortune" that have wrecked and weakened the foundations of mind. Meredith's way of encompassing this destruction and learning from it is once again to put at the service of his Modern Novelist a precise and complex prose style and an elliptical approach to dramatization that distances and organizes the violence while recognizing its presence—philosophy gripped hard to prevent disintegration while the mind's eye fastens on the awe-ful facts of reality. Nate, for instance, the first appearance of Gower Woodseer, the philosopher-tramp, in a passage strongly reminiscent of the opening of *One of Our Conquerors*, a deliberate piece of stylization whose complex rhythm and mosaic of images calls attention to the uses of language and the movement of mind in a way that controls, yet leaves basically uncontradicted, the violence stalking the novel's world:

> Three parts down a swift decline of shattered slate, where travelling stones loosened from rows of scree hurl away at a bound after one roll over, there sat a youth dusty and torn, nursing a bruised leg, not in the easiest of postures, on a sharp tooth of rock, that might at any moment have broken from the slanting slab at the end of which it formed a stump, and added him a second time to the general crumble of the mountain. He had done a portion of the descent in excellent imitation of the detached fragments, and had parted company with his alpenstock and plaid; preserving his hat and his knapsack. He was alone, disabled, and cheerful; in doubt of the arrival of succour before he could trust his left leg to do him further service unaided; but it was morning still, the sun was hot, the air was cool; just the tempering opposition to render existence pleasant as a piece of vegetation, especially when there has been a question of your ceasing to exist; and the view was of a sustaining sublimity of desolateness. . . . He would have enjoyed the scene unremittingly, like the philosopher he pretended to be, in a disdain of civilization and the ambitions of men, had not a contest with earth been forced on him from time to time to keep the heel of his right foot, dug in shallow shale, fixed and supporting. As long as it held he was happy and maintained the attitude of a guitar-player, thrumming the calf of the useless leg to accompany tuneful thoughts, but the inevitable lapse and slide of the foot recurred, and the philosopher was exhibited as an infant learning to crawl. The seat, moreover, not having been fashioned for him or for any soft purpose, resisted

219

his pressure and became a thing of violence, that required to be humiliatingly coaxed. . . . he lay back at his length and with his hat over his eyes consented to see nothing for the sake of comfort. Thus he was perfectly rational, though when others beheld him he appeared the insanest of mortals. *(Pp. 55-56)*

Really, the control exercised by the philosophic temperament in the face of possible imminent death seems a fine thing, like the Novelist's control over language in the treatment of what could have been a very pathetic scene full of "noisy enormity." But it has its limitations. If one is an airy enough philosopher—which is probably why he missed his footing in the first place—other people will simply have to endanger themselves rescuing him. As for his being of service to anyone else, his fastidious disdain for civilization renders him useless to it. Rescued from his mountain perch by Carinthia Kirby and her brother, Gower wishes to go to her aid after she has made her mysterious marriage with the Earl of Fleetwood and been abandoned by him; but he needs to borrow money from his father to do it, and on the way he muses shamefacedly: "Without [the money] he would have been useless in this case of need. The philosopher could starve with equanimity, and be the stronger. But one had, it seemed here clearly, to put on harness and trudge alone a line, if the unhappy were to have one's help." The Novelist adds: "Gradual experiences of his business among his fellows were teaching an exercised mind to learn in regions where minds unexercised were doctorial giants beside it" *(p. 205).*[2]

Much of this novel's "tenderness" is in its carefully modulated support of the philosophic attitude slowly brought down from its eminence and made to take an active

[2] "When will you understand," Gower's Nonconformist father harasses him earlier, "that this 'philosophy' is only the passive of a religious faith? It seems to suit you gentlemen of the road while you are young. Work among the Whitechapel poor. It would be a way for discovering the shallows of your 'philosophy' earlier" (p. 189).

role in the helping of "the unhappy." In this sense Gower is the Modern Novelist's hero, and he fights for the space to treat Gower thoroughly against the Dame, whose hero is whoever stirs up the most action. When in the second half of the novel Fleetwood—Dame Gossip's hero—begins rethinking his past actions, the Modern Novelist enters his consciousness too, and the Dame's impatience with the Modern Novelist's manner of presenting her hero points up the conflict in the subplot. Fleetwood is not "a person of no importance," as Woodseer is to the Dame; he is her hero, her property; and her anxiety to free him from the Modern Novelist's analytic presentation, to restore to him that dark mysteriousness of character out of which his most out-rageous actions come, parallels the anxiety in Fleetwood's own soul as he comes closer and closer to knowing himself.

That is why the treaty or convention between the two narrator-characters, Dame and the Novelist, has so much symbolic importance. In Meredith's view the impulses of romance and novel, action and analysis, mystery and understanding that these subplot characters represent ought not to be at war. Nor ought they to be at peace, exactly. Philosophy seems to say that in an integrated man (or writer, or reader) these impulses are united in a sort of dynamic interservice which includes a mutual probing for weak spots, a mutual pruning of excess ambitions, a tense and fruitful rivalry. The novel starts out peacefully enough in this convention, where the Novelist, speaking in the title of chapter 1, "Enter Dame Gossip as Chorus," hands to the Dame the task of narrating the old tale of the elopement and marriage of Countess Fanny and Captain Kirby. If after that calm interaction the novel breaks up into a bat-tlefield marked by the Dame's frequent attempts to "breach the Convention" or "abrogate the treaty," it is because in all fidelity to truth a story that contains so many violent people and so much internal and external conflict cannot be, perhaps ought not to be, left completely to the mercy of a distant ironic editorial voice, however shrewd, how-ever tender.

For now it is important to note that Meredith is picturing in this last novel, begun a decade after the Crimean War and published a few years before the Boer War, a world of "picturesque" violence where wars of one sort or another are always available if everyday life—in its symbolic context, marriage—is too oppressive. A Little Englander in most respects, Meredith was also a war correspondent in the 1848 Italian campaigns and an admirer of the liberal revolt everywhere, but all his life he maintained an equivocal love-hate relationship with the act of war itself. This equivocation holds both for the option of Carlist heroics open to the characters and for the act of war itself in the novel's climactic scene. Chillon, Carinthia, and Fleetwood meet to debate Carinthia's leaving for Spain to aid the Carlist cause, and meet, according to the Novelist's arrangement, in the gun-crammed workroom of the Counts Levellier, the building that striking workmen are later to blow up with its own products. The equivocal reverie is mainly Fleetwood's, with an assist from an analytic narrator who would scorn men unaware of the need for defensive war but does not quite know what to think of "men's bad old game" outside the attack situation:

> Contempt of military weapons and ridicule of the art of war were common in those days among a people beginning to sit with habitual snugness at the festive board provided for them by the valour of their fathers. Fleetwood had not been on the side of the banqueting citizens, though his country's journals and her feasted popular wits made a powerful current to whelm opposition. But the appearance of the woman, his wife, here, her head surrounded by destructive engines in the form of trophy, and the knowledge that this woman bearing his name designed to be out at the heels of a foreign army or tagrag of uniformed rascals, inspired him to reprobate men's bad old game as heartily as good sense does in the abstract, and as derisively as it is the way with comfortable islanders before the midnight trumpet-notes of panic have tumbled them to their legs. *(Pp. 455-56)*

Good sense inspires men to reject war, but that attitude may be abstract philosophy. In the concrete we may be forced to war. In the concrete, perhaps, we must put our hand to it, distasteful, nonsensical as it is. The Novelist is not sure. War is notoriously a bad teacher, as satire is. Treaties and conventions are proper to the comic look upon life. The difficulty remains unresolved; comedy, as everyone points out, is of Dionysiac and Bacchic origin, and Meredith wrote his civilized comedies for civilized readers in exactly that spirit. "He understands one important thing," says V. S. Pritchett of Meredith, "militancy and vigilance are the essence of comedy."[3] What is peculiar to Meredith, and to his Modern Novelist here, is not their aversion to violence as a fact of life but their refusal to use it as a tool of comic art. What he wishes to avoid is neither the reality of violence nor the examination of violence nor, entirely, the uses of violence but rather the depiction of violent action in fiction in ways that surrender to the human being's wish to be carried along by, rather than to carry, his consciousness. The trouble with violent clashes and social struggle, Meredith implies in the prelude to *The Egoist*, is not that their presence offends comic reality, but that noncomic writers, both realists and romantics, use only the outer skin of action—behavior, event—to present convincing impressions of reality and shirk the much harder task of presenting the core of action, which is psychology, the movement of mind.

For the Dame, of course, there is no difficulty. She likes war, revels in the romantic possibilities of "men's bad old game"; indeed, war needs romance to exist at all, the romance of "the cause of the queen" *(p. 452)* or of "her brother's military name" *(p. 476)*. She likes character in action; indeed she tends to think that character exists only in action. She asserts that action is the proper and only province of the writer partly because she thinks the public

[3] *George Meredith and English Comedy* (London: Chatto and Windus, 1970), p. 28.

likes it that way. But she thinks that the public is in fact wiser than anatomical novelists, because she feels, and they recognize, that "character must ever be a mystery." The Modern Novelist disagrees vehemently, and his response to the Dame's cry for more reporting of the action, the scenes, the events of the story, is to pare from his presentation several of the most important dramatic actions of the story. The outer skin of action that holds a narrative into a shape has been almost entirely withdrawn, especially at the beginning of the story of Fleetwood and Carinthia, where it would seem most important. As we move to examine the marriage, we meet increasingly the dilemma that Meredith has prepared for us: the narrator-gossip who wants to tell us what happened is not fully credible and is demonstrably uninterested in exactness, and the narrator-philosopher who is exact, penetrating, candid, and whom we do believe, does not care to tell us in so many words what happened. In fact, the Modern Novelist appears to believe that event, not character, is the mystery. For him, it almost seems, there are no events, only witnesses, and not even the deepest penetration of the witness, nor of a combination of witnesses, will ever reach all the way through character to the event. If the covenant between the Dame and the Novelist contained some compromise about her accepting his character "anatomies" while he accepts the need to dramatize the major events of the plot, then he is the culprit here, as he always intended to be: "An extinguisher descends on her, giving her the likeness of one under condemnation of the Most Holy Inquisition, in the ranks of an *auto da fe*: and singularly resembling that victim at the first sharp bite of the flames she will be when she hears the version of her story" *(p. 33)*. The Modern Novelist's weapon is not, like the Dame's, the heated, garrulous "irruption," but the "extinguisher," his perverse, principled, practically unforgivable silence about some major actions on the Dame's battlefield.

I. "The Amazing Baby"

In a long literary career of constructing plots with hidden scenes, undramatized crucial actions, "kiosks . . . which his people reach by their own impetus, and from which they emerge with altered aspect,"[4] Meredith surpassed himself in *The Amazing Marriage* by building and ruining the central relationship in the plot entirely on a hidden episode and its refractions. Critics objected, and still do. Lionel Stevenson reports sadly: "Some episodes of the story were melodramatic to the verge of fantasy. The birth of Carinthia's child was so unexplained that a wit said the title ought to be The Amazing Baby. . . . Meredith must have realized his mishandling . . . too late, for a copy of the book is in existence in which he has written additional paragraphs to suggest explanations" *(p. 321)*. The "additional paragraphs" (actually phrases inserted in four already quite suggestive passages, as Judith Sage's examination of the manuscripts makes clear)[5] were indeed added by Meredith in a revision of the fourth edition in 1896, now the standard text. But the move probably won him no plaudits from such readers as the anonymous reviewer in the *Pall Mall Gazette* (23 December 1895, rpt. *Critical Heritage, p. 442*), who recalled "to the best of our knowledge . . . the erring earl parted from his bride at the coach wheel on the wedding day," and put the birth down as "a deeply interesting case of spontaneous generation." More recently, Barbara Hardy has suggested tartly that "this instance of Meredith's obscurity seems to be an excellent instance

---

[4] E. M. Forster, *Aspects of the Novel* (New York: Harcourt, Brace and World, Inc., 1927), p. 90.

[5] Judith Sage ("The Making of Meredith's *The Amazing Marriage*," Ph.D. diss., Ohio State Univ., 1967) has explored two fragments and two editions of the novel to compare Meredith's early and late treatments of certain scenes, and I rely on long quoted sections of these manuscripts from her work for observations on Meredith's changes in the text of the novel.

of inattentiveness on the part of his readers."[6] Thus readers continue to disagree with each other over the effect of a commonplace in a Meredithian plot—the nondramatization of important actions—which was perhaps best described by Percy Lubbock in his review in 1911: "In his last three novels . . . the centre is found in a particular situation, the problem being to reason back from the facts, the objectively stated facts, to their inner history. Artistically speaking, [this method] is open to the destructive objection that the density of events is governed by no definite design. Vital aspects of the story become huddled and foreshortened" *(rpt. Critical Heritage, p. 510).*

This is the old argument about design, and Meredith's answer, like Fielding's, is to claim that every incident, or lack of incident, is purposeful according to *his* design. The purpose it seems to me is quite simply to draw as powerfully as he can in the first half of the novel the attractive, restless, fatalistic mysteriousness of Fleetwood's character and behavior so that when he comes in the second half to dramatize the Earl's tense, reluctant, almost successful journey through his memories to self-discovery and self-responsibility the reader will share that sense of discovery. Talking about the vagueness of outline of Carinthia's character in the early chapters, Gillian Beer adds, "It is as though the Reader must undergo Fleetwood's estrangement from her" *(p. 171).*

To understand what an effort Fleetwood must make to discover, understand, and assimilate his past so that he can shape his future, and to understand why he failed in that effort, we must go back to that controversially eccentric dramatization of his wedding day. For it is that day and night, whose meaning he, the Novelist, and the reader must actively struggle to apprehend, that shapes the marriage, the story, and the novel. The wedding day is dramatized from Fleetwood's point of view and contains two

[6] *"Lord Ormont and His Aminta* and *The Amazing Marriage,"* in *Meredith Now,* p. 308.

major elements, the wedding itself and the prizefight on the nearby meadow that Fleetwood gave "his word" to attend. The wedding is narrated in a few brief sentences; the fight is dramatized at length, and the structure of this narration clearly parallels Fleetwood's own willed preoccupations. But in taking his young bride to watch a gloves-off brutal fistfight on her wedding morning Fleetwood has more in mind than simply wiping out his marriage, more in mind even than simple arrogance and cruelty, although the onlookers at the fight have enough sense to remark on this aspect of the Earl's behavior. He drives to the meadow at a breakneck pace hoping to feel the thrill of Carinthia's fear. She disappoints him, as it happens, being, as he well knew, brave beyond any of the civilized women he has courted. But the true sensual thrill he has anticipated is that of sitting beside the bride he owns while his own fighter, Kit Ines, beats the challenger, a man of the people, into a bloody pulp. Exposed to that scene, Carinthia does not disappoint him; she agonizes for the fighters through sympathy with Ines's girl friend Madge, and her agony is Fleetwood's reward, the sadistic consummation of his marriage, much more a rape than an act of love:

> Her infant logic stumbled on for a reason while she repressed the torture the scene was becoming, as though a reason could be found by her submissive observation of it. And she was right in believing that a reason for the scene must or should exist. . . . Her one consolation was in squeezing the hand of the girl [Madge] from time to time.
>
> Not stealthily done, it was not objected to by the husband whose eye was on all. . . . the couple of them had . . . the tone of the women who can be screwed to witness a spill of blood, peculiarly catching to hear;—a tone of every string in them snapped except the silver string. Catching to hear? It is worth a stretching of them on the rack to hear that low buzz-hum of their inner breast. . . . By heaven! we have them at their best when they sing that note. *(P. 171)*

Fleetwood, of course, is thinking sensually, not symbolically. It is the Modern Novelist who invites the reader to consider the chapter following the prizefight "a shadow contest close on the foregoing."[7] The contest here is one of wills and glances, as Carinthia and Madge are deposited at a nearby inn while Fleetwood and Ines prepare to leave for a ball some hours' ride away. In a tingling, wordless farewell scene Carinthia expects her husband's first embrace, and Fleetwood, his senses reeling with the tension of "romantic devilry" and fear of entanglement, abandons her instead. But he glances up at her window as he rides off, and the ballroom at Canleys is not too far to ride back from, he calculates. Despite the separation that ends the chapter, Meredith has seen in this shadow contest the same motivation as in the first. Fleetwood planned the same rape. But this time Carinthia defeated him in a way he had never imagined when the two combatants, strangers to each other but not to the reader, found themselves married.

This is an oddly matched couple. The twenty-year-old Carinthia is notable for three striking qualities: a sort of ferocious spontaneity that makes her at once vulnerable to and a danger to the civilized; a disconcerting propensity

[7] Another shadow of this contest, of course, is the fight between the two narrators. The fight is between the Earl's man, the hard-drinking quick-acting Kit Ines, and the popular champion, "steady Benny" Todds. Kit is a boxer of "science," light on his feet, new to the game, flawed by pride and other modern vices; steady Benny has no science, no technique, but he has wind, bulk, and above all staying power. He is defeated, this time: "vanquisher and vanquished shook hands, engaged in a parting rally of good-humoured banter. . . . They drink of different cups to-day. Both will drink of one cup in the day to come. But the day went too clearly to crown the light and the tight and the right man of the two, for moralizing to wag its tail at the end. Oldsters and youngsters agreed to that. Science had done it: happy the backers of Science! Not one of them alluded to the philosophical 'hundred years hence,'" (pp. 173-74). The whole rhetoric of this novel, as we shall see, warns of the staying power of romance despite some superior and valuable qualities in the modern novel with its scientific analysis of character.

228

for brisk and straightforward action that veils but does not conceal an enormous capacity to dream and idealize; and an equally large capacity to suffer and bear suffering. It is this first quality that makes everyone, including her brother and protector Chillon, just a little too anxious to see her settled down into a marriage, however amazing. It is this second quality that accounts for her idealizing her brother and the mysterious lover of mountains who amazingly asks for her hand at their first formal meeting, that Fleetwood who, married to her, would no longer be a rival for her idolized Chillon's Henrietta. It is the third quality, that audible hum of suffering borne in silence that started at the double death of her parents and never ceases to sound all through the novel, which causes others to idealize *her*—some as a "haggard Venus"—with predictably ugly results for the idolized.

Fleetwood is also young, we should not forget, in his twenties, wealthy, in control of his wealth since his teens, and in control of the entourage that his wealth brings him. His central qualities are also three: a malignant restlessness deriving from his secret and voluptuous contempt for everything around him; a tendency to endless circular rational and "philosophic" discourse which veils, but does not conceal, his own great longing to worship and idealize; and a strange and ultimately fatal habit of externalizing and worshiping the warring "selves" of his character, a habit that is most strikingly symbolized in his notoriously slavish adherence to that unaccountable deity, his word. His will-to-contempt and his will-to-idealize hold alternate, rootless supremacy, and his fidelity to his word, given in whatever mood, makes him an absolutely dangerous man, particularly to women, who are the handiest, most sanctioned objects of idealization and who are easily tempted, forced, or maneuvered in their ignorance into those falls from grace that occasion a relieved and sensuous contempt in the breast of the "civilized male."

Married, these two are strangers to each other, but they are only too familiar with their idealized images of hus-

229

band and wife. Their task is to discard these abstract images and penetrate through to the real persons they have married, to know each other. The world, thinking that Fleetwood had abandoned Carinthia after the prize-fight that followed the marriage, is properly shocked nine months later. They had known each other. The question that the second half of the novel explores, the question that Fleetwood must answer is, What was it they knew?

Fleetwood, in the months between the marriage and the birth, behaves as though what he knows of her and himself is no more than that he went to a woman in the dead of night and consummated an act of "romantic devilry," one in a long line of such acts. The memory that clamors for attention after the birth of the child is that Carinthia received him not as a rake but as a husband:

> On the borders between maidenly and wifely, she, a thing of flesh like other daughters of earth, had impressed her sceptical lord, inclining to contempt of her and detestation of his bargain, as a flitting hue, aethereal, a transfiguration of earthliness in the core of the earthly furnace. And how?—but that it must have been the naked shining forth of her character, startled to show itself:—"It is my husband":—it must have been love. The love that they versify and strum on guitars, and go crazy over, and end by roaring at as the delusion; this common bloom of the ripeness of a season; this would never have utterly captured a sceptic, to vanquish him in his mastery, snare him in her surrender. It must have been the veritable passion: a flame kept alive by vestral ministrants in the yew-wood of the forest of Old Romance. . . . Love had eyes, love had a voice that night. *(P. 222)*

There, clearly, is the heart of the matter. Frequenter of the "jolly Parisian and Viennese bacchanals" *(p. 124)*, wor-shiper of innocence in the best tradition of the English gentleman, temperamentally "like the wandering spark in burnt paper, of which you cannot say whether is it chasing or being chased" *(p. 70)*, Fleetwood has every reason to take a night of "romantic devilry" in his stride, to add the

230

marriage bed to the round of gambling hall, prizefight meadow, yachting trip, and hiking trip that he follows with such furious aimlessness. But he does not. After this wedding night encounter he does have an aim, one that even the deadliest fear he knows, the fear of seeming ridiculous, will not serve to turn him from, the aim not to see his wife, not to speak with her or touch her in any way—above all, not to be alone with her. The gossip and ridicule that follows him relentlessly after his marriage is no one's fault but his own, brought on by his amazing behavior. Every inch of his suavity up to the very edge of the mask has deserted Fleetwood: instead of amicably arranging a quiet separation he bolts from his bride, leaving her exposed and solitary in the middle of the countryside; instead of paying Carinthia's price to leave Whitechapel, a simple meeting, Fleetwood has her kidnapped away from London in a desperate, clumsy move certain to bring ridicule upon himself; instead of accepting the accidental meeting the fates provided in Vauxhall Gardens he panics and starts a brawl, making the incident sweet wine to the thirst of London gossip: "Have you seen the kick and tug at the straps of the mettled pony in stables that betrays the mishandling of him by his groom? Something so did Fleetwood plunge and dart to be free of her, and his desperate soul cried out on her sticking to him like a plaster!" *(P. 241)*

What does he dread so? What is he fleeing? The birth of his child puts before Fleetwood in the most concrete and inescapable way the memory he and the narrators have been able to touch only in brief, painful allusions dipped in mystery, abstraction, and metaphors of Old Romance, the memory of the night that he and Carinthia made their child, made their love, made their marriage, lived as husband and wife. He went to enjoy a rape and stayed to learn from his raw mountain bride, his unashamed wifelover, a natural sexuality he cannot reconcile with his previous experience, with the artful coyness of a Henrietta or the gross mindless comforts of the jolly bacchanals. That experience is a memory, that night is a fact that can-

231

not co-exist with his romantic devil. One or the other must be destroyed.

Very slowly during the last third of the novel Fleetwood begins to drop his guard over the memory of that night, and the Novelist begins to penetrate and explore and understand the marriage just a few steps ahead of Fleetwood himself. But outside circumstances move more quickly than internal knowledge. Fleetwood's obstinate insistence on keeping some final part of himself free from the increasingly genuine light of his "penitential" reflections, plus Carinthia's own psychic flaw, the defensive transferral of her love from husband to child and then to her brother, account more than outside circumstances for the failure of the reconciliation that Fleetwood tries to make.

So the amazing marriage fails. But it is crucial to the pathos of the failure, it seems to me, to realize that there *was* a marriage, a consummation, a treasure achieved, briefly. The union of Carinthia and Fleetwood was not simply a perversion thankfully dissolved, or even simply an opportunity unfortunately missed, but a reality achieved and then destroyed, literally blasted, by those habits of mind, sentimentalism and egoism, with which man wars against reality. If we ask why Meredith lets the accomplishment of marriage take place in narrative darkness, while the destruction, the failure of the marriage, takes place in the full daylight of the interior monologue, we must find the answers in Meredith's habitual submersion of certain scenes in the swirl of the participants' reflections. If we never saw Willoughby's courtship of Clara, it is because by the time we meet Clara's mind at its full power to comprehend, to dramatize to itself those early scenes, the scenes themselves and the girl she was then and the man he seemed to be have become lost, invisible to her. If we never see Victor's mad proposal to Nataly, it is because that scene, in its idealized character as an explosion of ungovernable feeling, has become so crucial a prop to the couple's position and self-respect that it too has become lost, invisible except in its ideal character. If we do not see the marriage of Carinthia and Fleetwood consummated, it is because Fleetwood, not the Novelist, is fighting down the narration of the scene, the remembrance of it. Because she can dramatize it, Carinthia retains her love for a time in the memory of the reality of his. But this is Fleetwood's story, not Carinthia's; the story is of his efforts to avoid, abort, distort the scene. That he succeeds is his tragedy; that the reader is made to share Fleetwood's own ignorance of the most important act of his life is a typically aggressive Meredithian decision of composition, in the Jamesian sense, that is quite in harmony with the dramatic possibilities of the theme of the novel.

II. The Amazing Marriage

The theme, we recall, is the stormy relationship between romance and novel, which for Meredith is a reflection of the tension in the minds of men and women between action-producing abstractions and concrete, if paralytically complex, reality, between action and its wellspring, the movement of mind. That this tension is, or ought to be, expressive of a wholeness and not of a duality is one of Meredith's major tenets in art and in life. Thus all characters, all opposite qualities naturally seek marriage in Meredith: the act has universal symbolic significance, and his attempt throughout his fiction to hunt down and expose false marriage and to recognize and support true marriage parallels his affirmation of true romance, true realism, and the true philosophy that is the integration or marriage of all truths in nature. That is why the truly amazing marriage in this novel is not Carinthia and Fleetwood's but that of Dame Gossip and the Modern Novelist, a marriage to be made in the mind of the reader.

To assist him in the making of this marriage the reader has before him the instructive failures of Fleetwood and of Carinthia to unite their active and reflective energies, their sense of mystery and their power of understanding, in one self. He also has what looks like the failure of the author

233

to achieve that unity, since the Dame and the Modern Novelist, romance and philosophical analysis, remain separate characterized narrators from first to last. But the truth is that the whole dynamic of the subplot implies a fruitful if stormy intimacy between the male and female narrators that, if not marriage, is at least the closest thing to it, the closest thing to a real unity-in-diversity that Meredith could dramatize.

For all their diversity, it is not difficult to see what attracted this quarreling pair to tell this story together. The Dame, after all, can toss off a testy philosophical insight with the best of them: "Women should walk in armour as if they were born to it; for these cold sneerers will never waste their darts on cuirasses" *(p. 3)*, she remarks of the man anxious to comfort himself with the follies of women. Her problem is that instead of triggering thought or reflection, the insights she has evaporate in excess feeling: "Only to think of (the Countess of Cresset), I could sometimes drop into a chair for a good cry. And of him too! and their daughter Carinthia Jane was the pair of them, as to that, and so was Chillon John, the son!" *(pp. 3-4)*. The Modern Novelist is not totally immune to the Dame's contention that detailed analysis is a dangerous game:

> Things were so: narrate them, and let readers do their reflections for themselves, she says, denouncing our conscientious method as the direct road downward to the dreadful modern appeal to the senses and assault on them for testimony to the veracity of everything described; to the extent that, at the mention of a vile smell, it shall be blown into the reader's nostrils, and corking pins attack the comfortable seat of him simultaneously with a development of surprises. "Thither your conscientiousness leads." *(P. 367)*

His problem is that even after he has thus acknowledged a truth in her argument, he cannot stop analyzing it: "It is not perfectly visible. And she would gain information on the singular nature of the young of the male sex in listening to the wrangle between Lord Fleetwood and Gower Wood-seer. . . ." *(P. 367.)*

The two narrators need each other for the true exercise of their arts: she it is who has the story, the original documents, but he controls the "reading." In this day of the supremacy of the book over the tale-spinning in inns and gossip at firesides that the Dame remembers in the "old coaching days" *(p. 24)*, he brings her her audience: the Dame may narrate the first three chapters, but it is the stage-managing Novelist who made it all possible: "Chapter One. Enter Dame Gossip as Chorus" *(p. 1)*.

The Dame and the Novelist narrate the novel under treaty—they are, let us say, engaged to each other. The alliance is amazing, though, for the Modern Novelist is a product of schoolrooms and a man of "science," whereas Dame Gossip is a woman of the people, fresh from the country, scornful of your professional lecturers in the philosophy of art and your dryasdust anatomists and chemists of the human spirit. But she has the proverbial sneaking fondness for a lord, and while she may take time out to digress on the adventures of a peasant, Charles Dump, it is only as a witness to the events of the great, a "semaphore post" *(p. 26)*, that she will admit him to her art:

> The man is no more attractive to me than a lump of clay. How could he be? But supposing I took up the lump and told you that there where I found it, *that lump of clay had been rolled over and flung off by the left wheel of the prophet's Chariot of Fire before it mounted aloft and disappeared in the heavens above!*—you would examine it and cherish it and have the scene present with you, you may be sure; and magnificent descriptions would not be one-half so persuasive. And that is what we call, in my profession, Art, if you please. *(P. 28, the Dame's italics)*

Charles Dump was a witness to and a minor participant in the elopement of Countess Fanny and the Old Buccaneer; he is to them rather what Gower Woodseer is to Fleetwood and Carinthia, and the Modern Novelist, grousing that "the Dame will have him only as an index-post" *(p. 209)*, makes major use of Woodseer in the narration in a way that dramatizes clearly his own definition of art quoted at the beginning of the chapter:

> Her one idea of animation is to have her *dramatis personae* in violent motion, always the biggest foremost; and, indeed, that is the way to make them credible, for the wind they raise and the succession of collisions. The fault of the method is, that they do not instruct; so the breath is out of them before they are put aside; for the uninstructive are the humanly deficient. . . . The deuteragonist or secondary person can at times tell us more of them than circumstances at Furious heat will help them to reveal.
>
> *(P. 209)*

Thus the Modern Novelist defines his art to a great extent by the uses he makes of the characters around the main character, their attitudes toward the main character, their connections and parallels with him. It is a clear invitation to the reader to read Fleetwood by the light of Woodseer's progress toward philosophy.

The give-and-take between the Dame and the Modern Novelist is thus the give-and-take between circumstances at furious heat and the "revealings" that only a close reading of character against character will give, between the "credibility" that Meredith seems to admit is triggered in the "blood" of readers and the "instructive" that is triggered in the mind. This give-and-take is expressed in the subplot in two different ways. After her long opening narration of the adventures of Carinthia's parents, the Dame mostly makes her presence known by "thumps for attention" *(p. 469)* whose effect is to pull the Modern Novelist slightly away from his tendency to discourse at length on the inner mechanics of mind and move him toward the describing of actual events and their reception. At such thumps the Novelist may elbow her back with an ironic quotation of the sort of language he expects from her and wants to spare the reader: "The Dame is at her thumps for attention to be called to 'the strangeness of it,' that a poor, small, sparse village, hardly above a hamlet, on the most unproductive of the Kentish heights, part of the old forest land, should at this period become 'the cynosure of a city beautifully named by the poet Great Augusta, and truly indeed the world's metropolis' " *(p. 469)*. But call attention to the event he does, in his own sardonic, metaphorically exact way:

> The young nobleman of the millions was watched; the town spyglass had him in its orbit. Tales of the ancestral Fleetwoods ran beside rumours of a Papist priest at the bedside of the Foredoomed to Error's dying mother. . . . So thereupon, with the whirr of a covey on wing before the fowler, our crested three of immemorial antiquity and a presumptive immortality, the Ladies Endor, Eldritch, and Cowry, shot up again, hooting across the dormant chief city Old England's fell word of the scarlet shimmer above the nether pit-flames, Rome. *(Pp. 469-70)*

There are, however, three times when, to the annoyed ejaculations of the Modern Novelist, Dame Gossip takes over the narration summarily and completely. The first time she takes advantage of the Modern Novelist's reportage of Carinthia's romantic presentiment on entering England: "It is a dark land." The second time the Modern Novelist tries to pacify the Dame by narrating her event, the Londoner's reception of the fight in Vauxhall Gardens, in his own way, tries to outfox her by relegating one of her favorite stormy subjects, the lure of Rome for Fleetwood, to a mere terse report that Fleetwood had been seen with the Catholic Lord Feltre. He finds the story snatched from him: "We have Dame Gossip upon us." Thereafter, except for the burlesque episode of the Welsh Cavaliers and Fleetwood's Kentish drunkards which the Modern Novelist wisely invites Dame Gossip to make her own, the Modern Novelist is in control of the narrative, simply shifting technique to pacify the thumper, now and then, with good or bad grace, or quoting her documents and memories for short passages. The treaty seems back in force for the second half of the book, with both parties holding the compromise. For instance, having made brief but thorough mention of the London gossips' scarcely muted delight that "fate" had solved Chillon's last problem by arranging the explosion by death of the old curmudgeon Lord Levellier, the Modern Novelist gets in his own sardonic licks, but fairly, under the convention:

> Pitiful though it may seem for a miserly old lord to be blown up in his bed, it is necessarily a subject for congratulation if the life, or poor remnant of a life, sacrificed, was an impediment to our righteous wishes. But this is a theme for the Dame, who would full surely have committed another breach of the treaty, had there not been allusion to her sisterhood's view of the government of human affairs. *(P. 480)*

The third time the Dame takes over the story is to narrate its final pages. She does so because she is not satisfied with the Novelist's ending. He, concluding his examination of the epiphany of another "deuteragonist," Henrietta Kirby, chronicles her fall onto a burning oil lamp and subsequent intuition of her own weakness and her partial responsibility for Chillon's and Carinthia's dilemmas. He ends with a sonorous paragraph full of moral significance:

> Henrietta's prompt despatch to Croridge to fetch the babes, her journey out of a sick-room to stop Chillon's visit to London, proved her an awakened woman, well paid for the stain on her face, though the stain were lasting. Never had [Carinthia] loved Henrietta, never shown her so much love, as on the road to the deepening colours of the West. Her sisterly warmth surprised the woeful spotted beauty with a reflection that this martial Janey was after all a woman of feeling, one whom her husband, if he came to know it and the depth of it, the rich sound of it, would mourn in sackcloth to have lost. *(P. 507)*

Again, like the philosopher in *Sandra Belloni*, it was that one excitable metaphor that opened the door to his incurably and still charmingly loquacious enemy:

And he did, the Dame interposes for the final word, he mourned his loss of Carinthia Jane in sackcloth and ashes, notwithstanding that he had the world's affectionate condolences about him to comfort him, by reason of his ungovernable countess's misbehaviour once more, according to the report, in running away with a young officer to take part in a foreign insurrection; and when he was most the idol of his countrymen and countrywomen, which it was once his immoderate aim to be, he mourned her day and night, knowing her spotless, however wild a follower of her father's *Maxims for Men. (Pp. 507-08)*

The Modern Novelist ends his task with the cessation of mental change in his characters, the setting of attitudes. The Dame wants to follow the action to its end. The trouble is that with the Modern Novelist withdrawn the Dame is free to do her worst to the story, and she does, giving way to the flimsiest of conjectures and gossip about the behavior of Fleetwood after Carinthia's departure for Spain, until finally we do not know exactly what he did when he found his wife entirely departed and the dilemma of love and pride thus arbitrarily and "fatefully" resolved. "Monk of some sort he would be" *(p. 509)*, the Dame remarks quite truthfully, echoing Woodseer's earlier percipient observation. But whether Fleetwood returned to his estates, or joined a monastery, or created a false monastery and played at being Brother Russett (this last is appealing) is unclear. Carinthia went to Spain, returned with her brother, and married her dog-like Welsh squire after Fleetwood's death, but what were her deeds in Spain and her thoughts on second marriage we know better from our assessment of her character than from the thrilled enthusiasm of the Dame. Unchecked by caution, the Dame speeds to an ending of the subplot too, breathless in her denunciation of her fellow artist: "But the melancholy, the pathos of it, the heart of all England stirred by it, have been— and the panting excitement it was to every listener—sacrificed in the vain effort to render events as consequent to your understanding as a piece of logic through an exposure of character! Character must ever be a mystery," the Dame concludes on her favorite note,

> only to be explained in some degree by conduct; and that is very dependent upon accident: and unless we have a perpetual whipping of the tender part of the reader's mind, interest in invisible persons must needs flag. For it is an infant we address, and the story-teller whose art excites an infant to serious attention succeeds best; with English people assuredly, I rejoice to think, though I have to pray their patience here while that philosophy and exposure of character block the course along a road inviting to traffic of the most animated kind. *(P. 511)*

Recoiling from the Dame's assessment of him in the last paragraph of the novel, the fictional reader is drawn by the strongest personal motives to reject the Dame's central principle of art—character is not entirely a mystery, we irresistibly reply, and our interest in invisible persons depends exactly on how intimate with "character" in the broadest sense, which includes our own character, that philosophy and exposure has made us. Recoiling from the Dame of romance we are beckoned into identification with the Modern Novelist, who has both by his performance and by direct address given us the answer to her "endless ejaculations over the mystery of Life, the inscrutability of character,—in a plain world, in the midst of such readable people!" *(P. 209)*.

Conclusion

Readable people: here at the end of his career we are, I think, at the secret heart of Meredith's optimism as well as of his desperate, pugnacious, and tricky focus on the reader of and in his novels. His faith is that reality is, with effort, *readable*; what he wants to make of us all is *readers*, in the comprehensive, tough-souled sense in which he uses the word and construes the act of *reading*. His "readable people" are not only his characters, who can be read, but ideally his readers themselves, who are in a profounder sense read-able, able readers. And what enrages him beyond the limits of innkeeping politesse, or even sometimes beyond the limits of rhetoric where the Comic Spirit waits to smile at authors, is that we will not be made to *read*. To read is to put together those arbitrary and independently meaningless characters into words, to build those crowding perceptions into conceptions, to find for that lengthening line of meaningless acts in a person or society the grammar and syntax that will allow you to read those mysterious discontinuous units as character. For Meredith, reading is the name, not really the metaphor, for the primary human act of mind. When his Modern Novelist disdains Dame Gossip's "animation" as all act and no substance, all (one may say) fertilization and no incubation,[1] he is really condemning her art as all alphabet and no words, and her supporters as hurried leafers through bright picture books, not readers

[1] One may, that is, if one has in mind Meredith's opening to chapter 14: "Mention has been omitted or forgotten by the worthy Dame in her vagrant fowl's treatment of a story she cannot incubate, will not relinquish, and may ultimately addle. . . ."

241

at all. When he fancies himself spokesman for the future counterbalancing her nostalgic references to the past, when romance flashes living pictures before an audience sunk lovingly in "delicious dulness" *(p. 28)*, when he speaks of these "days of a growing activity of the head" *(p. 209)*, he is anticipating exactly that community of literacy called posterity which includes all men and whose name is reader.

There are numerous passages in Meredith that dramatize his conviction that to read, to think, to be human are forms of the same verb, names of the same reality. One of the most remarkable occurs in the important dialogue in *The Amazing Marriage* where Fleetwood is reluctantly revealing to Gower Woodseer his dawning recognition (or remembrance, rather) of the real quality of his wife—and of his deeds. The speaker, responding brusquely to Fleetwood's arrogant evasions of the truth, is the philosopher Gower Woodseer, and his speech, half-compliment, half-accusation, is exactly on target:

> "Why have me with you, then? I'm useless. But you read us all, see everything, and wait only for the mood to do the right. You read me, and I'm not open to everybody. You read the crux of a man like me in my novel position. You read my admiration of a beautiful woman and effort to keep honest. You read my downright preference of what most people would call poverty, and my enjoyment of good cookery and good company. You enlist among the crew below as one of our tempters. You find I come round to the thing I like best. Therefore, you have your liking for me; and that's why you turn to me again, after your natural infidelities. So much for me. You read this priceless lady quite as clearly. You choose to cloud her with your moods. She was at a disadvantage, arriving in a strange country, next to friendless; and each new incident bred of a luckless beginning—I could say more."
>
> Fleetwood nodded. "You are read without the words."
> *(Pp. 324-25)*

Eminently civilized, and a reader, Fleetwood is the hero of the novel. He is also the villain. First, because he allows

his contemptuous egoism and his abstract sentimental pos-
turing to interfere with his capacity to read character and
situation. Second, because he cannot act on his reading
until the mood strikes him. Here is the crisis peculiar to
Meredith. Latest in a long line of novelists who look for
the salvation of the world in the community of literacy, in
the equalization of posterity with reader, with all that reader implies, Meredith turns round to discover that his reader,
having withdrawn from act into reflection, manipulated
alphabet into sentence, shaped behavior into character,
cannot return into act again. The civilized reader seems
sometimes to like reading more than living; to act on life
in the light of its reading is not so easy a step. In fact, the
light of reading may freeze the reader into watchful contempt, as it did Fleetwood. Or it may pierce and dematerial-
ize the reader so that he ceases to have sufficient human
solidity from which to act, as it almost did with the quintessential reader in all Meredith, called (and from the
start, comically) philosopher, Gower Woodseer. Gower
has read nearly everything, on his own; he loves reading,
writing, and most of all reading his own writing. His
facility at reading in the Meredithian comprehensive sense
has made him independent of the earth, and as it has
helped him achieve general attitudes of great human value
—"his ardour for the life of the solitudes was unfeigned,
as was his calm overlooking of social distinctions"—so it
also tempts him to ruinous abstraction when he feels the
disturbing tug of a complex and powerfully human presence:

> Women are a cause of dreams, but they are dreaded
> enemies of his kind of dream, deadly enemies of the im-
> material dreamers; and should one of them be taken on
> board a vessel of the vapourish texture young Woodseer
> sailed in above the clouds lightly while he was in it alone,
> questions of past, future, and present, the three weights
> upon humanity, bear it down, and she must go, or the
> vessel sinks. And cast out of it, what was he? The asking
> exposed him to the steadiest wind the civilized world is

known to blow. From merely thinking upon one of the daughters of earth, he was made to feel his position in that world, though he refused to understand it, and assisted by two days of hard walking, he reduced Carinthia to an abstract enthusiasm, no very serious burden. His notebook sustained it easily. *(P. 73)*

What Gower wrote in his notebook and later read self-comfortingly ("he wrote her name . . . and some sentences, which he thought profound" [*p. 74*]) was his description of Carinthia as a "beautiful Gorgon . . . a haggard Venus," the description that "seized" Fleetwood in his sado-romantic soul, a reading productive of utmost human damage in its willful abstraction. It is this sort of reading that Meredith warns of in *Diana of the Crossways*:

> "So well do we know ourselves that we one and all determine to know a purer," says the heroine of my volume. Philosophy in fiction tells us, among various other matters, of the perils of this ultimate acquaintance with a flattering familiar in the "purer"—a person who more than ceases to be of use to us after his ideal shall have led men up from their flint and arrowhead caverns to inter-communicative daylight. For when the fictitious creature has performed that service of helping to civilize the world, it becomes the most dangerous of delusions, causing first the individual to despise the mass, and then to join the mass in crushing the individual. *(Pp. 19-20)*

It is maddeningly characteristic of Meredith, however, that when the reader has hacked his way through that complex sentence, that disturbing thought, that profound and subtle warning about the very act he, the reader, is performing; when the reader relaxes into that prepared attitude—watchful, thoughtful, keen-eyed for simple folly—he runs into the Meredithian undercut of his own philosophical method: "Wherewith, let us to our story, the froth being out of the bottle" *(p. 20)*.

Diana, of course, has only one narrative voice, and such undercuts can easily be ascribed to simple whimsy. Or they

244

may be ascribed to servility, Meredith saying cravenly to the "roast-beef reader" that he may forget or ignore what preceded, as the narrator of *The Egoist* does, opening the theory-laden prelude with the title, "A Chapter of which the last page only is of importance." Thackeray addressed the subscribing public similarly, "Come, children, let us shut up the box and the puppets." It is perfectly clear in all these cases, however, that the narrator has in fact attempted to create a fictional reader who knows that only false readers disdain or ignore the challenge of thought and personal reflection, the mystery of the precise apprehension of the fictiveness of fiction, which makes a very serious business, in the end, of reading. In the prelude of *Vanity Fair*, Thackeray includes himself among the "quacks" preying on man, and few novelists before or since have failed to worry about that particular possibility. Down in the hustle of Vanity Fair, in the fight for customers and the bustle of event, the excitement of feeling and the pull of story, of what happens next, of what goes on inside *this* booth, an author may very easily settle on romance as the quack-flaw in his makeup, and the romance-loving public as his nemesis. But the dragon is not so easily identified, let alone scotched, and Meredith, writing half a century later as the dream of universal literacy was beginning to assume strange and challenging shapes around the novelist, scents another danger in the kind of "purer familiar" authors have been presenting to the public. The most dangerous of these familiars, he sees, is not the character inside the story, but the one who controls the story, the narrator, who represents, in his comprehensive grasp, his necessarily arbitrary attitude toward the facts of the story, his godlike powers to condemn acts and even attitudes, a very flattering familiar indeed to the reader who has willingly become The Reader. There are two dangers in the use of this philosophical narrator, if he inclines to teach as well as delight. One, which Meredith sees from the start and, in his best moments admits whimsically, is narrative slowness, prosiness, he calls it. Meredith's excuse for stopping the action to highlight and explore the tableau is that, well handled, this method provides a lyric or poetic experience that is action of a vertical sort, as opposed to narrative's horizontal activity. Taking off on one of his favorite topics, the perniciousness of the love of mystery, Meredith's Novelist-narrator in *The Amazing Marriage* notes of men at large:

> Men uninstructed in analysis of motives arrive at this dangerous conclusion [of their inner mysteriousness], which spares their pride and caresses their indolence, while it flatters the sense of internal vastness, and invites to headlong intoxication. It allows them to think they are of such a compound, and must necessarily act in that manner. They are not taught at the schools or by the books of the honoured places in the libraries, to examine and see the simplicity of these mysteries, which it would be here and there a saving grace for them to see.
>
> *(Pp. 366-67)*

But a worse danger than simple prosiness is that danger noted in *Diana* and explored in *The Egoist, One of Our Conquerors*, and *The Amazing Marriage* in the persons of Willoughby Patterne, Colney Durance, and Lord Fleetwood that when fear of absorption or corruption drives one from Vanity Fair, from the center of the world, the resulting philosophic "purity" is all but certain to become contempt—first for the mass, then for the individual, then for the self.

The act of reading, specifically the act of reading fiction (which, Meredith wryly reports, occupies the dishonored places in the libraries) is for Meredith man's real school. That is where man learns to read the simplicity (here and there) of his own mystery. That is why the battle of the Dame and the Novelist for control of the story is vital to civilization itself. What is important about *The Amazing Marriage*, Meredith's final comment on the issue, is first that the battle, by its nature, cannot be won. The Modern Novelist has infinitely greater psychological subtlety, greater "science" than the Dame. The essentials of literate expression, the craggy graces of the printed page belong almost entirely to him, and on the frontiers of thought and analysis where the new stories are breaking he is supreme. But essentially the new stories are forms of the old, and the Dame controls the deepest impulses that produce story itself: memory ("We used to learn by heart the ballads and songs upon famous events in those old days when poetry was worshipped" [*p. 10*]), ideal feeling ("But supposing I took up the lump and told you that there where I found it, *that lump of clay had been rolled over and flung off the left wheel of the prophet's Chariot of Fire before it mounted aloft*" [*p. 28*]), and, paradoxically, a very solid appreciation of reality, or at least of a certain aspect or moment of reality ("And all the while the windows of the lecture-room are rattling, if not the whole fabric shaking, with exterior occurrences" [*p. 133*]). The Modern Novelist has the edge, but the Dame has the primitive energy that makes for staying power, and "we are so far in her hands that we have to keep her quiet" *(p. 367).*

The Modern Novelist, of course, can no more keep romance quiet than he can write clearly with half a hand or read truly with one eye. This final novel we are invited to read with two eyes, we have *in* it two eyes, two characterized narrators working in an uneasy but necessary partnership that requires the interpenetrating activity but the separate identity of romance and novel. Meredith is counting on his reader somehow to embrace both identities without giving way to the contempt for life that an extreme adherence to either way of seeing would give. A victory in the battle between romance and novel inevitably ends in contempt on the part of the reader for the other side, and with that contempt comes the dislocation or the atrophy of some vital quality he needs in order to "read." A total victory for novel, philosophy, the analytic power denies the "tender part of the reader's mind," that elemental, sentimental, egoistic, blindly energetic force that can destroy an individual, as Meredith has shown, but that also somehow supplies a part of the necessary energy for loving

247

and hating invisible persons. If romance wins, it is the sterner part of the mind that is denied, the waiting judge, distanced, analytical, civilized, philosophical, and cool, sometimes harshly critical yet somehow supplying the necessary molding firmness by which consciousness grasps those invisible persons, the characters of fiction, as "instructive"—tools, that is, for making judgments about ourselves. Most instructive of all from the point of view of this reading of Meredith are the characters who make fiction, the contradictory impulses governing narration and reading, fractious yokefellows whose marriage is proposed by the author and accomplished by the reader: "The posterity signified will, it is calculable, it is next to certain, have studied a developed human nature so far as to know the composition of it a not unequal mixture of the philosophic and the romantic, and that credible realism is to be produced solely by an involvement of those two elements" *(p. 396).* The civilized reader of *The Amazing Marriage* is not deceived by the Modern Novelist's sly metaphor about posterity, as he was not deceived by the allusion in *Richard Feverel* that a new audience "will come." Human nature is here. The novel is in his hands. Posterity is himself. The production is involvement. The marriage is now.

Meredith's confidence is not without its shadow of doubt. Even for a reader of goodwill there are too many temptations to false romance and false philosophy for the marriage of contradictory impulses, the integration of blood, brain, and spirit to be a certainty. But it is calculable; it is next to certain.

That was in 1895. On 5 January 1909, six months before his death, Meredith was still trying hard to see the unity he believed in, and still analyzing quite shrewdly the distance yet to be covered: on the subject of a unified national army he wrote his friend H. M. Hyndman that "one may fear that a landing on our shores alone will rouse the mercantile class. Doubtless also there is an apprehension as to the prudence of schooling the toilers in the use of arms. We are not yet a people" *(Letters,* III, 1612).

The years ahead were to give wry and disturbing evidence of the efficiency of armies to make a people. Meredith, one feels, would not have been too amazed. But during those final years of liberal ascendancy in Britain, this century's first decade and Meredith's last, he pinned his personal faith on the Book, not the Army, on the capacity of men to read, not fight, their way into community. His hope was that Gower Woodseer the philosopher-reader would inherit the earth from the likes of the Conquerors Victor Radnor and Buccaneer Kirby. But underneath the irony he was finally not unappreciative of the role of Chillon and Carinthia in trying to salvage the international patrimony of liberalism in Spain. He was saddened, though, by the romantic haste, the personal flaws, and lack of preparation that resulted in the doom of that expedition to fight for the Queen's cause. A little more reflection on the part of the chiefs of action, one feels him murmur, might have brought a victory. It is calculable. It is next to certain.

Index

251

Library of Congress Cataloging in Publication Data

Wilt, Judith.
   The readable people of George Meredith.

   Includes index.
   1. Meredith, George, 1828-1909—Criticism and
interpretation. I. Title.
PR5014.W55   823′.8   74-25610
ISBN 0-691-06275-7

99119

Ohio Dominican College Library
1216 Sunbury Road
Columbus, Ohio 43219

DEMCO